Prof. Lev Ginsburg's

Edited by Dr. H.R. Axelrod
Translated from the Russian by X. M. Danko

"Art is the result of a perfect harmony between thought and feeling."

Eugène Ysaÿe

"M. Ysaÿe's greatest merit is not superficial brilliance but an incomparable wealth of feeling and expression...."

Nikolai Kashkin

Л. ГИНЗБУРГ

Эжен Изаи

ГОСУДАРСТВЕННОЕ
МУЗЫКАЛЬНОЕ ИЗДАТЕЛЬСТВО

МОСКВА · 1959

Original Russian title page.

ISBN 0-87666-620-9

© 1980 by Paganiniana Publications.

Front Cover: A photograph of Ysaÿe with color restoration by Tom Hamilton.

Back Cover: Drawing of Ysaÿe by Marie Pilat, 1980.

Frontispiece: Drawing of Ysaÿe by Robert Florczak, 1980.

Published by Paganiniana Publications, Inc.
211 West Sylvania Avenue, Neptune City, N.J. 07753

Contents

1. The Early Years 18
2. The Middle Years 92
3. Ysaÿe and Debussy 152
4. The Berlin Concert:
   1912 162
5. The Concert Season:
   1912-1914 186
6. The Latter Years 202
7. The Style of Ysaÿe:
   The Performer 256
8. The Style of Ysaÿe:
   The Composer 306
9. Russian Music Critics
   On Ysaÿe's Art 354
10. Conclusion 434
11. Addenda 466

Dr. Herbert R. Axelrod and Prof. Josef Gingold (1979).

Editor's Foreword

The name of Prof. Dr. Lev Ginsburg is synonymous with the highest ideals in ethical reporting and musical integrity. I was honored to be able to meet the professor, a well-known and highly published musicologist, and convince him that this, of his many masterpieces, should be translated into English, enlarged to include more illustrations, and brought up to date with Ysaÿe's American experiences.

During the 1978 Tchaikovsky Competitions held in Moscow, I was fortunate enough to convince the professor and the Copyright Agency of the U.S.S.R., and the English edition of the Ysaÿe book began.

In a few months I received the English translation of the work from X. M. Danko. The translation is exceptional in all respects and required a bare minimum of "Americanizing."

My function, as editor, was to organize the material, search out pertinent illustrations, and to interview experts and Ysaÿe students to round out the Ginsburg material. All of this new editorial material appears in the last chapter, Addenda.

Without the extremely generous assistance of I. S. Arazi, nearly 30% of the illustrations would have been left out. Marianne Wurlitzer, of the famed Wurlitzer family, and her musicologist husband have formed a firm, "Wurlitzer-Bruck" of New York, which specializes in the sale of musical antiques, especially violin material; they also made rare photographs and letters available to me. A special thanks to Paul Paradise whose research talents have been fully utilized by the editor to obtain photographs and the identification of obscure personalities and obscure facts.

Finally, I must thank the most wonderful of all living violinists—Josef Gingold. He gave me everything he had: photos, original manuscripts and time. He read the translation and helped in so many ways. He has a speaking knowledge of Russian and this helped immensely. More than anything else, he has the same brilliant technique and the same warm manner as Ysaÿe, and he was the model upon which I based my image of the great master.

Dr. Herbert R. Axelrod

Lev Ginsburg

Professor Lev Ginsburg, Mus. D., (b. 1907) received his musical education at the Moscow Conservatoire from which he graduated in 1931 (Professor Semyon Kozolupov's class of cello); he had studied ensemble playing with Alexander Goedike and history of music with Valentin Ferman and Konstantin Kuznetsov.

After a few years of concert appearances Ginsburg devoted himself to teaching, music criticism and research. He has worked at the Moscow Conservatoire since 1936, teaching, in addition to cello, the history, theory and methods of bowed-instrument playing, the courses which he has done much to elaborate and perfect.

Ginsburg is the author of numerous works on the history, theory and aesthetics of musical interpretation: about twenty scores of books and pamphlets, many critical articles and investigations of musical culture, Russian and foreign. Some of his works have been translated into foreign languages.

Of Ginsburg's books mention should be made of *Luigi Boccherini* (1938), *Karl Davydov* (1950), *History of the Art of the Violoncello-Playing* (Vols. I-IV, 1950, 1957, 1965, 1978), *Ferdinand Laub* (1950), *Anatoly Brandukov* (1951), *Working on a Piece of Music* (1953, 3rd edition, 1968), *Hanus Wihan and the Czech Quartet* (1955), *Joseph Slavik* (1957), *Pablo Casals* (1958, 2nd edition, 1966), *Eugène Ysaÿe* (1959), *Mstislav Rostropovich* (1962), *Giuseppe Tartini* (1969), *Researches and Articles* (1971), *Maurice Maréchal* (1972), *On the Musical Interpretation* (1972), etc. In the Soviet and foreign press have appeared articles on the instrumental works of Myaskovsky, Gliere, Shostakovich, Shaporin, Khachaturyan, Kabalewski, Chrennikow, Wlassow, Rakov, Weinberg, Haydn, Beethoven, Mussorgsky and other composers. Many of Ginsburg's articles deal with the art of outstanding Soviet performers, for instance, David Oistrakh, Mstislav Rostropovich and Leonid Kogan.

Professor Ginsburg has to his credit the first publications of some of Tchaikovksy's letters and of instrumental pieces by N. Afanasyev, Alexander and Mikhail Vielgorsky, Sergei Vasilenko, Zoltan Kodaly and other composers. He has edited and arranged

Prof. Dr. Lev Ginsburg, musicologist and cellist.

The author, Prof. Dr. Lev Ginsburg, with the editor, Dr. Herbert R. Axelrod, in Moscow, 1978, preparing this book for publication. Below: Josef Gingold with Paul Paradise and Pavel Kogan.

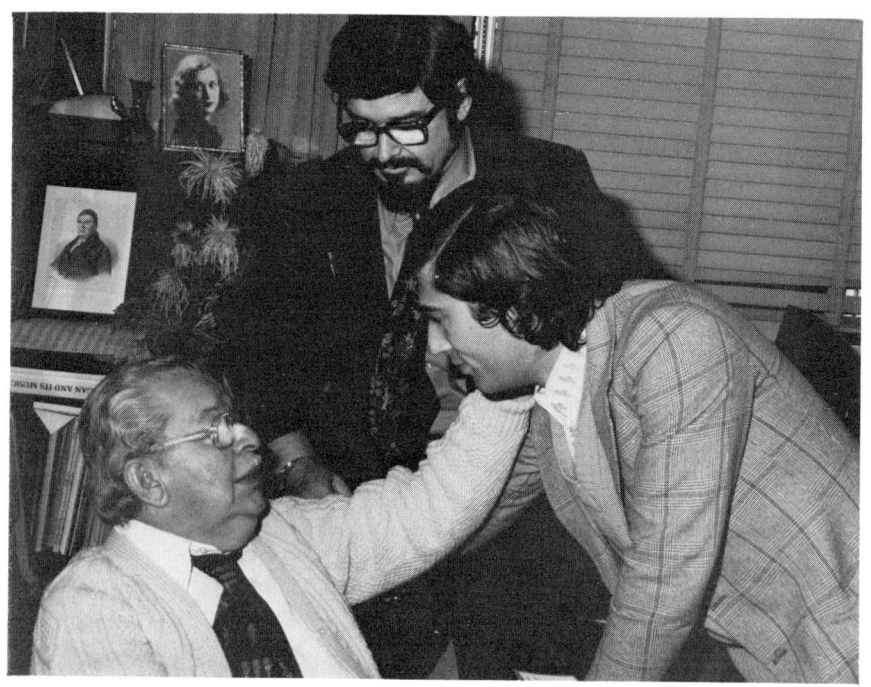

works by various composers, including Sergei Taneyev (Trio, Op. 31), Boccherini and Chopin.

Lev Ginsburg is Vice-President of the Music Association of the Union of Soviet Societies for Friendship and Cultural Relations with Foreign Countries. He has repeatedly taken part in international music conferences, competitions and festivals. Here are the titles of some of the papers he presented at such gatherings: *Some Problems of the Aesthetics of Musical Performance* (Janacek Academy, Brno, 1958), *Czech Contemporaries of Mozart in Russia* and *Mozart, Laub, Tchaikovsky* (Bertramka, Prague, 1960 and 1966), "Mozart in Russia," (Mozarteum, Salzburg, 1961), *Russian and Soviet-Italian Musical Contacts* (Italy-USSR Society, Rome, 1964), *Music Education in the USSR* and *New Works of Soviet Composers* (Vienna, Academy of Music; Salzburg, Mozarteum; Graz, Academy of Music; Innsbruck, Conservatoire, 1966), Frankfurt a/M, Mannheim, Hannover (1976), *On the Interpretation of Music for Stringed Instruments in the 18th Century* (Brno, Colloquium on the Interpretation of Old Music, 1967), *Zur Geschichte der Aufführung der Streichquartette Beethovens in Russland* (Bonn, Beethovenkongress, 1970), *Russische und sowjetische Violinschule* (Graz, Violinkongress, 1972), *Die Grundsätze der sowjetischen musikpädagogischen Schule* and the seminar *Methodik des Streichinstrumentenspiels* (Akademie J. Sibelius, Helsinki, 1975), *Neuheiten der sowjetischen Musik* (Universitat, Helsinki, 1975), *Zur Interpretation von Bachs Werken für Streichinstrumente in unserer Zeit* (Bachs Konferenz, Leipzig, 1975).

Professor Ginsburg's articles have appeared in the *Beethoven-Jahrbuch, Hudebni rozhledy, Slovenska hudba, Österreichische Musik-Zeitschrift* and other foreign periodicals.

Ishaq Arazi, violinist, conductor and writer was awarded the Ysaÿe Medal and Diplome D'Honneur by the Ysaÿe Foundation in Brussels on September 5, 1969 for his researches and writings on the life, times, and influences of the King of the Violinists, Eugène Ysaÿe. Many of the photos in this book are through the combined courtesy of the Ysaÿe Foundation and Mr. Arazi.

Introduction

Eugène Ysaÿe, the eminent violinist, conductor and composer, is deservedly regarded, along with Grétry, Gossec, Vieuxtemps, Servais, Franck and Lekeu, as one of the greatest figures in Belgian music, which is considered the pride of the Belgian people.

His significance as an artist-violinst and composer for his instrument, however, goes far beyond his native Belgium. The inspired art of this unsurpassed performer and talented composer, symbolizing truth and sincerity, poetry and inspiration, heartfelt lyricism and vivid romanticism, has left a lasting mark in the history of world violin playing.

Ysäye's art, which aroused the admiration of audiences in the major musical centers of Europe and America, still lives in the recollections of his contemporaries. It also remains alive in his recordings (Alas! very few in number) and in the violin compositions written by him, which combine high artistic merits with brilliant virtuosity and to this day grace the repertoire of the world's best violinists.

The author has made a number of minor alterations and additions in preparing his book for publication in the USA.

Eugène Ysaÿe, age 17, when he was awarded a gold medal in Liege, Belgium in 1875. Photo from Arazi.

Chapter 1

The Early Years

The descendant of an old peasant family in the Ardennes, Eugène Ysaÿe was born in Liège on July 16, 1858. His great-grandfather and grandfather were village nailsmiths, his uncle was a mason and his father a tailor. All of them, besides, were good musicians who would often oblige their neighbors by playing the fiddle or some other instruments at village fêtes and weddings, in the tavern and in church. The musicians themselves enjoyed the music as much as they did the extra money which it brought them, of which there was always a shortage.

The violin had taken a permanent place in the large Ysaÿe family, which maintained close ties with the cultural traditions of their people. There was a legend which, with variations and embellishments, was handed down from father to son in the old Ysaÿe family, whose members had for many generations been famous in the Ardennes both as craftsmen and musicians. The legend tells of a boy whom some woodcutters found in the forest and brought to the village. The boy grew up to be a blacksmith. Once he appeared at a village feast with a viol and astonished everybody by his playing on that simple folk instrument. He became a general favorite and the villagers took pleasure in singing and dancing to the strains of his viol. One day an illustrious traveler stopped in front of his smithy to have a horse shod. The count's servant saw the viol inside the smithy and told the young

A panorama of Liege, circa 1970, the birthplace of Ysaÿe. Photo from Arazi.

smith that he had heard a new Italian instrument played by some minstrels at the count's court. That instrument, called the violin, was much better than the viol—its tone was like the human voice and it could sing and express every feeling and passion.

From that moment the young man lost his peace of mind. He no longer took pleasure in his viol and had become indifferent towards his beloved Biethline. Day and night he was thinking of that wonderful new instrument which could express joy and sorrow and whose tones went straight to the human heart.

Then he had a dream: he saw before him a young woman of indescribable beauty who had a vague resemblance to his Biethline. She came up to him and kissed his brow. The young man awoke, looked at the wall where his broken and neglected viol used to hang, and could barely believe his eyes: there, instead of the viol, was a perfectly new instrument of beautiful proportions. That was the violin. He snatched it, put it against his shoulder and drew the bow over the strings, producing sounds that were truly divine. The violin sang in a heartwarming tone, it rejoiced and wept from happiness—as did the musician. Thus, says the legend, the first violin came to the Ardennes.[1]

The violin, a traditional instrument like the viol and the rebec[2] which possesses greater expressive resources than either, replaced other bowed instruments in the course of the 16th-18th centuries, quickly gaining popularity and becoming a universal favorite. As Nikolai Cherynshevsky, the great Russian publicist, wrote: "The violin is prized above all other musical instruments, because its sound is more akin to the human voice than that of any other instrument."[3]

Many nations have contributed toward the art of violin playing. The classical Russian school, in particular, has figured prominently in this development, while the achievements of the Soviet violin school, many of whose representatives proudly bear the title of winner of the Prix International Eugène Ysaÿe, are well known.

The Belgian school of violinists, adorned with the names of de Bériot and Vieuxtemps, Prume and Léonard, Massart and Marsick, Thomson and Ysaÿe, holds a place of honor in the history of the violin. Especially outstanding are the achievements of two eminent Belgian violinists—Henri Vieuxtemps, who for a number of years was active in St. Petersburg, and Eugène Ysaÿe, his best pupil.

The future "hero of the violin" grew up in a musical atmosphere. His father, Nicholas Ysaÿe, left his native village of Soumagne as a young man and settled in Liège in order to get a musical education. For some time he attended the Conservatoire but the lack of means prevented him from completing the course of studies. He gradually made a name for himself as a good orchestral violinist and conductor of theater and ballroom orchestras. Little Eugène eagerly absorbed musical impressions from his father's lessons, from the small orchestras which played under his father's direction and from the Ysaÿe family ensemble, which consisted of Nicholas, his brother Jean-Pierre and their sons. This little group of musicians would play on Sundays in nearby villages where they were always welcome. Then there was music at the parish church, too.

When Eugène was four, his father began teaching him to play the violin. He was a severe and demanding master and although

In 1923 Bloomfield designed this bookplate for Ysaÿe. The reproduction here is double the original size

Ysaÿe was baptized in Soumagne in the church of St. Lambert which was built in 1686.

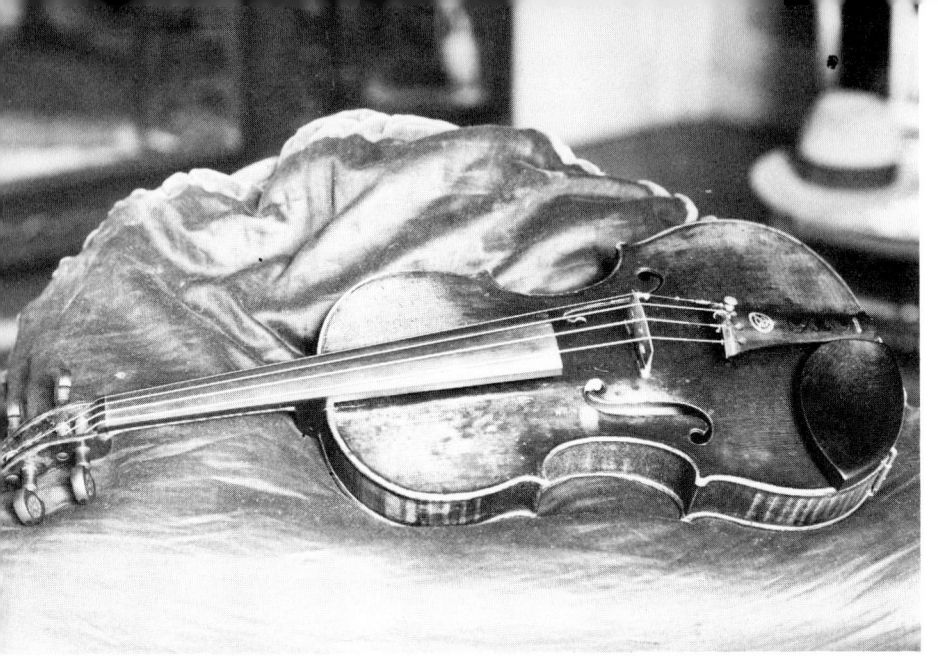

The Guarnerius del Gesu of Ysaÿe. It is now the property of Isaac Stern. Photo from Arazi.

Eugène Ysaÿe subsequently received an excellent training under the guidance of first-rate violinists, he always spoke with gratitude of his father. It was his father who, in the course of three years, had taught him the natural position of the hands, correct bowing and developed in him a taste for a singing and expressive tone— qualities which largely determined the future evolution of the young violinist. "His hand was heavy, but without his strict attitude I should never become what I am today," wrote Eugène Ysaÿe in later years. "My father was indisputably my real teacher. True, Rodolphe Massart, Wieniawski and Vieuxtemps opened up new horizons for me in the realm of technique and interpretation, but it was my father who taught me how to make the violin speak."

Eugène's childhood was anything but carefree. In 1865, when at the age of seven the boy had already played in the theater orchestra, he became a pupil of Désiré Heynberg at the Liège Conservatoire. Although he received a second prize for violin playing in his second year at the Conservatoire, his progress there was less spectacular than was expected from a boy of his gifts. This might have been due to his master's lack of understanding, but was mostly because Eugène had to work much more strenuously than a child should. His father had a large family of five children to provide for and so his two elder boys—Joseph, also a violinist, and

Nicholas Ysaÿe, father of Eugene. Born 1826. Died 1905.

1. OTTOKAR ŠEVČIK. 2. TOSCHA SEIDEL. 3. LOUIS SPOHR. 4. IRMA SEYDEL. 5. CAMILLO SIVORI. 6. HENRY SCHRADIECK. 7. HANS SITT. 8. ACHILLE SIMONETTI.

Famous violinists.

Eugène—were obligated to combine their studies with work. In 1868, Nicholas lost his wife and the children were left motherless. Besides studying at the Conservatoire, Eugène Ysaÿe played in two orchestras—a theater orchestra and a church one—and not infrequently he would spend whole nights playing at village balls. All this led to his leaving the Conservatoire in 1869.

The talented young musician, however, did not stop studying: he worked assiduously and mastered the violin repertoire by himself, learning the caprices of Locatelli and Paganini and the concertos of Bach, Beethoven, Viotti, Spohr, Wieniawski and Vieuxtemps. His general education was not neglected, for Eugène was an avid reader and showed particular interest in history and the natural sciences.

Eugène Ysaÿe accompanied his father on his concert trips to various cities of Belgium, France, Germany and Switzerland. Playing in the orchestra under his father's direction, the young violinist got to know not only Strauss waltzes and operetta potpourris but also the symphonies of Mozart and Beethoven, the overtures of Wagner, and other orchestral works.

With so much time spent traveling and at the desk in the orchestra, it is astonishing how Eugène managed to perfect his skill on the violin. This is where his unusual gifts stood him in good stead, not just musical gifts in general, but the specific talent for, and love of, the violin. The often-repeated statement that "Eugène Ysaÿe was born to play the violin" seems not the least bit exaggerated.

There came a moment when his father and elder brother realized, all of a sudden, that Eugène had become an accomplished violinist. Then Henri Vieuxtemps (1820-81) happened to hear the fourteen-year-old Eugène play. Vieuxtemps was a famous Belgian violinist, a brilliant representative of the virtuoso-romantic trend in interpretative art and who, incidentally had made several tours of Russia and had even lived there between 1845 and 1852. He was Eugène Ysaÿe's long-cherished idol. He was struck by the boy's performance of his Fifth Concerto and *Fantasia appassionata* and was quick to appreciate his outstanding talent.

Vieuxtemps arranged for Eugène Ysaÿe to be readmitted to the Liège Conservatoire, where he became a pupil of Rodolphe Massart. His wonderful progress won for him a Premier Prix and a

Facing page: Henri Vieuxtemps, Ysaÿe's major violin professor. He was born in Verviers in 1820 and died in 1881. Above: Vieuxtemps arranged for Ysaÿe to be admitted to the Liege Conservatoire where he studied with Rodolphe Massart, shown above.

Martin Pierre Joseph Marsick, a contemporary of Ysaÿe.

Gold Medal. Professor Théodore Radoux, the director, greatly admired the naturalness of Eugène's playing and said: "He plays the violin as a bird sings."

At the age of sixteen, Ysaÿe studied with Henryk Wieniawski (1835-80). The famous Polish violinist had recently returned from America after a concert tour with the world-famous Russian pianist Anton Rubinstein[4] and replaced Vieuxtemps, who had become paralyzed, at the Brussels Conservatoire. Two years later, Eugène Ysaÿe went to Paris to continue his studies under Henri Vieuxtemps, his compatriot and a master of equal standing with Wieniawski.

Both Wieniawski and Vieuxtemps were superb musicians whose style of playing, for all the individual peculiarities, had much in common: it was distinguished for consummate artistry, romantic élan, brilliant virtuosity and an expressive singing tone. Young Ysaÿe inherited all these qualities and became one of the best interpreters of the masters' music.

He always spoke with profound reverence and affection for his great teachers whose artistic aspirations were so congenial with his own. He became especially close to Vieuxtemps at the time that he mastered his instrument. Vieuxtemps continued what had been begun by Wieniawski and exerted a strong influence on Ysaÿe's aesthetic views and taste. "He opened the way for me, he opened my eyes and my heart,"[5] said Ysaÿe at the Vieuxtemps centenary celebrations in Verviers.

Once a week the most illustrious musicians of the time would gather at Vieuxtemps' house and young Ysaÿe had many an occasion to hear great artists and to play before them. On one such musical evening in February 1876, Eugène Ysaÿe met Franz Liszt and Anton Rubinstein. The great Russian pianist, then at the peak of his fame, left an indelible impression on the young violinist, who later referred to him as his "master of interpretation." In spite of a considerable difference in their ages (Rubinstein was nearly 30 years older than Ysaÿe), the two musicians became good friends.

Like Vieuxtemps, Rubinstein, too, had the highest opinion of the talent and artistic proficiency of the young violinist and encouraged him in every way.

After Eugène's appearance at one of Vieuxtemps' parties in 1877, a Paris newspaper wrote: "M. Ysaÿe possesses precious

Henryk Wieniawski, one of Ysaÿe's first violin professors. Facing page: Anton Rubinstein.

Three young violinists from Liege playing in the Orchestra in the resort city of Ostende in 1873: Ovide Musin, Eugène Ysaÿe and Arthur Guidé at the far right.

qualities: a beautiful tone, a broad bow, a fine style and warmth; his technique certainly meets the requirements of modern virtuosity."[6]

In one of his letters of recommendation Vieuxtemps spoke of the eighteen-year-old Eugène as a very capable pupil, one who would become a great artist. As early as 1877, the master noted his original way of playing, a taste for what is natural and simple, an excellent tone and an exceptional technique.

When, paralyzed and unable to play the violin himself, Vieuxtemps was working on his Sixth and Seventh violin concertos a few months before his death, he wrote to Radoux (on October 15, 1880): "Unfortunately there is nobody I can call on to play them for me and advise me on the changes and cuts to be made. I need someone and this someone is Ysaÿe who would do well to spend the winter here so that he could learn my new works with me. I can still hear his *chanterelle* and I want so much to hear it again. Find out where he is and send him to me as soon as possible."

His old master saw Eugène not only as a friend and a brilliant pupil, but also as one destined to continue the fine traditions of his school, to develop a trend in art to which he had devoted his life.

Eugène Ysaÿe's road to the concert stage and to world recognition did not prove to be an easy one. While studying at the Conservatoire and upon graduation he continued to play in various orchestras (at Spa, Ostend and other towns). From 1879 to 1882, Ysaÿe was first violin in the well-known Benjamin Bilse orchestra, which played at a large Berlin beer-hall called the Konzerthaus. The repertoire of his orchestra, made up of excellent musicians (before Ysaÿe, his post had been held by the well-known Czech violinist Karel Halir) contained, along with Strauss waltzes and potpourris from Lecocq and Offenbach, works by Bach and Beethoven, Mendelssohn and Schubert, Brahms and Tchaikovsky. Nevertheless, neither the nature of the concerts nor his work in the orchestra could satisfy young Ysaÿe, who longed for a serious concert career.

His appearance in Berlin in October 1881 attracted the attention of local musicians, and the press warmly praised the Belgian violinist. Ysaÿe never missed an opportunity to play in public, and in the early 1880's he gave some successful concerts in Leipzig and Paris. His repertoire at that time included *Adagio and Fugue* from

Peter I. Tchaikovsky. On the facing page: The class of Rodolphe Massart, 1873. Sitting from left to right: O. Dossin, L. Charlier, R. Massart, A. Marchot, E. Ysaÿe. Standing in the back row—only Musin, Guide and Voncken are identifiable. Photo courtesy of Arazi.

Franz Liszt, at a late age. Below: Liszt with students and colleagues.

Liebling   Siloti   Rosenthal   Friedheim   Sauer   Reisenauer   Mannsfeld   Gottschalg

Franz Liszt.

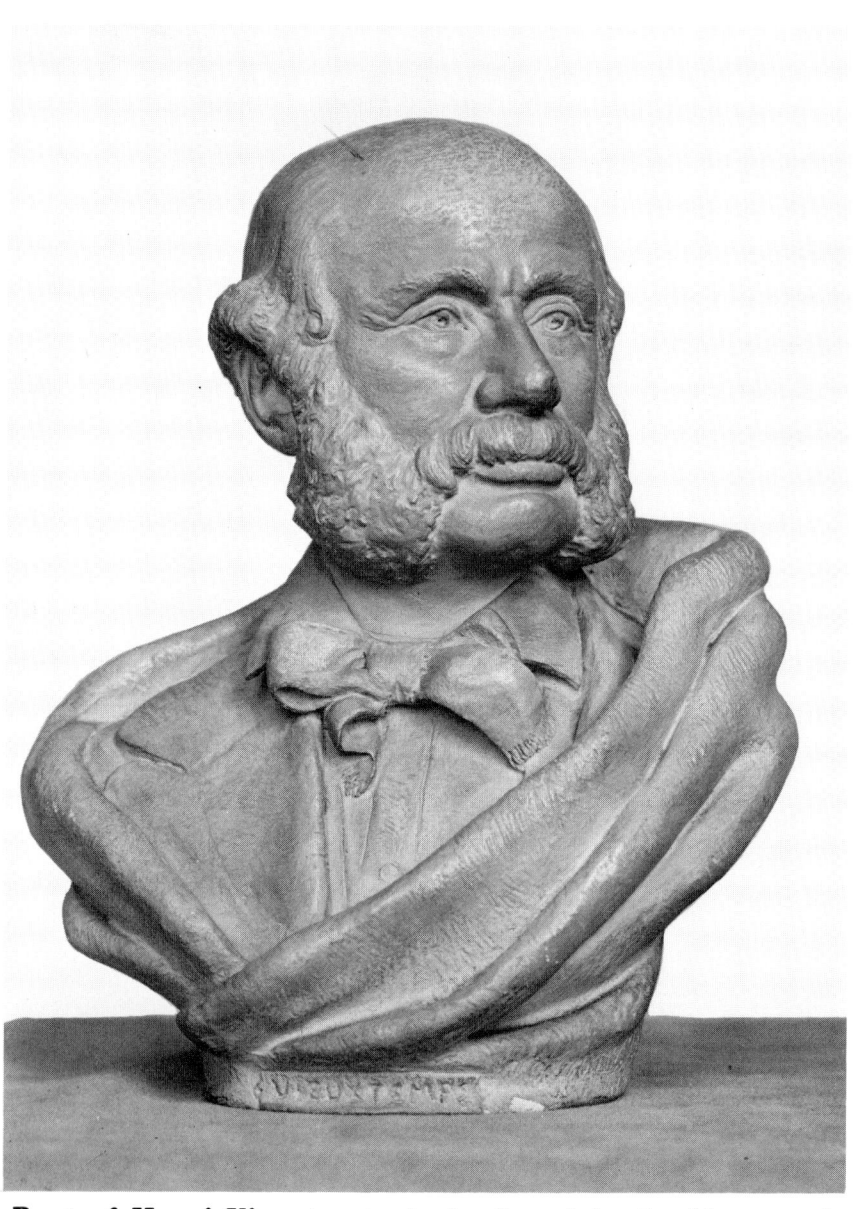

Bust of Henri Vieuxtemps to be found in the Museum in Liege. Photo from Arazi.

Bach's *First Sonata for Solo Violin,* the Beethoven *Romances,* pieces by Wieniawski and Vieuxtemps, *Rondo Capriccioso* by Saint-Saëns, his own Variations on Caprice No. 4 of Paganini, and some other works. The press noted that the young artist possessed great control, breath-taking virtuosity and played with perfect assurance, precision and expressiveness.

Although Ysaÿe was not wholly satisfied with his work in the Konzerthaus, he had frequent opportunities there of playing solo with orchestral accompaniment, arousing the admiration of the numerous patrons of the Prussian capital's beer-hall. The Konzerthaus was often visited by prominent musicians, some of whom were attracted primarily by Ysaÿe's playing. (It should be noted that his participation in the Bilse orchestra lent to it greater prestige, and was largely instrumental in its transformation, in 1882, into the Berlin Philharmonic Orchestra.) Among the famous visitors was Joseph Joachim, who brought his pupils to the Konzerthaus so that they could hear Ysaÿe play.

In recalling his meetings with Eugène Ysaÿe, Andreas Moser, one of Joachim's pupils, later wrote: "The first time I heard him was at Joachim's shortly after his arrival in Berlin. He came with his friend, sixteen-year-old Krezma,[7] my countryman and a very gifted violinist who was also a member of the Bilse orchestra. When Joachim asked him to play something from the music lying about, Ysaÿe said that Krezma would accompany him on the piano without music. He then took one of Joachim's Stradivari violins and played, first, Vieuxtemps' *Fantasia appassionata* and, after that, Wieniawski's *Concerto in D minor.* Joachim greatly admired the excellence of each young musician's performance. The following day he took his pupils to the Flora Café where Bilse's orchestra played during the summer to listen to what he called 'Die zwei famose Kerle' play with orchestra and to once more express his admiration for them."[8]

Other celebrated artists who heard Ysaÿe play with Bilse's orchestra were Franz Liszt, Clara Schumann and Anton Rubinstein, to mention just a few.

Anton Rubinstein realized at once that if Eugène Ysaÿe was to become a real artist he must leave the orchestra at once. He arranged for Bilse to release the young musician from his contract and invited him to join him in a tour of Norway.

Joseph Joachim.

Henri Vieuxtemps autographed this lithograph to one of Wolfgang Amadeus Mozart's relatives in Vienna.

Eugène Ysaÿe in 1879.

"You must not stay here," Rubinstein told him. "You have mastered all the secrets of the violin and deserve better surroundings than those you have here. They are certainly not bad, but not adequate to your talent. Take my advice and I will set you on the road along which you should proceed."[9]

This tour[10] proved an excellent start for Eugène Ysaÿe. The communion with Anton Rubinstein and joint appearances with him in sonatas (in particular, Rubinstein and Ysaÿe played the sonatas by Grieg, whom the young violinist met in Bergen),[11] the friendly support of his elder Russian colleague who arranged for Ysaÿe's concerts in Russia—all this Ysaÿe gratefully recalled in later years when he was at the summit of world fame.

The deep solicitude which Anton Rubinstein felt for his young and somewhat headstrong friend can be seen from the words which he addressed to Eugène Ysaÿe at the period of the latter's first dazzling successes. This is what he wrote: "Do not let the outward manifestations of success turn your head . . . Always keep before you the one goal, which must be to interpret the music according to your understanding, your temperament and feelings. Do not try merely to give pleasure to the public. You have acquired the art of giving pleasure. You should now singe your wings against the flame of success and taste the pungent wine of triumph. When you have realized the vanity of success, when you have understood that the true role of the interpretative artist is not to receive but to give, you will then have realized the sacred nature of your mission, and after having conquered the public you will have overcome yourself."[12]

Ysaÿe took these words to heart. In the future, he never was satisfied with his achievements, and placed the highest demands upon himself and his art. His playing was the voice of his heart, sincere and inspired, and this he shared with his listeners naturally and convincingly.

Working ceaselessly to perfect his art, Ysaÿe gradually overcame his youthful infatuation with virtuosity and became increasingly interested in the music of the old Italians Corelli, Vivaldi and Tartini and in the great creations of Bach. He also showed a growing interest in chamber music—quartets and sonatas.

While working in Bilse's orchestra Ysaÿe read a lot, dividing his sympathies between the romantic and poetic images of Victor

Eugène Ysaÿe in Kiev, Russia, 1882. Photo courtesy of Leslie Sheppard.

Hugo and the forceful realism of Honoré de Balzac. His close creative contacts with Franz Liszt, Camille Saint-Saëns, Sophie Menter and Anna Yesipova (Essipova), whom he met at the festival of interpretative artists in Zürich in honor of Liszt, prompted him to take the decisive step in leaving the Bilse orchestra. (Sophie Menter was the wife of David Popper, and Anna Yesipova, one of Theodore Leshetizky's seven wives, was according to some authorities, a great pianist in her own right).

At that period Eugene Ysaÿe was closely associated with Paris, where he resided until 1886. He was beginning to make a name for himself and soared to fame overnight after his triumphant appearance as soloist with the orchestra at one of the *Concerts Colonne*, whose director engaged him on the recommendation of Saint-Saëns.

The symphonic concerts, which were established in 1873 under the direction of Edouard Colonne (1838-1910), had a far-reaching educational significance: their programs presented the finest works of classical and contemporary music (incidentally, Tchaikovsky and Rimsky-Korsakov appeared with this orchestra as guest conductors). They played a prominent role in democratizing the French capital's musical life, especially since 1874 when the concerts were held at the vast auditorium of the Châtelet theater, seating 3,600. "It was at the Châtelet that the public preserved to the last the hottest musical passions," wrote Romain Rolland at the beginning of the present century. "Thanks to the size of the theater, one of the largest in Paris, and the great number of cheap seats, there emerged a constant young audience of men and women students, that is, the most sensitive public in the world. For many of them music was more than a mere pleasure—it was a necessity. No such public had existed in France prior to 1870."[13]

So it was before this large, sensitive and highly discriminating public that Eugene Ysaÿe made his debut. At this concert, held in 1885, he gave a magnificent performance of the *Symphonie espagnole* by Lalo and *Rondo Capriccioso* by Saint-Saëns. The music of the two works was in perfect harmony with Ysaÿe's style. Even though some time previously the celebrated Spanish virtuoso Pablo Sarasate had also appeared with Lalo's *Symphonie* (which the composer had dedicated to him), Ysaÿe, according to witnesses, was not only successful, he was triumphant. For an encore, Ysaÿe

ugène Ysaÿe's wedding to Louise Bourdau, 28 September, 1886.

In 1887 when the Liege Conservatoire moved to a new building, the students and faculty gave a performance. The violin section played a concerto for four violins by Maurer. From left to right: Martin Marsick, Rodolphe Massart, César Thomson and Eugène Ysaÿe.

Camille Saint-Saëns.

Eugène Ysaÿe and Theofile Lindenlaub on their Russian tour, 1883.

played a prelude of Bach for solo violin, demonstrating his rare gift for transformation and an exceptional sense of style.

The young violinist resumed old acquaintances in Paris and struck up a close friendship with the prominent French composers Saint-Saëns, Fauré, Debussy, Vincent d'Indy, Chausson, Chabrier and, naturally, the outstanding Belgian composer and organist César Franck, who was intimately associated with the French school of composition. They often met to discuss all kinds of musical problems, new compositions, their interpretation, and simply to make music. The friendship with these Paris musicians proved to be of immense value for Ysaÿe's artistic development.

His inspired playing prompted many outstanding Belgian and French composers to write a large number of violin concertos, sonatas and other works for Ysaÿe. Among these works are the *Sonata for Violin and Piano* by Franck, a string quartet by Saint-Saëns, the *Sonata for Violin and Piano* by Lekeu, the *Piano Quintet* by Fauré, the *Quartet* by d'Indy, the *Quartet* and the original—violin—version of *Nocturnes* by Debussy, the *Poème* by Chausson, the *Sonata for Violin and Piano* by Dukas, and the sonatas by Jongen and other composers—altogether, more than 50 compositions. This brief list gives a good idea of the exceptionally wide range of Ysaÿe's contacts and the immense prestige enjoyed by the great artist who tirelessly popularized the work of these composers for several decades.

César Franck (le Père Franck to his intimates) was a particularly close friend of Ysaÿe, who was filled with admiration for Franck's music at a time when that composer was insufficiently appreciated. Franck dedicated his *Sonata for Violin and Piano* in A Major, that masterpiece of chamber music, to Ysaÿe. He received it on the day of his marriage to Louise Bourdau from the composer Charles Bordes, who, on Franck's commission, brought it to the small Belgian town of Arlon where the ceremony was held. Ysaÿe looked through the manuscript and, deeply moved, said: "Nothing in the world could have done me greater honor or given me more pleasure than this gift. But it is not for me alone. It is for the whole world. To interpret it, I shall do my very best as an artist and the warmest admirer of César Franck, whose genius has not been sufficiently recognized up until now. I shall play this Sonata for you the way I understand it and feel it in my heart."[14] Ysaÿe then played

César Franck, perhaps Ysaÿe's best friend, shown at the organ in 1880. This portrait by Rouvien was supplied by Arazi.

Vincent d'Indy, a composer and well-rounded musician, was an accepted member of the group which included Saint-Saëns, Fauré, Debussy, Franck and Chausson.

Program advertisement showing Eugène Ysaÿe performing with his brother. The concert was played at the famous Twenty Club of Brussels.

the Sonata with the French pianist Marie Bordes-Pène, who had come to the wedding with her brother-in-law. It would be in place to remark here that recognition came to César Franck soon after Eugène Ysaÿe performed this *Sonata*.

Eugène Ysaÿe's activities as a soloist of the first rank, member of chamber ensembles and conductor proved highly beneficial for the cause of contemporary composers, especially French and Belgian composers. He clearly realized the educational mission of the interpretative artist. This is what he said: "Is not the popularization of important new or unknown works one of the most profound joys of the interpretative artist? It is in offering such works to the judgment of the public, without a thought of his own success, that the interpretative artist fulfills his highest mission."[15]

Settling in Brussels in 1886, Eugène Ysaÿe provided a strong impulse to the development of Belgian music by his manifold activities, his creative initiative and the force of his artistic personality.

During the last decades of the past century, a very prominent part in Belgium's artistic life was played by *Le Cercle des XX*, in 1893 renamed *La Libre Esthétique*. Its members were outstanding Belgian artists and art patrons. In spite of its initial appellation suggesting a limited sphere of action, the Twenty Club, as it was familiarly called, stimulated the work of many national artists (mainly Impressionists) and musicians and was instrumental in popularizing their achievements. At this inception (*Le Cercle des XX* was founded in 1884) it consisted chiefly of painters and sculptors. Work in this field formed the focus of its attention, with the holding of exhibitions by such prominent artists, predominantly French and Belgian, as Constantin Meunier, Claude Monet, Auguste Rodin, Camille Pisarro and Paul Cézanne, but when Eugène Ysaÿe joined it, the Twenty Club became a major musical center and the fame of the concerts sponsored by it spread beyond the borders of Belgium.

Ysaÿe drew towards himself a large group of Belgian musicians, young and not-so-young, who made a sizable contribution to the development of their country's music, and thereby acquainted the audiences with the work of composers from other countries.

In the Twenty Club's concerts of chamber music, a leading part was played by the Ysaÿe String Quartet. Besides Ysaÿe, the quartet

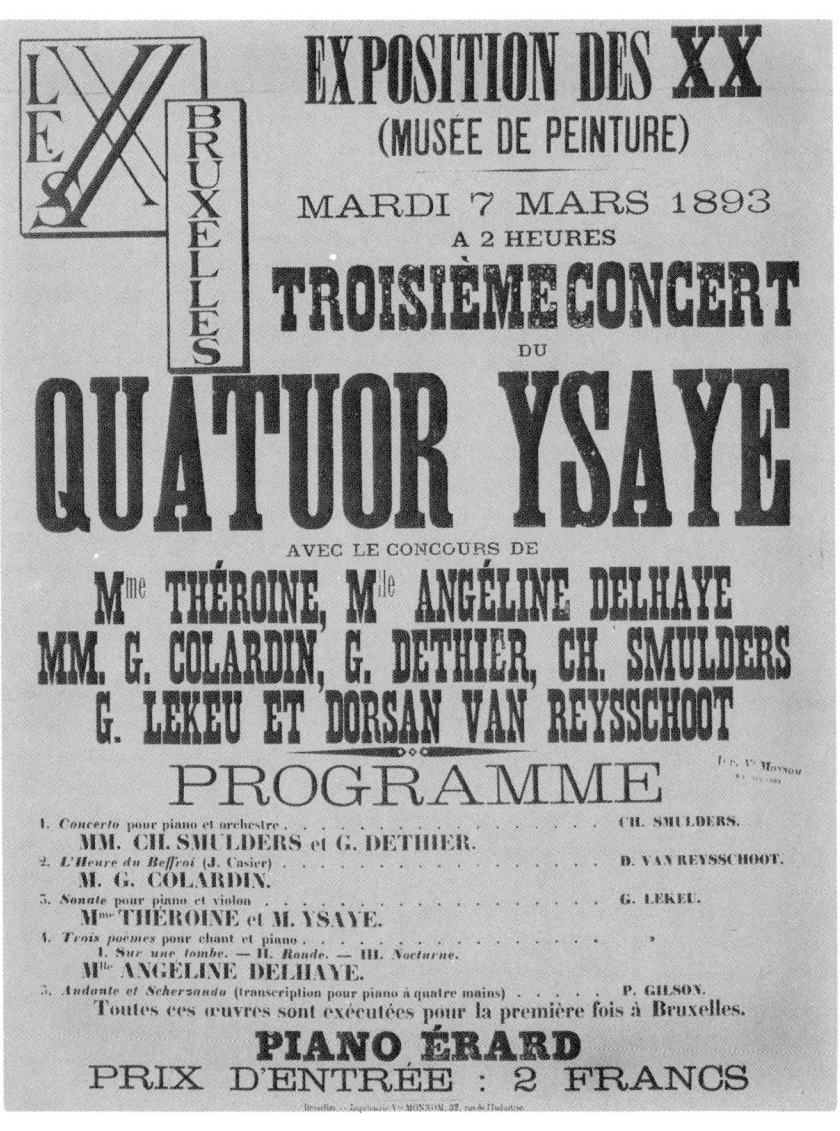

Another Twenty Club concert, this one in March, 1893 features the Ysaÿe Quartet.

Eugène Ysaÿe, 1884. Photo from Arazi.

Le Major Bourdau et Madame Bourdau ont l'honneur de vous faire part du mariage de leur fille Louise avec Monsieur Eugène Ysaÿe, Professeur au Conservatoire Royal de Bruxelles.

Arlon, le 28 Septembre 1886.

Monsieur Nicolas Ysaÿe
a l'honneur de vous faire part
du mariage de son fils Eugène
avec Mademoiselle Louise
Bourdau.

Arlon, le 28 Septembre 1886.

The wedding invitation to the Ysaÿe and Bourdau affair dated 28 September, 1886.

The menu at the wedding party celebrating Ysaÿe's marriage to Louise Bourdau includes a dish "Danse d'écrevisses á la Paganini." Photo from Arazi.

consisted of Mathieu Crickboom, his pupil and subsequently a professor of the Brussels Conservatoire, Leon van Hout and Joseph Jacob. The repertoire of this quartet, famous for its perfect ensemble and artistic performance, consisted not only of works by contemporary French and Belgian composers, but also of classical masterpieces by Mozart, Beethoven, Schubert, Mendelssohn, Borodin and Tchaikovsky.

Another potent educational factor were the Ysaÿe Concerts, which he established in 1895 with the aim of initiating the public into the best musical works, classical and contemporary. These concerts were given regularly until 1914. In his work with the orchestra, Eugène Ysaÿe proved himself no ordinary conductor; he trained an excellent body of musicians and presented to the public a whole series of symphonic compositions in skillful and highly artistic interpretations. Besides Ysaÿe, the orchestra gave concerts under the direction of Camille Saint-Saëns, Artur Nikisch, Felix Mottl, Felix Weingartner, Willem Mengelberg and other celebrated musicians.

The repertoire of the Ysaÿe Concerts was varied, featuring classical and romantic music along with works by contemporary composers, not only French and Belgian such as Franck, d'Indy, Fauré, Chausson, Debussy, Dukas, Lalo, Lekeu, Gilson and Jongen, but also foreign—Grieg, Svendsen, Wagner, Strauss, Elgar and, in particular the Russian masters Tchaikovsky, Balakirev and Glazunov. Among the outstanding soloists who willingly appeared with the orchestra were Fritz Kreisler, Pablo Casals, Alfred Cortot, Jacques Thibaud, Karel Halir, Lucien Capet, Raoul Pugno, Ferruccio Busoni, to name but a few. Recitals were resumed after World War I and attracted as soloists Sergei Rachmaninov, Nikolai Orlov, Jascha Heifetz, Bronislaw Hubermann and Andrés Segovia.

From 1886 to 1898 Eugène Ysaÿe held a professorship at the Brussels Conservatoire, training a whole galaxy of excellent violinists. It may be added here that in later years, after leaving the Conservatoire, when he dedicated himself wholly to concert appearances in Europe and America, Ysaÿe never refused to give lessons or advice to violinists who flocked to him from all parts of the world.

The inspired artistry of his interpretation, spirit and temperament of his playing, sincerity, perfection and technique of his

An old faded photograph showing Ysaÿe performing with Vincent d'Indy in 1893.

Gabriel Fauré, composer and great friend of Ysaÿe.

Ferruccio Busoni. Facing page: Jacques Thibaud.

Fritz Kreisler. Facing page: Ysaÿe and Raoul Pugno.

Georges Enesco. Facing page: Pablo Casals.

Louis Persinger

CRITICAL OPINIONS

EUGENE YSAYE:
"A virtuoso of a *superior order*—one of my best pupils."

ARTHUR NIKISCH:
"One of the most talented pupils the Leipzig Conservatory has ever had."

JACQUES THIBAUD:
"A very remarkable *artist*, in addition to being a great violinist."

DR. OTTO NEITZEL (in *Koelnische Zeitung*, Cologne):
"Among those whom we have heard on the concert platform during the past few years, he is the most finished, and sympathetic. One could call him a new-born Ysaye, if at the same time his bowing—especially the elegance of his staccato—did not awaken memories of Sarasate."

ROBIN H. LEGGE (in *Daily Telegraph*, London):
"Not since Sarasate have we heard violin playing more neat in the left hand or more masterly in the bow hand."

Louis Persinger ran this advertisement in **The Violinist** *to obtain concert engagements.*

phrasing attracted to Ysaÿe, for nearly four decades, many of the world's best violinists, who were eager to study under the great artist.

The list of Eugène Ysaÿe's pupils includes Josef Gingold, Mathieu Crickboom, Carlo Van Neste, René Benedetti, William Primrose, Alfred Marchot, Dany Brunschwig, Alberto Bachmann, Louis Persinger, André de Ribaupierre and many others. Ysaÿe gave advice to some musicians who had been educated at the Russian conservatoires, among them the outstanding Russian violinists, graduates of the Moscow Conservatoire, Michael Erdenko, Michael Press and some others. Ysaÿe exerted a considerable influence on many contemporary violinists of world fame, including Fritz Kreisler, Georges Enesco, Joseph Szigeti, Jacques Thibaud, Carl Flesch and Albert Spalding.

Beginning with 1902, violinists of various schools and nationalities visited Eugène Ysaÿe for many years at his villa "La Chanterelle" on the Meuse where the master spent his summers. When on holiday, Ysaÿe enjoyed nature and music, without which life for him was unthinkable. He practiced, gave lessons and consultations and played in string ensembles with such musicians as Fritz Kreisler, Jacques Thibaud, Georges Enesco and Pablo Casals. He liked to play the viola (incidentally, Ysaÿe could play the cello, too). In their performances of chamber music with piano, Ysaÿe's partners were Raoul Pugno, Ferruccio Busoni[16] and Alfred Cortot. The artists were so absorbed in the beautiful music that they would often play into the small hours. These friendly sessions usually ended with Ysaÿe playing Bach's *Chaconne* or some of his own compositions.

Even while he was associated with the Brussels Conservatoire, Ysaÿe's concert activities were assuming an ever increasing scope. He appeared with triumphant success in various Belgian and French cities, in Russia,[17] Italy, Austria, Germany, Switzerland, Britain, the USA, Spain, Portugal, Sweden, Norway, Finland and other countries of the world, one tour succeeding the other. Despite the hardships of a touring artist, which affected his health, in particular, his hand (which had been injured in the artist's early years), Ysaÿe was perfectly satisfied, even happy.

In the autumn of 1894 Ysaÿe came for the first time to the USA, where his tour was an uninterrupted succession of triumphs. But

First page of a letter to Ysaÿe's wife, the following two pages shown on the facing page.

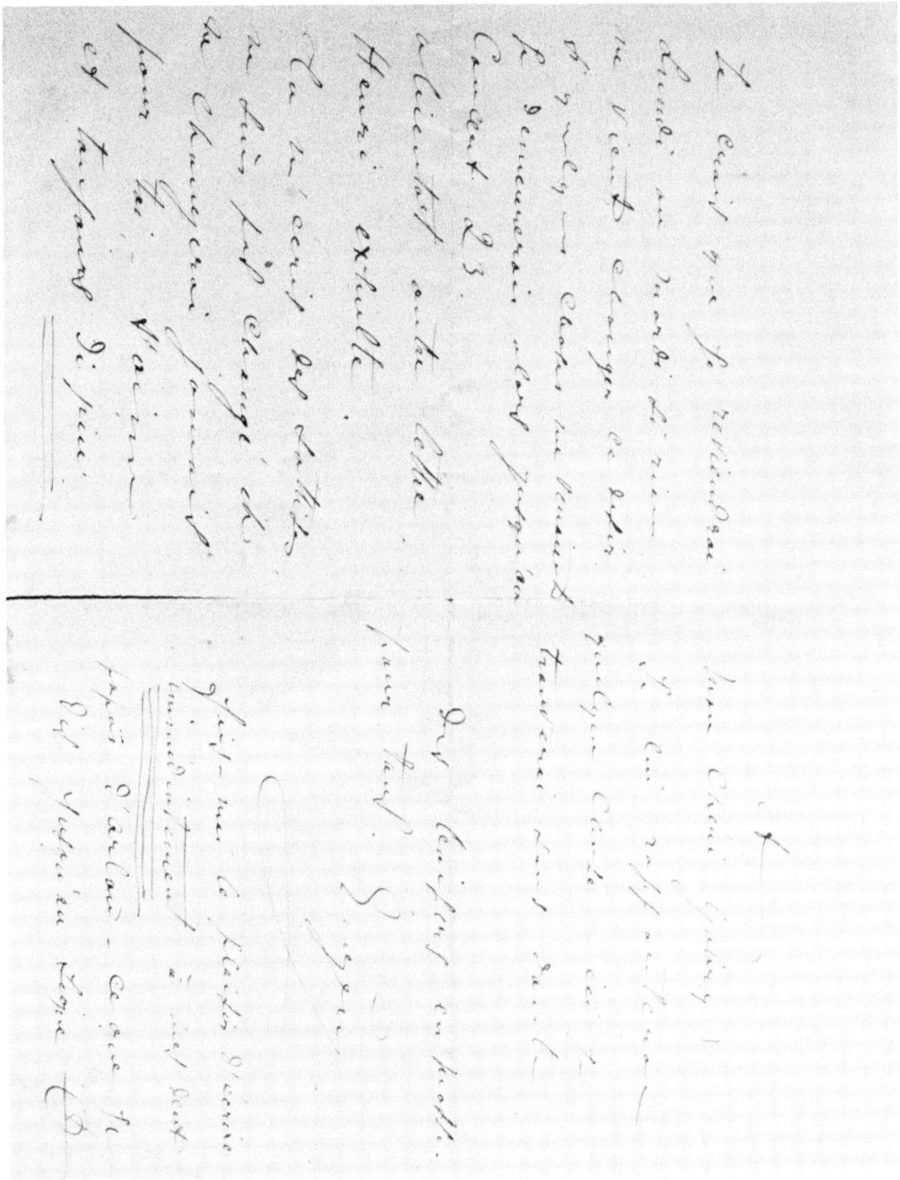

+

Mon chéri Gaby!

Je lui rapporterai quelques cartes ... je traverserai sans doute.

Des baisers en masse pour tous.

Eugène.

Fais-moi le plaisir d'écrire immédiatement à mes deux papas d'Arlon - ce que je dis jusqu'au signe (D

Je crois que je reviendrai Lundi ou Mardi si rien ne vient changer ce désir. Si quelques choses me venaient je demeurerai alors jusqu'au Convent 23.

A bientôt autre lettre.

Henri exulte.

Tu m'écris des bêtises je suis pas changé et ne changerai jamais pour toi. - t'aime et toujours de pire.

A sketch of Albert Spalding.

Madame Louise Ysaÿe in 1894.

in spite of the tempting offers, he refused to renew his contract. One of the reasons is clear from the letter he wrote to his wife, in which he said that the artists established in America "earn good money, but socially they receive little consideration."

Eugène Ysaÿe was the interpretative artist first and the teacher second, and although he could impart much that was valuable to his pupils and could derive immense satisfaction from teaching, the artist in him demanded unlimited freedom to devote himself to artistic activity. In order to be his own master and dispose of his time as he saw fit (the annual holidays were not enough for his concert tours), Ysaÿe decided to leave the Conservatoire.

He became free to spend the greater part of the year touring and giving concerts. In letters to members of his family he repeatedly complained of exhaustion. Sometimes he had to give 14 or 15 recitals in as many days, each in a different town. This constant strain and lack of sleep, on account of travel, were very tiring.

He complained also of the reprehensible behavior and dishonesty of some of his managers. This seems to have been a fairly typical state of affairs: the impresarios and managers were unscrupulously exploiting the artists' labors—suffice it to recall similar complaints of Anton Rubinstein on tour in America and the experiences of Sergei Rachmaninoy.

And yet Ysaÿe was happy. "It is when I play that I am happiest," he wrote in a letter to his wife. "Then I love everything in the world. I let go my feelings and my heart." The only thing that caused him anxiety was the state of his hands, especially his left hand. He was afraid that he would have to curtail his appearances or eventually give up his artistic career altogether. In 1899 he wrote in one of his letters: "All other misfortunes would be just nothing compared to that which might be caused by an incapacitated hand."

Nevertheless, he tried hard not to worry even after his hand made him interrupt the playing of the Lalo *Concerto* in Paris. He had sufficient strength of character to overcome his fears and score fresh successes. In the letter referred to he said: "Art, with all its setbacks, its smiles and its tears, animates me and gives me new life; it opens up unlimited horizons to my eyes. I love activity, I love the contrasts of light and shadow, I love life in all its manifestations."

Joseph Jacob, a cellist in the Ysaÿe Quartet. Circa 1893. Photo from Arazi.

Ysaÿe's studio in Brussels. Note the beautifully sculptured

urn which contains Ysaÿe's heart.

This important poster for the Twenty Club in Brussels advertises the second concert for the benefit of Fauré. Ysaÿe did everything possible to help popularize the music of his friends.

The Ysaÿe Quartet with friends: Left to right are Van Hout (viola), Jacob (cello), Ysaÿe, first violin, Crickboom, second violin and Braud, piano. Seated in the middle is César Franck.

Clipping of César Thomson's appearance in America.

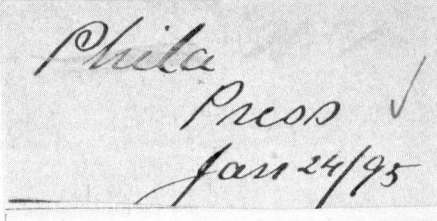

YSAYE IS A DARLING, TOO.

The Girls in Danger of Forgetting Paderewski for Him.

"This violinist, Ysaye, will outrank Paddy himself" [the man referred to Paderewski when he said 'Paddy'] "as a matinée idol. It was one of the few men in Carnegie Hall yesterday afternoon during the third recital of Eugene Ysaye. The hall was filled, nine women to one man, and the enthusiasm began when the violinist had finished the fourth movement of the first number, Raff's "Finale Confuoco," and culminated in a hysterical storm which brought Ysaye out on the stage six times after he had played the last thing on the programme, Greig's "Allegro Guerriero." If he had been kindly disposed he would have had excuse for continuing to appear and bow until hunger drove his admirers home, for it was not until the ante-room door behind which he had disappeared had remained unresponsively closed for five minutes that the sighing multitude of women slowly and regretfully left the hall.

The picture which accompanies this is Ysaye's favorite, and the illustrating department used it out of respect to his feelings, doubtless. It gives an idea of how the violinist looked when he made his first great success. He is fatter now. His cheeks have encroached so much upon his eyes that there is not much of the eyes to be seen, especially when he is in the ecstacy of playing. He is a much more manly looking man than Paderewski. Ysaye seems to take the adoration of the fair sex with considerable surprise; not as a matter of right, as "Paddy" did. It may be a difference of hair. The pianist, as all the world knows, manipulated his hair, or his valet did, until it stood out like a sunset cloud agitated by the evening breeze. Ysaye's hair is almost in the present style.

It is only a little longer than the locks of the smart young men, but he does not part it in the middle as they do. He parts it far down on the left side, and from there it loosely crosses his forehead and dances, as to its ends, when he fiddles.

Yesterday the most persistent and the loudest applauders were girls; really girls, from 14 to 18. One, between those ages, 16, shredded her gloves in the violence of her applause, and when the idol would not appear and bow any more she turned to her mother and sighed:

"Is he not supreme, mamma?"

"Button up your coat, Ethel," responded mamma, who looked as if she was thinking of a good dinner. They were going home. She had been sleeping placidly.

When the last of the programme had been played, a hundred of the women crowded to the edge of the stage, and leaned there facing the ante-room door, and soulfully longing until their applause brought Ysaye forth. Then they looked as if they were inclined to throw things at him—flowers and ribbons and gloves—as they did at "Paddy," but the craze has not quite reached that point yet.

"It will, though," said the man in the lobby. "He's fit to beat Paddy in a walk, but the girls are a little shy yet."

A SUN reporter saw Mr. Ysaye. He found the violinist interested in just one thing, and that seemed a curious thing, too. Ysaye said:

"I am instructor, you know, in the Brussels Conservatory. Now there are always there and coming and going a lot of clever Americans—oh, yes, very clever—excellent performers, men with technique and feeling. Well, then, what becomes of them? So! Where do they go, eh? I see in your orchestras here only a lot of bald-headed Dutchmen. Where are those Americans? So! Do they not learn to play as a profession? No! It is strange and too bad. A lot of bald-headed Dutchmen, eh?"

YSAYE, WHEN HE WAS MORE BEAUTIFUL.

From the Ysaÿe scrapbook made available by Marianne Wurlitzer.

A view of the Ysaÿe Studio recreated for the Ysaÿe Museum in Liege. Photo from Arazi. On the facing page is a sketch commissioned by R. E. Johnston, Ysaÿe's first agent in America, and the real discoverer of Ysaÿe. In Benoist's memoirs The Accompanist, *there is a marvelous story about the first meeting between Johnston and Ysaÿe.*

After prolonged travels Ysaÿe was especially glad to return home to spend the summer months in the country, surrounded by his family, friends and pupils.

The music at the Ysaÿe home—sometimes performed by a whole orchestra—would attract listeners from the neighboring villages. Antoine Ysaÿe, the artist's son, in his book dedicated to his father, gives a graphic description of the village fête which took place at

When the modern violin genius Eugene Fodor played the Ysaÿe Sonatas, Antoine Ysaÿe, son of Eugene, was so impressed with Fodor's rendition of the "Sonata to Szigeti" that he sent Fodor an autographed photo of his father with an American flag.

Sainte-Marie, in the Ardennes, in the summer of 1899. Eugène Ysaÿe spread a lavish entertainment on the lawn for his friends and the villagers. Then there were fireworks and after that the host came out with his Guarnerius to the lawn lit with oil lamps and, just like his remote ancestor the village blacksmith used to do, played an inspired improvisation in the style of the Ardennes minstrels before a spellbound audience.

NOTES

[1] The legend is adapted freely from: A.Ysaÿe, *Eugène Ysaÿe. Sa vie—Son oeuvre—Son influence. D'après les documents recuellis par son fils*. Bruxelles, 1947; Antoine Ysaÿe and Bertram Ratcliffe, *Ysaÿe. His Life, Work and Influence*, London, 1947. These books, largely identical regarding material and presentation, contain numerous passages from Eugène Ysaÿe's correspondence collected by his son, Antoine Ysaÿe, many of which are quoted here. When quotations are borrowed from other sources, the latter ones are indicated.
[2] Cf. B.A. Struve, *Protsess formirovaniya viol i skripok (The Process of Formation of the Viols and the Violins)*, Moscow, 1959.
[3] N.G. Chernyshevsky, "Esteticheskiye otnosheniya iskusstva k deistvitelnosti" (dissertation), 1855, *N.G. Chernyshevsky ob iskusstve, (The Aesthetic Relationship between Art and Reality*, a dissertation, in *N.G. Chernyshevsky on Art)*, Moscow, 1950, p. 58.
[4] Wieniawski and Rubinstein became friends in Russia: the Polish violinist visited it more than once and from 1862 to 1868 held a professorship at the St. Petersburg Conservatoire, and was soloist to the Czar.
[5] Quoted from: Ernest Christen, *Ysaÿe*, Genève, 1947, p. 35.
[6] Le *Revue et Gazette musicale*, 1877 (quoted from Edouard G.-J. Gregoir. *Les artistes-musiciens belges au XVIII-me et au XIX-me siècle*. Bruxelles . . . , 1885, p. 250).
[7] Franz Krezma, a fine violinist, died in an accident at the age of nineteen.—*L.G.*
[8] Andreas Moser, *Geschichte des Violinspiels*, Berlin, 1923, pp. 453-4.
[9] Quoted from A. Ysaÿe, *Eugène Ysaÿe. Sa vie—Son oeuvre—Son influence. D'après les documents recueillis par son fils*, Bruxelles, 1947, pp. 63-4.
[10] The tour took place in the spring of 1882.
[11] Eugène Ysaÿe spent three weeks in Bergen. He gave one of his concerts in aid of the Ole Bull Foundation. That celebrated artist (1810-80) was also a prominent leader of the Norwegian National movement. During his stay in Bergen, Ysaÿe received a photograph from Grieg with the following inscription: "A Eugène Ysaÿe avec remerciement et admiration de Ed. Grieg. Bergen 1 mai 1882."
[12] Quoted from A. Ysaÿe, *op. cit.*, p. 65.
[13] Romain Rolland, *Musiciens d'aujourd'hui* (Russ. transl., Moscow, 1938, p. 281).
[14] Quoted from A. Ysaÿe, *op. cit.*, p. 97.
[15] Quoted from A. Ysaÿe, *op. cit.*, p. 281.
[16] An interesting caricature of Eugène Ysaÿe and his constant partner, Raoul Pugno, by F. Busoni is found in Edith Stargardt-Wolf's book, *Wegbereiter grosser Musiker*, Berlin, 1954.
[17] Ysaÿe's appearances in Russia are described in a special chapter.

Another view of Ysaÿe's studio.

Eugène Ysaÿe, circa age 21.

Chapter 2

The Middle Years

Eugène Ysaÿe's appearances on the leading concert platforms of the world, which lasted for nearly forty years, comprise an epoch in the history of musical interpretation at the turn of the century. Ysaÿe began at a time still alive to the fame of his great teachers Henryk Wieniawski and Henri Vieuxtemps, when his elder colleagues Joachim and Sarasate were at the peak of their fame. Inspired by the friendly contacts and joint appearances with Anton Rubinstein, Camille Saint-Saëns and César Franck, Ysaÿe's career proceeded alongside those of Leopold Auer, August Wilhelmj, Emile Sauret, Frantisek Ondricek, César Thomson and Jenö Hubay, as well as of his illustrious younger contemporaries Fritz Kreisler, Georges Enesco, Jacques Thibaud, Jan Kubelik, Willy Burmester and some others. Finally, in the first decades of the present century Ysaÿe had numerous occasions to get to know the art of young violinists representing the Russian school, from which Michael Erdenko, Miron Polyakin, Mischa Elman, Efrem Zimbalist and Jascha Heifetz were quickly gaining world recognition.

His manifold gifts as soloist, chamber musician and conductor, his astonishing capacity for work, his rare sociability and lively interest in new impressions—all widened the sphere of Ysaÿe's artistic contacts and creative friendships with his outstanding contemporaries. Ysaÿe's art was a model for many artists of his time

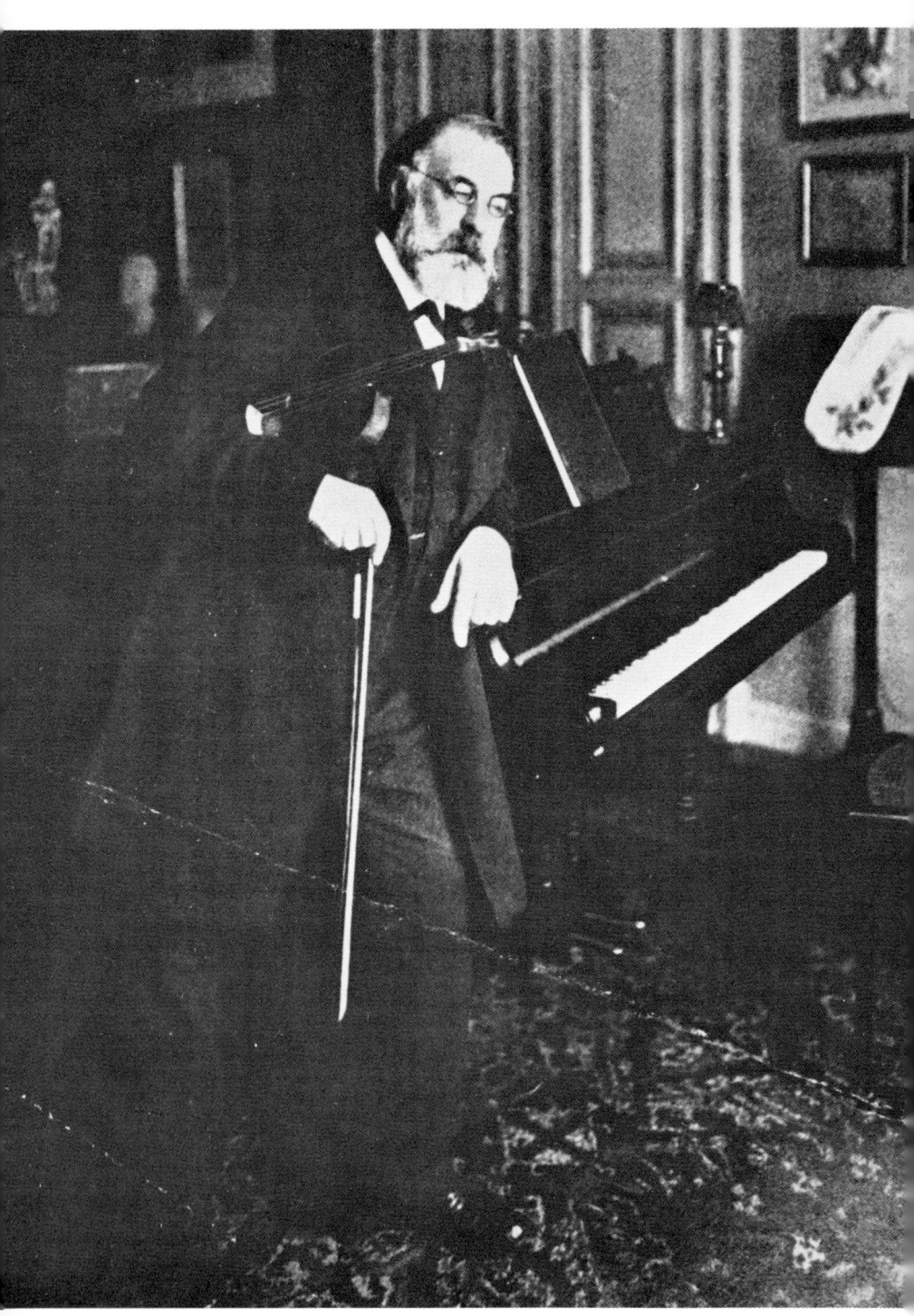
Joseph Joachim.

Pablo de Sarasate.

and, as has already been remarked, inspired many composers to create musical masterpieces.

In this book we can but briefly touch upon some of the more memorable episodes from the rich and varied life of the great artist.

We have described elsewhere the circumstances in which, in September 1886, Ysaÿe received the manuscript of the Sonata, a work of ineffable beauty, nobility, poet expressiveness and romantic fervor, completed by César Franck shortly before then.

César Franck (1822-90) who, like Ysaÿe, was born and educated at Liège, subsequently graduated from the Paris Conservatoire (he studied composition there with Antonin Reicha, a well-known Czech musician) and at a comparatively early age became a member of the French composition school on which he, in turn, exerted a marked influence. Romain Rolland said that there was "no name more pure than the name of that great and simple soul. Almost all who were near Franck experienced his irresistible magnetism."[18] Eugène Ysaÿe was no exception, and Romain Rolland was perfectly right in asserting that it was not only Franck's pupils (among whom were Vincent d'Indy, Ernest Chausson, Henri Duparc, Alexis de Castillon, Guillaume Lekeu, to name but a few) who experienced his influence, but also virtuoso artists, for example, the violinist Armand Parent[19] and Eugène Ysaÿe.

Long before he became known as composer (he has written, besides the Violin Sonata, a symphony, several symphonic poems and many chamber, organ, piano and vocal works), César Franck had been enjoying the reputation of an outstanding organist with a unique gift for improvisation. The penchant for improvisation is in evidence in many of his works, in particular, in the third movement (*Recitative-fantasia*) of the Sonata dedicated to Ysaÿe. Elements of the recitative and improvisatory style, expressive melodies in the Franck manner and perfect skill in contrapuntal writing are all present in Ysaÿe's own compositions.

Franck's music was in many respects in harmony with Ysaÿe's aesthetics, which explains his interest in the work of that venerable composer. Ysaÿe took upon himself the praiseworthy, but at the same time hard mission of acquainting the musical world with Franck's creations. There was a strong opposition on the part of the Wagner admirers and of those of the Belgian and French musicians and critics who were suspicious of the new school. Even the

Mischa Elman with Prof. Leopold Auer, circa 1923. Elman and Ysaÿe played a concert in New York's Hippodrome at the same time Jascha Heifetz was playing in New York. Both concerts filled their respective houses of over 3000. For details read **Heifetz** *by Dr. Herbert R. Axelrod.*

Emile Sauret, most famous now for his cadenza to the first Paganini Violin Concerto.

August Wilhelmj.

Boston Courier.

SUNDAY MORNING, JAN. 27, 1895.

The features of the Thirteenth Symphony concert would undoubtedly be considered the first appearance in Boston of Mr. Cesar Thomson, who has been dividing public attention with Mr. Ysaye as a solo violinist. He is an elder man, thick set, and with a physiognomy which suggests Du Maurier's drawings of Svengali in "Trilby," although he has a far pleasanter and more reasonable face, with the expression upon it of a scholar and not of a cynic. It is a quiet, concentrated face, over which pass few changes; the beard is slightly grizzled, and the hair is thick, heavy and black. Altogether the man's appearance interests and his passionless devotion to his task commands a respectful attention wherewith will be soon blended a great admiration and much astonishment. For when they who understand something of the difficulties of violin technique hear and see him perform such feats as he executed in the last movement of the concerto which he had chosen, they realize that they have before them an executant who cannot at present be surpassed. Because he meets and conquers the most stupendous problems of execution as if he were playing a simple exercise. There is absolutely no trickery, no display to catch the eye and no intimation but that all is plain and easy and might be so for any virtuoso of approved proficiency. There is not much depth to his art, if it be fair to judge him by this one hearing, nor is there much resplendency. He does not lack animation, incisiveness, emphasis or decision, and he has often a tender and gentle tone. But it is as a philosopher and not as a poet that he renders his music, and the dramatic quality seems to be quite lacking in his style. Beautiful perfection of method and unstrained command of all complexities have their value and their influence, and Mr. Thomson will be accepted and heard gladly and appreciatively as an artist of peculiar and eminent power. He took for this occasion Goldmark's concerto in A minor, opus 28, of which the first movement is dull, labored and unfavorable for a soloist's debut; the second contains a genial sostenuto air and the third with its tremendous cadenza offers a chance for all the virtuosity which the player possesses, thus bringing in a sensation along with the conclusion.

The Symphony was Dvorak's "From the New World," a second hearing of which confirms our previous impression that this composition must be considered as only theoretically and not illustratively relevant to the life and character of America, and as typical conditions in historical development instead of suggestive of musical forms and ideas. The allegro hints at the barbaric freedom of un-tutored peoples in its rhythms and phrases, which are at least as Oriental as Western, and might dropped consistently enough into a new "Lakme The larghetto breathes the native peaceful of a prin tive and unperturbed state. The scherzo is like t stirring up of irregular and vagrant forces, and t finale is an orderly confusion of diverse elemen characterized alternately by erratic excitement a prideful pomposity. The band played it all wel the wooden wind did wonders of grace and finis and Mr. Paur actually conceded a pianissimo at t end of the larghetto.

A short symphonic poem by Smetana was t novelty of the night, and created a fairly favoral impression. It is supposed to depict an episode in war between vengeful Amazons and guilty Man. I in the form of a knight, is smitten with compassi for the fair and injured Sarka (whose name t music bears) and she in return summons her sis after he and his comrades have fallen asleep bivouac, and remorselessly extirpate them.

Beethoven's second "Leonore" overture ended t concert. But although it was well played, it ma comparatively little effect, for want of contrast w the heavy and engrossing music which had gone fore. A light overture, preferably of the Fren school, would have been better and more encours ing.

For next Saturday are announced,—the overtu to "Don Giovanni," a suite by Lachner a Mendelssohn's "Italian" symphony.

The programme book for this last concert w one of the most indiscreet and unhelpful which I yet been printed—and that is saying a good de About the Dvorak symphony, concerning wh people would gladly have been informed, the were just three valueless lines, while upon familiar overture were expended five pages analytic academic details. Last year many pa were expended by the editor on reprints from works of Berlioz; this year many are being wast on the egotistical and inconsequential an biographic chatter of Mr. Martin Roeder, who manuscripts apparently do not find other acc easy to printers' ink. If this gentleman's c fessions and experiences had been "left in pen" of the translator and transcriber, a something inserted about Mr. Thomso life, education, work and success, the program book would have deserved well of the people w take it up expectantly from week to week. then its chief object seems to be to tell what peo do not need or desire to know and to avoid w might interest or inform them.

A favored few had an opportunity on Tues afternoon to hear the eminent New York baryto Powers, who sang at a private musicale arrange a Mt. Vernon street residence by Mrs. S. B. Fi Six times have public appearances been arran for Mr. Powers- with the Apollo and other club but some accident has always prevented. Now t one chance has been favorable, it is to be hoped t he will try again to make himself heard in Bost for he has a voice of rare fulness, resonance a brilliancy, mastered by a simple, sterling style earnest, truthful expression. Miss Marguerite F contributed in the charm and sympathy to the pl ure of the distinguished company, and Mrs. F herself was at the piano for the proper accompa ments.

HOWARD MALCOM TICKNO

Reviews from a scrapbook mentioning Ysaÿe and Thomson.

César Thomson, from a review in a New York paper.

Henri DuParc, one of César Franck's most capable students. Photo from Arazi. On the facing page: Jenö Hubay.

Sonata did not win immediate recognition. Ysaÿe later said that he had had to give many public performances before the Sonata took its fitting place in the world of music.

The Franck Sonata was given its first public performance at the *Cercle Artistique* in Brussels on December 16, 1886, in the presence of the composer. The all-Franck program included his Quintet, Prelude, Chorale and Fugue, and the Sonata for Violin and Piano played by Eugène Ysaÿe and Marie Bordes-Pène. As Alfred Marchot[20] writes in his reminiscences, Franck "was at a loss how to thank his interpreters, especially Ysaÿe, for revealing to the world

The famous violinist Armand Parent (1863-1934). See footnote 19 at the end of this chapter.

the masterpieces that had been hitherto unknown or not appreciated."

When Armand Parent, who was present at the concert, turned to Franck remarking that Ysaÿe's playing, although really wonderful, did not conform to the composer's directions, Franck replied: "This may be so, but from now on it will be impossible to play it in any other way. Don't worry, it is Ysaÿe who is right." This shows the esteem in which the composer held Eugène Ysaÿe, and how highly he prized the young artist's comprehension of his work.

Shortly afterwards Ysaÿe played the Sonata at the *Société Nationale de Musique* in Paris, and early in 1888, at the Twenty Club in Brussels, after which he often performed it in all musical centers of Europe and America. His partners in the Sonata were his brother Théophile Ysaÿe and afterwards, for many years, Raoul Pugno. He played it with other pianists as well; in Russia Ysaÿe's partner in the Franck Sonata was Alexander Goldenweiser.

The venerable composer was filled with happiness at hearing his work performed with such perfection. Vincent d'Indy (1852-1931), a pupil and one of the most important of Franck's followers (he dedicated his first quartet to Ysaÿe), wrote that Ysaÿe "carried the Sonata round the world like a torch and gave Franck one of the few earthly joys he knew."[21]

Ysaÿe's playing was so sincere, so full of feeling and so convincing, he personalized it to such an extent that the inspired music acquired new colors and captivated the listeners. The Franck Sonata, as interpreted by Ysaÿe, influenced even contemporary painting, sculpture and literature (Proust, Mauclair and others). According to one of Ysaÿe's biographers, Constantin Meunier, the famous Belgian painter and sculptor asked the artist to extemporize on themes from the Franck Sonata while he was working on Ysaÿe's bas-relief. Eugène Ysaÿe and Ernest Chausson are known to have played the Sonata in Rodin's studio.

Eugène Ysaÿe and his quartet repeatedly played Franck's Quartet and Quintet.[22] He also conducted the master's Symphony in D minor in London. This time, using the baton as he had the bow, he succeeded in conveying with equal conviction the dramatic contrasts, romantic fervor, agitated lyricism and improvisatory essence of that work. The grateful composer gave him a copy inscribed: "To my ideal interpreter."

The haut relief of Ysaÿe executed by Constantin Meunier in silver. It is to be found in the Museum of Ysaÿe in Liege. Photo courtesy of Arazi.

In 1901-4, Ysaÿe, then at the zenith of his powers, made frequent trips to England where his concerts were a series of brilliant triumphs. He appeared as soloist, in sonatas with his friend and constant partner Raoul Pugno,[23] and also as conductor (in particular, he conducted Beethoven's *Fidelio* at the Covent Garden Theatre several times).

Celebrations in honor of Camille Saint-Saëns (1835-1921) were held in London in March 1901 and Ysaÿe was invited to participate. In the presence of the composer, Ysaÿe performed his Third Violin Concerto and *Rondo Capriccioso*. This is what he wrote to his wife: "I shall always remember this concert as one of the supreme moments of my career. Saint-Saëns was wildly applauded and after the concert (it may be assumed from this that Saint-Saëns himself conducted the Concerto with Ysaÿe as the soloist.—L.G.) we had to come back six times holding hands. My own hands behaved well and my head was remarkably clear. Colonne, who was present, told me that he had never heard me play so well. There was similar enthusiasm after the *Jeunesse d'Hercule*.[24] In fact the whole thing was a triumphant success for that great-hearted French musician, Saint-Saëns, and at the same time it was a great pleasure for me to feel that I had contributed toward it."

Then Ysaÿe went on: "This morning at the station, the aged master embraced me affectionately, and when I realized the warmth of his feelings for me I felt immensely proud, far more proud than all the applause of the crowd or the praise of silly journalists could ever make me."

Shortly after this concert the Royal Philharmonic Society awarded Ysaÿe its Gold Medal. Among the great musicians who had this honor conferred on them by the Society (founded in 1813) were Beethoven, Brahms, Saint-Saëns, Grieg and later Dvorak, Bruch, Casals, Cortot, Toscanini, Stravinsky, Rachmaninov, Glazunov, Prokofiev and Shostakovich. Of violinists only Joachim had received the Gold Medal before Ysaÿe and after him—Sarasate and Ondricek, Kubelik and Kreisler.[25]

It has already been mentioned that at the time young Ysaÿe was staying in Paris he became friends with Saint-Saëns, "that incarnation of the classic French spirit," to quote Romain Rolland.[26] The eminent French composer, who had lent the welcome moral support to the young Belgian violinist at the outset of the latter's

Franz Ondricek was responsible for having Paganini's grave opened so he could view the corpse.

Raoul Pugno.

Jan Kubelik, and on the facing page, Fritz Kreisler, both recipients of the Gold Medal awarded by the Royal Philharmonic Society.

The photograph used for promotion of the Joachim Quartet.

Above: An Ysaÿe letter signed in 1904 with the Godinne-Chanterelle postscript. On the facing page: an excerpt from a review of Willy Burmester's Berlin recital.

WILLY BURMESTER.

BURMESTER IN BERLIN.

When Willy Burmester, violinist, plays in Berlin the house is almost invariably sold out in advance. Such was the case on the occasion of his last Berlin recital. Mr. Burmester played the Schubert D Major Sonata, the Paganini D Major Concerto, a group of his own arrangement (Beethoven Minuet, Mehul Gavotte, Haydn Minuet and three waltzes by Clementi, Hummel and Weber respectively), a Järnefelt "Berceuse" of his own arrangement and the Saint-Saëns "Rondo Capriccioso." The enthusiasm was so great as almost to border upon frenzy, and yet the audience was made up largely of the fashionable element.

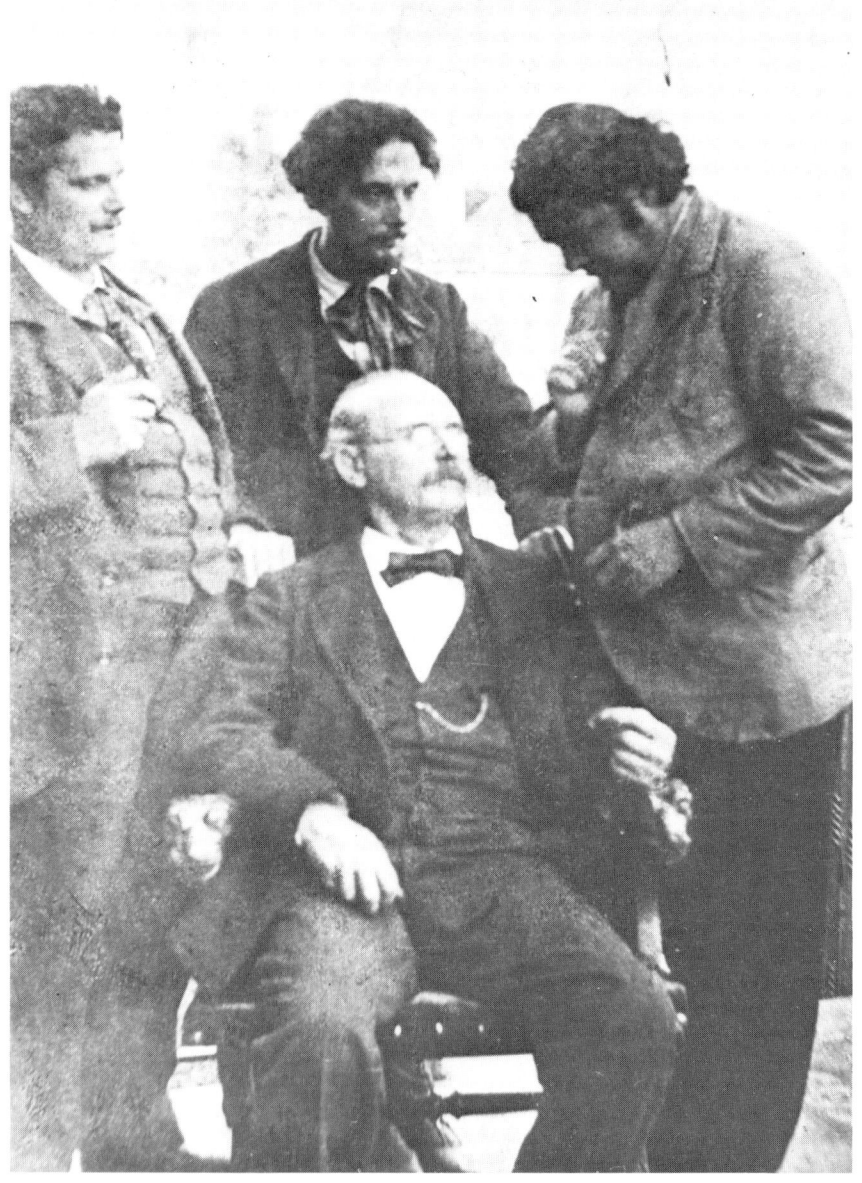

"Accord parfait" shows Nicolas and his three sons: Joseph (1852-1929), Eugène (1858-1931), and Theophile (1865-1918). Photo courtesy of Arazi. On the facing page: An advertisement from **The Musical Courier.**

New York, January 28, 1898.

VICTOR THRANE

wishes to announce that he has assumed the SOLE and EXCLUSIVE Management of

YSAYE,
PUGNO and
GÉRARDY.

YSAYE.

PUGNO.

GÉRARDY.

Address all communications relative to these ARTISTS to

VICTOR THRANE,

33 Union Square, West
(Decker Building),

: : : : : : NEW YORK.

Telephone: No. 2693
18th Street.

Charles Camille Saint-Saëns preferred to leave out the "Charles."

Johannes Brahms.

career, revealed to Ysaÿe the intentions embodied in his Third Violin Concerto, one of his instrumental masterpieces,[27] and had in turn found in Ysaÿe an incomparable interpreter of his creations, one whom he esteemed very highly.

This is clear from Saint-Saëns' letters to Ysaÿe[28] in one of which, written on September 20, 1899, he said:

"My dear friend,

"You were divine, marvelous—that's all one can say, but it is not all: the publisher now would like to hear the quartet[29] and you yourself have said that you wanted to play it. I suggested next Tuesday and he readily agreed. So if you can do us this great honor, we shall meet at 19 avenue de l'Alma (it is high up but there is a lift) at 4 o'clock; you will work with your bows and then everybody will meet again for dinner at my house at 7 o'clock.

"I am really ashamed at the inconvenience I am causing you with my vile music.

"Please let me hear from you.

"Give my best regard to Mme. Ysaÿe.

Affectonately yours,

C. Saint-Saëns."

The composer expressed his gratitude to Eugène Ysaÿe by dedicating this quartet to him; Ysaÿe in turn assured the quartet's success on the concert stage by his performance of it.

According to Antoine Ysaÿe, Saint-Saëns dedicated to his father two more compositions: *La Muse et le Poète* for violin, cello and orchestra, Op. 132, and Sonata for Violin and Piano.[30] The first performance of *La Muse et le Poète*, composed in 1909, was given by Eugène Ysaÿe and Joseph Hollman,[31] and it was with these two artists that Saint-Saëns played his Piano Trio.

This is what Saint-Saëns wrote to Ysaÿe about his performance of the *Muse* and the brilliant *Rondo Capriccioso:*

"Paris 24 Oct., 1910

"You were marvelous, my great friend! You expressed the idea of my *Muse* as though you yourself were its author. And the *Rondo* which all the world plays well you managed to play better than all the world.

"What miracle made your tone still more beautiful than it was before!? That wonderful tone which had never been heard until then. I was not the only one who noticed it.

Pablo Casals autographed this photo to the author.

Efrem Zimbalist and his son, the famous television personality, Efrem Zimbalist, Jr. in 1978.

Igor Stravinsky.

Thrilling in their power and purity of tone, and true to every vibration of the strings, Ysaye's Columbia recordings are dramatically *natural* presentations of the art of the fiery Belgian genius. And Ysaye's records are representative of all

COLUMBIA DOUBLE-DISC RECORDS

Whatever class of music you prefer: vocal, instrumental; solo, ensemble; concert, operatic, dance, orch stral, you get splendid, rich, *natural* reproductions on Columbia Double-Disc Records. They will play—*perfectly*—on your machine. You can get them—*everywhere*—at Columbia dealers'. Listen to them *today*. "Hearing is Believing."

New Columbia Records on sale the 20th of every month.

A Columbia Record promotional advertisement.

Alexander Glazunov.

EUGENE YSAYE
THE GREAT BELGIAN MASTER, AS A GUEST OF
The Rudolph Wurlitzer Company
AT THE RECENT OPENING OF THEIR
OLD VIOLIN STUDIOS
115 W. 40th Street, just East of Broadway
NEW YORK

Said: "*The truly remarkable thing about your collection is the fact that there is not even one mediocre violin in it.*"

THE RUDOLPH WURLITZER COMPANY
115 W. 40th Street   NEW YORK

Ysaÿe endorsed Wurlitzer in this advertisement. 1917.

Eugène Ysaÿe with Ernest Chausson in Lusancy about 1899.

"It is a real happiness to have such interpreters.
                    Yours, grateful and devoted,
                    C. Saint-Saëns."

Strong ties of friendship and creative interests united Ysaÿe with Ernest Chausson, a pupil and adherent of Franck, who was older than Ysaÿe by a mere three years. Chausson was a more prominent representative of that trend in French music which set itself against Wagner's influence and which Romain Rolland defined as "The Renovation."

Thanks to Ysaÿe's tireless efforts, the name of this talented composer was becoming increasingly popular in France and Belgium beginning with the 1890's. His works were performed many times with Ysaÿe's participation at the Twenty Club's concerts in Brussels. Thus on March 4, 1892, Eugène Ysaÿe, the Ysaÿe

The Ysaÿe family, left to right: Carry; Louise, his wife; Thesey; Ysaÿe; Theo; and Antoine with an American flag. The photo was taken in Godinne in 1904. On the facing page, Ysaÿe and his wife sent out this autographed photo inscribed "Andante amoroso . . . for two violins without accompaniment."

When he was 37 years old Ysaÿe still used a bicycle. Photo courtesy of Arazi.

The Ysaÿe Chamber Music Ensemble in the 1890's. Left to right: Victor Thrane, Ysaÿe's earlier manager; Ysaÿe; Jean Gerardy, cellist; Henri Marteau, violinist, and Lachaume, French pianist.

Quartet (with his pupil Biermasz) and August Pierret, pianist, played for the first time Chausson's *Concert* for violin, piano and string quartet, one of his finest works. This highly successful premiere at the Twenty Club may be said to have marked the beginning of Chausson's popularity. Shortly before this Chausson wrote to Ysaÿe:

"My dear Ysaÿe:

"D'Indy told me that if your trip to Berlin did not take too much of your time you would agree to play my *Concert* at the second concert of the Twenty Club. I needn't tell you how glad I should be in such a case. It is always a joy for a composer when you play his works and I had an occasion to experience this joy a few years ago when you consented to perform my trio at Mme. Borde's concert. This time, however, the work in question is of much more importance to me. I worked on it very long and have a firm conviction that it is the best thing I have written up to now. You understand how necessary it is for me to have this work presented to the Brussels public in the best possible way. I cannot imagine better performers than you and your splendid quartet. I shall not conceal from you that it was with you and your faultless interpretation in mind that I was writing the *Concert*. Consequently, something in it belongs to you for, without you, I probably should not have written it. I hope you will let me dedicate it to you and that you will fulfill your role of coworker to the end by finally breathing artistic life into a work that has been inspired by you.

Cordially yours,
Ernest Chausson."[32]

After the performance of Chausson's *Concert* in Brussels, the Ysaÿe Quartet was invited to Paris where four concerts were given at the Salle Pleyel, whose programs featured, besides the Chausson *Concert*, the Quartet and Quintet by Franck, the String Quartet (dedicated to Ysaÿe) and the Piano Quartet by Vincent d'Indy, two Piano Quartets by Fauré (1854-1924) and the Quartet by Alexis de Castillon (1838-73).

While the music of these composers, Franck's followers, was criticized in the Paris press, the performers won unqualified praise: "These four most excellent artists made a great impression by their impeccable ensemble, they were perfect in every respect. The Ysaÿe Quartet, a quartet of virtuosos, merits all the praises

Kreisler and Ysaÿe celebrate together in Brussels, 1907. Photos courtesy of Arazi.

Eugène Ysaÿe was an ardent cyclist. Circa 1904. Courtesy of Arazi.

which are lavished on it and the memory of these artists will long remain in the hearts of the lovers of chamber music who applauded them with such enthusiasm."[33]

Chausson had promised to write something for Ysaÿe, so he tried to master the nature of expressive media best suited to the violin by studying the Violin Sonatas of Bach. Ysaÿe reminded his friend of his promise and advised him to read a collection of Walloon Farandoles. The composer liked the material in it and intended to use it for a violin concerto.

Chausson chanced to hear the *Poème Elégiaque* just then composed by Ysaÿe. He was struck by this music and decided that his work for Ysaÿe should follow the same style. It seemed to him that the form of a poem was best suited to the artist's character and style of performance. In 1896 he completed his *Poèm* for violin and orchestra (or piano), which he dedicated to Ysaÿe and which has been adorning the violin repertoire ever since.

This is what Debussy wrote about this work of Chausson:

"It shows the best qualities of his music. Its formal freedom in no way contradicts its harmonious proportions. Nothing can be more touching than the tender reverie of the ending of this *Poème* where the music is beyond anything external and descriptive and is the expression of pure feeling.[34]

On receiving the long-awaited piece Ysaÿe wrote to Chausson: "I have received the *Poème*. I like it very much and I am quite certain that it will be a great success. I am also sure that this work is one of the finest things you have written."

Chausson's *Poème* was first performed at Nancy on November 27, 1896, under the direction of Guy Ropartz (who had dedicated to Ysaÿe a Sonata for Violin and Piano, his First Quartet and First Symphony). Subsequently Eugène Ysaÿe gave brilliant performances of this work with Emile Jaques-Dalcroze on their tour of Germany. (Incidentally, Albeniz arranged with the Leipzig publisher, Breitkopf, to have the *Poème* published.) This work became one of Ysaÿe's greatest favorites, and in his letters the composer referred to it as the "Mon-Ton poème." Indeed, the Belgian violinist's magic bow, his unforgettable art of a true poet, had served as the impulse for the appearance of this inspired piece. And, on the composer's request, Ysaÿe had marked in the score the bowing and phrasing, the great artist's interpretation, beginning with the

Elman, Enesco, Heifetz, Spalding, Morini, Francescatti.

Famous violinists.

Paganini, Bull, Vieuxtemps, Joachim, Wieniawski, Sarasate.

Famous violinists.

1. FRANZ VON VECSEY. 2. JACQUES THIBAUD. 3. CÉSAR THOMSON. 4. CAMILLA URSO. 5. RAOUL VIDAS. 6. GIUSEPPE TARTINI. 7. ANTONIO VIVALDI. 8. PAUL VIARDOT.

Famous violinists.

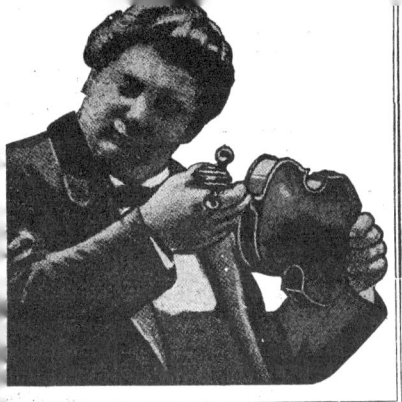

YSAYE
And the House of
WURLITZER

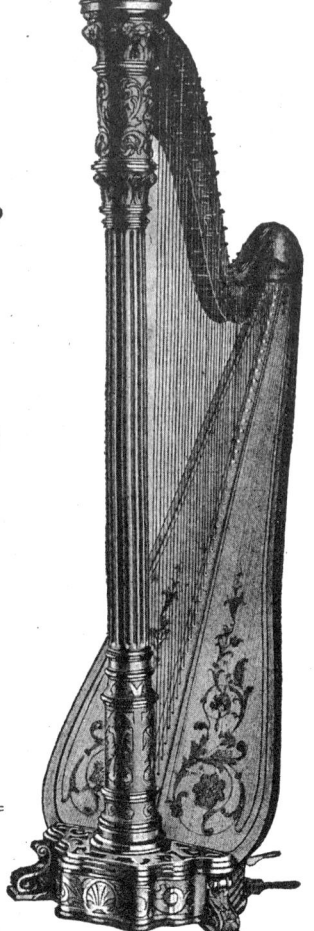

WHEN in January, 1917, the great master Eugene Ysaye was present at the opening of the Wurlitzer Old Violin Studio in New York, he wrote in the golden book of the Wurlitzer House:

"*The most marvelous thing about your collection, my dear Wurlitzer, is that there is not even a mediocre violin amongst them.*"

We will send our book of the master pieces of Old Violin Makers upon request.

Builders of
**HIGH GRADE PIANOS
HARPS AND ORGANS**

The
Rudolph Wurlitzer Co.
CINCINNATI   NEW YORK   CHICAGO
121 E. Fourth St. 115 W. 40th St. 239 So. Wabash

Ysaÿe endorses Wurlitzer in this 1918 ad.

BERLIN

**LUITPOLD ST. 24,
BERLIN W.,
OCTOBER 30, 1904.**

YSAYE was the magnet that drew an audience which overflowed the Philharmonie at the second Nikisch Philharmonic concert Monday evening. His numbers were Bach's E major concerto, Chausson's "Poem" in E flat, and his own arrangement of Saint-Saëns' "Etude in Form of a Waltz." Ysaye played the concerto with wonderful breadth and repose. In the adagio he was enchanting! Such nobility of tone! Such warmth! Such esprit! And yet some of the Berlin critics did not like him in the concerto; they said it was too sentimental and "weichlich." What absurdity! If a violinist does not "scratch" and play out of tune, and does not reveal such a tedious conception of the work that the audience goes to sleep, then in the eyes of the critics it is not Bach playing.

Chausson's "Poem," for violin and orchestra, affords the soloist much opportunity, for it abounds in cantilena and recitative. As a composition it is handicapped by poverty of ideas. The Saint-Saëns waltz etude, an effective piece, was played with remarkable virtuosity and with many subtle touches, but after all it is not idiomatic violin music, nor is it very grateful, and I should not care to hear anyone but Ysaye play it. His success was, of course, immense, as usual.

Nikisch, besides accompanying Ysaye matchlessly, led Beethoven's "Coriolan" overture, Vincent d'Indy's "Istar" variations, and the Mendelssohn "Italian" symphony. Vincent d'Indy's "Istar" was given here for the first time. I heard the work with the Ysaye orchestra under the composer's direction in Brussels seven years ago. The underlying poetic idea is taken from an old Assyrian-Babylonic epos called "Istar's Descent Into Hades." As program music it cannot be called a remarkable illustration of the text, but as absolute music it is an interesting piece, although its charm lies more in its piquant harmonies and rhythms than in the value of the musical thoughts. "Istar" and the symphony were admirably done by Nikisch.

Tuesday evening Mischa Elman, the new violin prodigy, gave his second concert in the Singakademie to a sold out house. He played the Mendelssohn concerto, the Saint-Saëns "Rondo Capriccioso," the Beethoven G major romance, and Paganini's "Moto Perpetuo." Some things Elman plays like a great artist; in others, as, for instance, the first movement of the concerto, he shows a lack of maturity. His playing of the Saint-Saëns rondo and the Paganini piece would have done credit to any living violinist. The appearance of Elman and Vecsey has settled one thing to my mind, and that is that the Berlin public loves a sensation just as much as the New York public or any other public. That is, the Berlin public at large, for the concerts of Elman and Vecsey are attended by people that otherwise never go to concerts. I have been an habitué of the Berlin concert halls for ten years, and am perfectly familiar with the concert audiences. There were many people at Elman's last concert that were never in a Berlin concert hall before. They heard his first class violin playing, but would they have paid their five marks to hear the same or better playing by a full grown man? No.

Do they go when Ysaye or Burmester plays? Never. The masses the world over can be drawn out only by something sensational. They will not pay five pfennigs to hear the best violin playing the world affords, but they will willingly pay five marks to hear a boy of twelve do what few men of forty can do. It is not a question of violin playing or music at all, for these audiences are not musical and do not care for music. They go to see the sensation of the day. As a down East farmer who attended an Ole Bull concert in New York over fifty years ago put it: "Ole Bull? Why that's the man wot I gin a hull dollar to see."

It is said that Elman will return to his teacher, Leopold Auer, January 1, and retire to private life for further development. It is to be hoped that this is true. It would be a deplorable thing if such a genius as Elman were to be systematically exploited in public. That must mean his ruin. Already he looks worn and sallow. How can a child undergo the excitement attendant upon frequent public appearances and ovations, and how can he play with such feeling without wearing out his little body? It is physically impossible. After all, this public exploitation serves generally only to enrich some manager, the child rarely being the chief beneficiary.

Joachim sat an attentive listener in Elman's concert. His thoughts must have wandered back to the time when he,

THE VIOLINIST OF THE FUTURE.

over sixty years ago, as a boy of Elman's age, achieved a similar triumph in a Philharmonic concert under Mendelssohn's direction in London. Luckily for Joachim, Mendelssohn saw to it that such a public performance did not recur for several years. Joachim undoubtedly could have made a sensational career as a prodigy, but Mendelssohn prevented it and the world is the gainer. It is to be hoped that Auer will prevent Elman's further public career at present and so save this genius to the world.

Marie Berg, the well known soprano, sang on Thursday evening at the concert given by Dr. Reimann in the Emperor William Memorial Church. The lady has a sweet, flexible voice which is under good control, and she has a whole sound, warm delivery. Her style of singing at once reveals the artist, the true musician, and that is something that cannot be said of all singers, to put it mildly. Miss Berg produces a good, pure tone, she sings in perfect tune, she phrases artistically, and she puts an individual note into everything she does.

Lula Mysz-Gmeiner gave an evening of "Lieder" at Beethoven Hall Tuesday. This lady is justly one of the most popular singers in Germany today. She has a beautiful mezzo-soprano voice, which she uses with consummate skill, and she sings with great warmth and intelligence. There is a frank, breezy air of largeness and naturalness about her whole personality that is refreshing. She had a full house and a big success.

The same evening Alexander Petschnikoff played at Bechstein Hall a new sonata by Hermann Zilcher, with the composer at the piano. The work does not call for extended comment. Petschnikoff also played works by himself, by Mozart and by Tschaikowsky. He has the same sweet, singing tone as formerly, and he plays with much warmth, but manly vigor is lacking. It is perfumed and monotonous playing. Petschnikoff seems to have lost his hold on the Berlin public.

The Hekking Trio gave their second concert Thursday evening. I heard Hekking and Schnabel play the Saint-Saëns C minor sonata for 'cello and piano, and a most finished performance it was, far more so than the composition deserved, for it is one of the most uninspired things the illustrious Frenchman ever penned.

A new Swedish soprano, Signe von Rappe, a very tall, good looking girl from Stockholm, made her Berlin début at this concert in a group of Schumann songs. She has a pretty, sweet, fresh voice, and she has learned a good deal, but she seemed to be suffering from stage fright, for she failed to enter into her work with that mastery which bespeaks conscious power and carries conviction.

The same evening a new American pianist, Ethel Newcomb, of New York, a Leschetizky pupil, made her début with the Philharmonic Orchestra at the Singakademie, playing no less than three concertos, the Schumann, the Chopin E minor and the Saint-Saëns C minor. Miss Newcomb is a very talented girl, and she evidently has made the most of her opportunity during the years she spent in Vienna. She has a very clean, crisp, accurate technic, a big tone, a decided sense of rhythm and much brilliancy. Miss Newcomb played the romance of the Chopin concerto with genuine poetry. Her passage work in the finale was very clear and telling. The Saint-Saëns C minor concerto is not a grateful task for the pianist, being far inferior both as music and as a display piece to the G minor concerto by the same composer. Miss Newcomb had more than average success with the audience.

Jean Oppenheim, a fourteen year old 'cellist from Paris, made his initial bow to a Berlin audience in the hall of the Royal High School. He was accompanied by the Berlin Tonkünstler Orchestra, the orchestra Strauss formerly conducted. Oppenheim played the Saint-Saëns and Goltermann concertos with orchestra and the Bach "Air" and Davidoff's "Am Springbrunnen," with piano.

Oppenheim is a lad who deserves encouragement. He has already acquired a remarkable dexterity on his unwieldy instrument. Such a technic on the 'cello in one of his years is far more difficult than on the violin, on ac-

THE MUSICAL COURIER.

count of the big intervals and the great strength of finger required. The boy has a pure tone of good quality, although it is quite small as yet. He has plenty of assurance, and if he develops and acquires more depth of mind and soul he will become a 'cellist of the first rank.

≈ ≈

Emma Calvé made her début in "Carmen" at the Royal Opera Friday night. The house was sold out at three times the ordinary prices. It is said that Calvé received 5,000 marks for the one appearance. Opera goers in America know far better than we do here how this fascinating Frenchwoman sings "Carmen," for over there she sang the role scores of times when in her prime. The best years of her life were spent in America, for it cannot be denied that she now is passé as a singer. Her voice shows unmistakable signs of wear. Her acting was superb. She gives many characteristic and wholly individual touches to the role, yet her acting seems to be prompted by her head and not by her heart, notwithstanding that she makes the impression of being a very impulsive woman. It impresses the keen observer as being all cold calculation for effect. Calvé clearly is too accustomed to the "starring" system of America, for she sang at and to the public for the most part, and paid too little attention to the ensemble, forgetting (or not knowing) that in Germany the ensemble is everything. Calvé was called out innumerable times, but the applause was by no means general, and she failed to impress a large part of the audience. Berlin is apt to be a little cool to celebrities who have made their reputations before appearing here.

≈ ≈

At its first concert the Singakademie Oratorio Society gave three works, Cherubini's "Missa Solemnis," and "Sehnsucht" and "Totenklage" by the conductor Georg Schumann. Cherubini's work sounds strange to modern ears. Parts of it are quite antiquated and shallow, but there are other parts of great interest. Some of the choruses are beautiful, particularly the "Crucifixus," in which the simple melody of the voices is most ingeniously and effectively accompanied by the muted strings and the woodwind. The chorus sang finely, but the soloists were not so good.

Schumann's "Sehnsucht," for chorus and orchestra, is well conceived and well written work. It opens with an unaccompanied chorus, which does not make a very favorable impression, but there is a steady crescendo in the work until it closes with a pompous and effective employment of the entire orchestral apparatus and the full chorus fortissimo. I wrote about Schumann's "Totenklage" when it was performed at the Frankfort Music Festival last May.

George R. Tillson, a young American organist, gave a concert at the Luther Church, playing works by Bach, Max Reger and Liszt. He is a gifted youth and played exceedingly well. He is studying organ with Franz Grimcke and composition with Stillman Kelly.

≈ ≈

Willy Burmester celebrated the tenth anniversary of his first Berlin success with a concert in the Singakademie last night. It was just ten years ago that the great violinist created a sensation with a Paganini program in the same hall. I well remember that memorable evening. Yesterday Burmester played a classical program, very much in contrast to his program of a decade ago. His selections this time were the E major concerto, the "Chaconne," "Air" and a gavotte by Bach; the Beethoven G major romance, a gavotte by Padre Martini and menuets by Handel and Mozart, the last three pieces being arranged by Burmester.

It was interesting to hear two such great violinists as Ysaye and Burmester play the Bach concerto during the same week. Burmester took the first allegro at a much faster tempo than his Belgian colleague, and the finale, on the other hand, considerably slower. Both played the adagio at about the same tempo. Burmester makes a real allegro of the first movement, while Ysaye plays it quite moderately and with great breadth. Burmester played the entire work and the "Chaconne" with wonderful clearness and plasticity. His infallible technic, pure tone, energetic accent and healthy conception revealed his absolute command of the composition and the instrument, and bespoke a potent mentality.

≈ ≈

The same evening Arrigo Serato, the Italian, played a new violin concerto in B minor by his countryman, A. d'Ambrosio. It is well written for the violin and fairly well instrumentated in Wagnerian style, but it contains no ideas of importance. The first movement is bombastic and shallow in the orchestra, and the solo violin has meaningless recitatives. The andante is commonplace, but the spirited finale shows some originality in the themes and passage work of the violin, as well as in the employment of the orchestra. It is not a concerto that will find its way into the repertory of violinists.

Serato played it admirably. He has a beautiful, warm cantilena, and his tone is larger than formerly. He has a good left hand and a supple bowing. But a little more esprit in his interpretation would not be amiss.

≈ ≈

The twin sisters Christman, of the Moscow Imperial Opera, have been singing with great success at the Magdeburg Opera. They will make their first public appearance in Berlin at the Philharmonie tomorrow night.

Georg Schnéevoigt, the gifted Finnish conductor, led a Kaim concert in Munich recently with enormous success. The Munich Neuste Nachrichten of October 19 writes: "Schneevoigt is a conductor of the very first rank, who combines all the qualities, without exception, that go to make up a great orchestral leader." The critic then enumerates the Finn's artistic virtues in detail, and winds up by saying: "I must confess that I have not for years heard the 'Leonore' overture, No. 3, so enchantingly played, with such dramatic power and such wonderful finish of detail." This, from the pen of one of the leading critics of Germany, in the city where they are continually hearing Weingartner and Mottl, means a good deal. It is praise of which Schneevoigt may well be proud.

Georg Fergusson, the Scotch-American baritone, has achieved one of the most remarkable successes in Berlin as a singing teacher that ever came to my notice. He started in here some eight years ago in a very modest way, without any influential friends, without "pull," introduction or anything to help him but his own merit. Even his public appearances in Berlin were not in his favor, as he was in bad voice each time, and could not do himself justice. Yet he has taught so thoroughly and so conscientiously his exhaustive knowledge of voice production that he has gained an enviable reputation for accomplishing results with his pupils. Today he has far more applications for lessons than he can accept, notwithstanding the fact that he is one of the highest priced vocal teachers in Berlin. Fergusson's success is solid and well deserved. He has gained a strong and permanent foothold in the German capital.

≈ ≈

Fergusson's chief assistant is Kirk Towns, who was a teacher at the Chicago Musical College the past two years. Mr. Towns, with his wife, has lately settled in Berlin, having rented a nice apartment in the Münchner strasse. Besides preparing pupils for Fergusson, Towns has also quite a large private class of pupils, and is doing well here. He will remain in Berlin several years at least, and possibly permanently.

≈ ≈

Weber's "Oberon" was revived at the Bremen Opera October 16, and made a fine impression. It was given in the same form as at the gala performance in Wiesbaden before the Emperor a few years ago. This arrangement unquestionably is a great improvement over the original, which Weber composed expressly for Covent Garden, and with which he was not satisfied himself, because too many concessions had to be made to the English public. In the new form the dialogues have been rewritten and treated melodramatically, the number of changes in the scenes reduced, and the dramatic effects heightened, so that the work as a whole makes a much more vivid impression.

≈ ≈

The Bohemian Quartet have made a permanent repertory number of Kaun's new piano quintet.

≈ ≈

A new Roumanian music paper has been started in Bucharest. It is called the Revista Musicala si Teatrala, and the publisher is Jean Feder.

≈ ≈

Mrs. Wilhelm Eylau, a new piano teacher, has recently settled in Berlin, and she evidently came with serious intent, for her influence is already beginning to be felt. She started here in August with two pupils, and now she has fifteen. Mrs. Eylau is an American and a very charming and very energetic young woman. There is surely room for her here, as she does what no other piano teacher in Berlin does—she makes a specialty of so called hopeless cases. Anyone with large, flexible hands, strong fingers and loose wrists can acquire technic and tone with comparative ease, but with those unfortunate aspirants who have small, stiff hands, and weak fingers, it is a different matter. Mrs. Eylau makes a specialty of loosening and strengthening the wrists and fingers and of imparting to pianists who have a hard touch and tone the art of acquiring an elastic touch and a soft, round, full tone. Although Mrs. Eylau makes a specialty of these things, she is an artist and not a one sided specialist. After she has prepared a pupil for a composition technically she gives her attention to the interpretation just as thoroughly. Mrs.

D. RAHTER, LEIPZIG.
Works of **P. Tschaikowsky.**
Catalogue, with Portrait and Biography, 23 pages, sent post free on application.

GEORG
FERGUSSON
BARITONE.
Vocal Instruction.
KLEIST STRASSE 27, BERLIN W.

Prof. RUDOLF SCHMALFELD,
Mme. MARGARETHE SCHMALFELD-VAHSEL,
Kammersaengerin,
VOCAL INSTRUCTION.
Voice building by means of concentrated tone.
Specialty made of Restoring Lost and Injured Voices and of Wagner singing.
Lessons given in German, English, French and Italian.
Bamberger St. 4, BERLIN, W.

Clifford **WILEY**
BARITONE.
"THE STANLEY," PHONE:
124-126 West 47th Street. 4249 38th Street.

LENA DORIA DEVINE
Vocal Instruction.
METHOD OF FRANCESCO LAMPERTI.
Teacher of BLANCHE DUFFIELD, Coloratura Soprano, Soloist Sousa's Band several seasons; MARIE SIERSDORFER, Soprano with Conried Metropolitan Opera Co.; JOSEPHINE MILDENBERG, Soprano; MARIE LOUISE GEHLE, Contralto; LOUISE TOMPKINS, Coloratura Soprano; WILHELMINA MUENCKE, Soprano; JOSEPH MILLER, Basso; FRED'K BUTTERFIELD ANGELL, Baritone; EDWARD W. GRAY, Tenor, and other successful singers.
STUDIO: 136 FIFTH AVENUE, NEW YORK.

New York College of Music
128-130 East 58th Street.
(Formerly ALEX. LAMBERT.)
Directors: Carl Hein, August Freemcke.
Private instruction in Piano, Singing, Violin, 'Cello and all branches of music, by a faculty unsurpassed for its excellence.
SPECIAL DEPARTMENT FOR BEGINNERS.
All instrumental and vocal students receive free instruction in harmony, counterpoint, vocal sight reading, ensemble playing and free admission to concerts, lectures, etc., etc.
Students received daily. Catalog sent on application.

A reprinted pair of pages from The Musical Courier *of 1904. It reports of Ysaÿe's success in Berlin. It also mentioned Burmester's concert as well as information on Elman and other famous artists. Berlin was, at that time, one of the music capitals of the world.*

deepest penetration into each phrase and ending with the modifications he considered necessary in order to make the music better suited to the violin in the solo cadenzas. The genuinely creative work resulting from the composer's and the interpreter's efforts impressed the listeners as a well-integrated whole.

Ysaÿe popularized the Chausson *Poème* in various ways. When Ysaÿe was invited to appear at one of Colonne's concerts, Ysaÿe consented on the condition that he would play the *Poème*. The talented composer was in a dejected mood at the time: his work was not going as he wished it and nobody would play his music. The news of the projected concert buoyed Chausson up and he wrote to Ysaÿe:

"I am so pleased that you are going to play my *Poème* at the Colonne concert. It is the first time that my name will appear on the program of the Châtelet, which makes your news more than welcome. It has reached me at the precise moment when I am rather depressed, and am working without obtaining the slightest result. I can produce absolutely nothing which gives me any satisfaction. Your news has cheered me considerably . . . your confidence in me gives me courage."

Chausson's hopes, however, were not to be realized: on June 10, 1899, his life was tragically cut short in a street accident. A week later the concert took place and Ysaÿe, deeply grieved at the death of his friend, wrote to his family:

"Today on the 18th of June, 1899, three thousand people who were told of the composer's death listened to the *Poème* in concentration, with awe and deep emotion which I sensed to become more tense as its sad, exalted and plaintive melodies were wringing tears from my own heart."

The artistic results of this friendship between the two great musicians were, besides the *Poème*, the *Poème de l'Amour et de la Mer* and the *Concert* in D *(Sextour)*, written for Eugène Ysaÿe.

NOTES

[18] Romain Rolland, *Musiciens d'ajourd'hui* (Russ. transl. Moscow, 1938, p. 131).

[19] Armand Parent (1863-1934), a noted violinist, also a native of Liège and graduate of the Liège Conservatoire, was leader of the Bilse and the Colonne orchestras. In 1892 he was first violin of a string quartet in Paris, and since 1900 taught the violin class at the Schola Cantorum.

Dalcroze's autographed photograph he gave to Ysaÿe.

FRANCIS MACMILLEN

VIOLINIST
FIRST AMERICAN TOUR

Beginning December, 190[6]

New York Debut December 7 with MR. WALTER DAMROSCH and the New York Symphony Orchestra

"No wonder, then, that it moved the American artist to score a genuine triumph, and the audience to regard him with perfervid applause. But he played everything well—with beauty of tone, accuracy of intonation, and phrasing worthy of being described as immaculate."—*London Daily Telegraph, May 20, '06.*

Direction: LOUDON CHARLTO[N]
CARNEGIE HALL, NEW YORK

Francis Macmillen, typical of many talented violinists who were contemporaries of Ysaÿe and whose fame faded because they never composed or recorded anything worth-

while. This double page spread appeared in **The Musical Courier** *in 1906.*

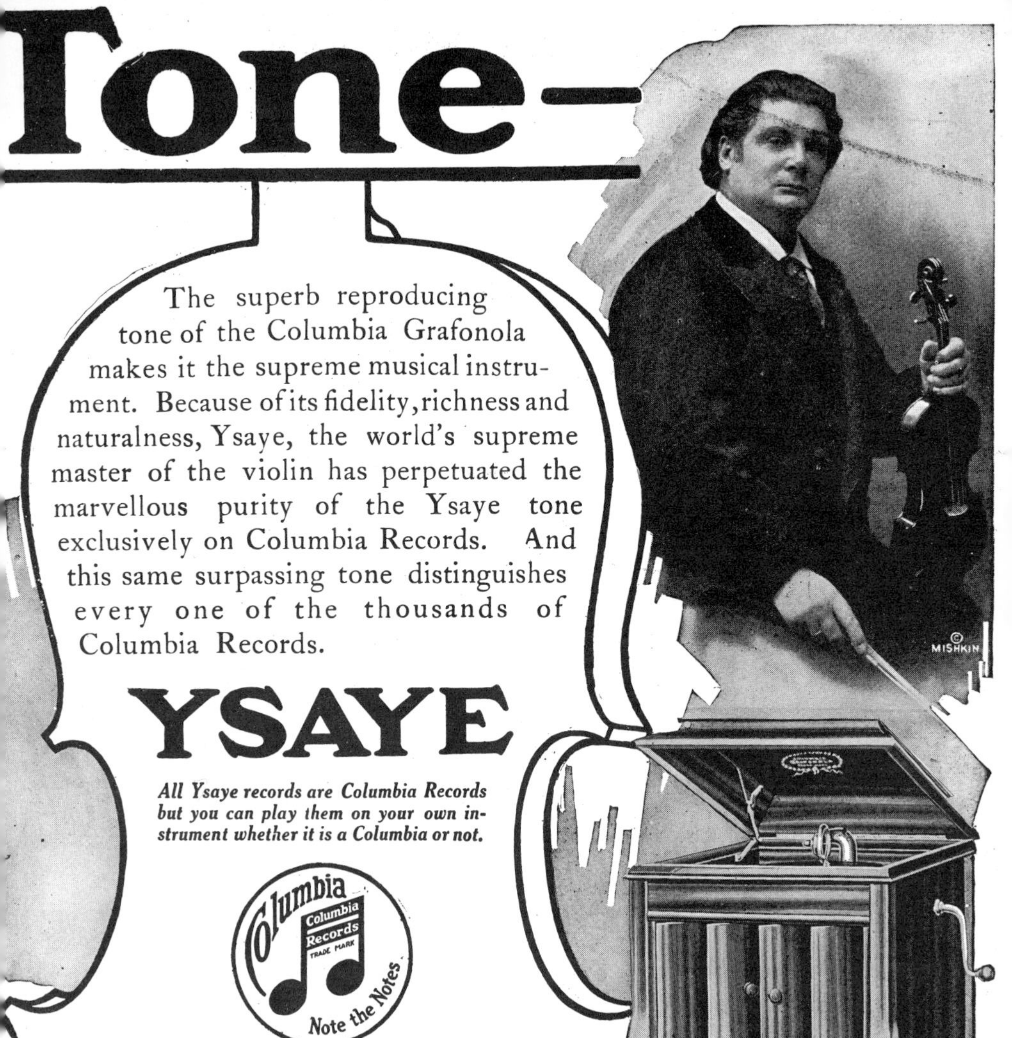

Tone —

The superb reproducing tone of the Columbia Grafonola makes it the supreme musical instrument. Because of its fidelity, richness and naturalness, Ysaye, the world's supreme master of the violin has perpetuated the marvellous purity of the Ysaye tone exclusively on Columbia Records. And this same surpassing tone distinguishes every one of the thousands of Columbia Records.

YSAYE

All Ysaye records are Columbia Records but you can play them on your own instrument whether it is a Columbia or not.

Any one of 8500 Columbia dealers is waiting to demonstrate to you Columbia Grafonolas and Columbia Records. He will gladly play any records you choose including the Columbia Dance Records, which are personally supervised in the making by Mr. G. Hepburn Wilson, the world's greatest authority on modern dancing. Your dealer will send any model of the Columbia Grafonola and any list of records to your house on approval—and for your convenience easy terms of payments may be arranged.

Columbia

GRAPHOPHONE COMPANY

Box F 636 Woolworth Building - New York
Toronto: 365-367 Sorauren Ave.   Prices in Canada Plus Duty
Dealers wanted where we are not actively represented.
Write for particulars.

Columbia Grafonola "Leader." Price $75
Easy terms. Others from $25 to $500.

Columbia Graphophone Company, later to be Columbia Records, promoted the whole company through Ysaÿe.

[20] From the reminiscences of Alfred Marchot in A. Ysaÿe, *op. cit.,* pp. 289-9. Marchot (1861-1939) was Eugène Ysaÿe's fellow-student in Massart's class at the Liège Conservatoire. Later he studied with Ysaÿe and in his work as professor of the Brussels Conservatoire adhered to the principles of the Ysaÿe school.
[21] Vincent d'Indy, *César Franck,* deuxième édition, Paris, 1907, p. 31.
[22] Franck's Quartet dedicated to Camille Saint-Saëns was written in 1878-9; his Quartet, in 1889.
[23] Raoul Pugno (1852-1914) was a prominent French pianist; he visited Russia several times, appearing with Ysaÿe and with Casals. He died in Moscow on January 3, 1914.
[24] *The Youth of Hercules,* Op. 50, a symphonic poem by Saint-Saëns.—L.G.
[25] Eugène Ysaÿe had many honors and decorations from Belgium, France, Rumania, Great Britain, Italy and other countries.
[26] Romain Rolland, *Musiciens d'aujourd'hui* (Russ. transl., Moscow, 1938, p. 111).
[27] This Concerto dedicated to Pablo de Sarasate was written and first performed in 1880.
[28] Quoted in the article by José Quitin, which appeared in the brochure issued by the Liège Conservatoire for the Ysaÿe centenary in 1958 *(Centenaire de la naissance de Eugène Ysaÿe, Liège, 1958),* pp. 32-33.
[29] The quartet in question is Saint-Saëns' No. 1, Op. 112, written in 1899.
[30] The works published by Durand, however, bear other dedications. *La Muse et le Poète* is inscribed "A la mémoire de Mme. J. Henry Carruette;" the dedication of the first Sonata for Violin and Piano (Op. 75, 1885) is: "A Monsieur M. Marsick" and of the Second (Op. 102, 1896)—"A Monsieur et Madame L. Carembat." It would seem that the composer had changed his dedications before handling the works to the publisher.
[31] Joseph Hollmann (1852-1927) was a noted Dutch cellist, a pupil of François Servais.
[32] *La revue musicale,* 1-e Décembre, 1925, p. 127.
[33] Quoted from A. Ysaÿe, *op. cit.,* p. 314.
[34] Quoted from Julien Tiersot, *Un démi-siècle de la musique française (1870-1919),* Paris, 1924 (Russ. transl. in *Frantsuzskaya muzyka vtoroi poloviny XIX veka,* Moscow, 1938, pp. 123-4).

Ysaÿe joined forces with colleagues and went on a chamber music tour for six weeks.

'SAYE.　　　MARTEAU.*　　　GERARDY.　　　LACHAUME

NSEMBLE CONCERTS.

Tour begins April 15 at Washington, D. C., and closes April 30 at Chicago, Ill.

Heifetz and Piatigorsky, above. On the facing page, the editor of this book, Dr. Herbert R. Axelrod congratulating Heifetz on the celebration of his 76th birthday at Heifetz' Malibu Beach home.

Antoine Ysaÿe, son of Eugène, sent this original photograph

suitably inscribed, to Prof. Dr. Lev Ginsburg.

Claude Debussy, original drawing by Robert Florczak.

Chapter 3

Ysaÿe and Debussy

Of Eugène Ysaÿe's numerous creative contacts with contemporary composers, his relationship with Claude Debussy (1862-1918) deserves special consideration. Their friendship, dating from mid-1880's was put to a test and nearly broke off at the turn of the century. But even while their relations were strained, they continued to respect each other as artists who had much in common. Ysaÿe was saddened at Debussy's abandon of the classical principles of Franck, Debussy's organ master.[35] The work of this distinguished composer, the founder of Impressionism in French music, was complex and somewhat contradictory: he was capable of appreciating, at one and the same time, the great Russian realists Mussorgsky and Rimsky-Korsakov and the French symbolist poets, but his music appealed to Ysaÿe by the striking talent of its creator and by its vivid colors and picturesque force.

These qualities are in evidence in Debussy's *Nocturnes*, a cycle in three movements—*Nuages, Fêtes, Sirènes*—the preliminary version of which, scored for violin and orchestra, was intended for Ysaÿe and dedicated to him.

This is what Debussy wrote to Ysaÿe in a letter of September 22, 1894:

"My very dear Friend, I am working on three nocturnes for violin and orchestra. In the first the orchestra consists of strings, in the second of flutes, four horns, three trumpets and two harps.

The third is the combination of the two. It is in fact an attempt at research into various musical arrangements which result in the same color, as, for example, in painting one might make a study in gray.

"I hope it will interest you, and your reaction to it is what matters most to me . . .

"I wish you all success—it is so much your right.

"Your faithful and devoted friend,
                                    Claude Debussy."

In another letter which Debussy wrote to Ysaÿe in October 1896, he mentions ". . . three *Nocturnes* for violin and orchestra written for Eugène Ysaÿe, a man whom I like and admire."

A few years previously, Debussy had dedicated to the Ysaÿe Quartet his wonderful String Quartet, written in 1893. "I am anxious to learn your opinion of my Quartet and to know what fate is reserved for it?" He went on to say that he had read in the *Art moderne* that a quartet by C.A. Debussy was to be performed at a concert of *La Libre Esthétique* and asked Ysaÿe if he was responsible for this as he hoped was the case.

Debussy's String Quartet was first performed by the Ysaÿe Quartet at the *Société Nationale de Musique* on December 29, 1893, and subsequently at *La Libre Esthétique* in Brussels. Since then Ysaÿe became a tireless propagandist of this work, one of the best in contemporary French chamber music.

Ysaÿe continued to play the Quartet with his friends even at the time when his relationship with the composer had become strained, and Debussy withdrew the original dedication to Ysaÿe of his opera *Pelléas and Mélisande*, which had its premiere on April 30, 1902.

And yet eight years previously Debussy wrote to his Belgian friend:

"Your opinion of *Pelléas and Mélisande* has given me tremendous encouragement and I only hope that you will be as pleased in having that work dedicated to you as I have been in dedicating it."

The two musicians preserved respect for each other in the future, which is proved by the fact that Ysaÿe constantly performed Debussy's music. Also, in the letter which the French composer wrote to the Belgian violinist on December 30, 1903, it is clear that he was eager to have their friendship renewed. Upon learning that

Claude Debussy.

A portion of the letter from Claude Debussy to Ysaÿe.

The Ysaÿe Quartet performing at the Salle Pleyel in Paris. Claude Debussy is seated at the piano.

Ysaÿe in his studio in 1906.

Claude Debussy.

Ysaÿe was going to conduct his three *Nocturnes*, Debussy wrote: "My dear friend, I have received a letter from Lindenlaub telling me that you are going to conduct the three *Nocturnes*. I need hardly tell you how pleased I am. My only regret is that I shall not be able to be present at this performance which, I am sure, will be such as I have dreamed of, being prevented by quite futile reasons. It is a long time, dear friend, since I have had the pleasure of seeing you, but whatever people may have said to you about me (one's friends sometimes have an extraordinary way of going about things), I hope you will believe me when I say that I have never forgotten all that I owe you in the realm of art and beauty. I shall ever feel the warmest admiration for you.

Claude Debussy."

NOTES

[35] Besides, Ysaÿe and his family could not forgive Debussy for divorcing his first wife, whom they all loved and respected. And, as is often the case, there were mutual "friends" who fanned the misunderstanding.

Eugène Ysaÿe at the time of one of his concerts in Berlin.

Chapter 4

The Berlin Concert: 1912

An interesting episode in Ysaÿe's career is associated with his playing of the Elgar Concerto at the sixth Philharmonic Concert, under the direction of Artur Nikisch, in Berlin on January 8, 1912. The concert attracted most of the distinguished violinists of the time—Fritz Kreisler, Carl Flesch, Henri Marteau, Willy Burmester, Michael Press, Alexander Pechnikov, Mischa Elman and many others. They all were keenly interested in the inspired art of their famous Belgian colleague and in his interpretation of the Violin Concerto by Edward Elgar, written in 1910 and little known at the time.

That was a period when Ysaÿe, aged 53, was not feeling well. He was worn out by his intense concert activities. His diabetes had grown worse, his heart and—causing him the greatest anxiety—his hand, were giving him trouble. The doctors were unanimous in advising him to stop traveling, keep a strict diet and reduce his appearances to a minimum or give them up altogether. But, as Ysaÿe wrote to his wife from Rome on January 7, 1911,

"This proposed remedy constitutes a living death. No, I shall not give up my life as an artist until I have no strength left, until I feel the weakening of the will within me, of the power of my fingers, of my bowing, of my brain."

His extraordinary willpower, love for his profession, need to communicate with the public and realization of the absolute im-

Artur Nikisch. A charcoal sketch by Coschell.

Fritz Kreisler.

Carl Flesch.

Artur Nikisch.

Henri Marteau.

Willy Burmester posed for this photo in 1914 for his American tour. He had absented himself from America for 16 years before that time.

Mischa Elman attended Ysaÿe's performance of the Elgar Concerto, in Berlin in 1912.

Eugène Ysaÿe and Michael Press in Berlin, 1912.

Mischa Elman.

Carl Flesch with his students.

1. HENRI WIENIAWSKI. 2. AUGUST WILHELMJ. 3. HENRI VIEUXTEMPS. 4. JOHANNES WOLFF. 5. EFREM ZIMBALIST. 6. JEAN BAPTISTE VIOTTI. 7. JOSEPE WHITE. 8. RODERICK WHITE.

Famous violinists.

Fritz Kreisler often sent his photo on Christmas greetings.

Ysaÿe and a group of musicians in Moscow (1910). Included

in the group are A. Brandukov, M. Casadesus, and Fauré.

possibility to cease being an artist—these proved Eugène Ysaÿe's supports in the most trying moments of his life and urged him to devote himself wholly to his beloved art. He remained a great artist capable of awakening an emotional response in the hearts of his listeners, of addressing them in the language of his exalted art.

After his triumphant concerts in Vienna and other European cities in 1911, a tour of Germany, Russia, Austria and France followed in the first months of 1912.

When Ysaÿe heard from his manager that the best violinists of the world would attend his Berlin concert in January 1912, and that Fritz Kreisler postponed leaving Berlin just to hear him play, he was at first somewhat disconcerted. But his consummate professionalism and skill enabled him to hold his own. At the dress rehearsal he was not at all nervous, and he aroused the admiration of his colleagues—friends and rivals alike. As he wrote from Königsberg to his wife:[36]

"It may have been that the number was too large to bother about, or it may have been my keen desire to ensure appreciation for the work, or again emulation . . . Perhaps it was a combination of all these things. In any case the fact is I do not remember that my fingers or my bowing or my interpretation have ever been better throughout my career as an artist. It was a great victory for the work and a great joy for the interpreter. On Monday night, the concert took place, and although I feared I might not be able to do as well, I played with more calm and conviction, in full possession of all technical and mental powers. I played 'happy.' I played allowing my thoughts to flow like a stream, limpid and fresh.[37]

"After the rehearsal Kreisler was delightful. He was full of admiration, both for me and for the work. He has a rare nature, perfect tact and also great sincerity. All he said to me went straight to my heart. Coming from him, who first performed the Elgar Concerto—which he played so well, with so much poetry and in so masterly a manner—[38]his words had double their value."

After the rehearsal Carl Flesch gave a lunch for Ysaÿe, Kreisler and young Mischa Elman, a recent graduate of the St. Petersburg Conservatoire where his master was Leopold Auer. At Ysaÿe's request, Elman played the first movement from Tchaikovsky's Violin Concerto, which filled the Belgian artist with admiration for the beauty of its music and the excellence of Elman's performance.

Kreisler on Ysaÿe's right. The third gentleman is unknown.

Sitting: Dwight J. Partello holding the Duke of Edinburg Strad, 1722; Ysaÿe with a Carlo Bergonzi, 1733. Standing, left to right; Louis Seigel holding a 1690 Strad; Mrs. Abel

holding a Joseph Guarneri, 1742; Mr. Abel holding the Irish Amati, 1648. This photo was taken in Berlin just before World War I.

The Partello Collection of Violins. *Dwight J. Partello, an American living in Berlin, Germany around the turn of the century (1900) had accumulated the greatest collection of Cremonese violins and bows the world had ever seen. With Partello it was not a question of money and just buying violins; it was quality that counted and he wanted the best examples that were available. He had a Gagliano which was never used; he also had a collection of 17 Tourte bows which were brand new and perfect examples of the Master's work. Just how large his collection was is unknown, but he had at least 27 Strads and Guarnerius del Gesus. The photos on the facing page show a sample which was on display in Washington. It contained 22 violins, 2 violas, 2 cellos and 31 bows. This photograph merely shows the Strads in the collection, top and bottom view with the dates that the instruments were made written underneath. Photo by Muenzer.*

Eugène and Louise Ysaÿe celebrated their 25th wedding anniversary in Godinne, 1911.

Then Kreisler and Elman played Bach's Concerto for two violins, Flesch rendered a Sonata by Nardini and Mischa Elman, accompanied by Kreisler, played some of the latter's smaller compositions.

This memorable meeting of violinists concluded with the eldest of them, Eugène Ysaÿe, (who was persuaded to play by his younger colleagues), giving them an inspired performance of Vieuxtemps' Fourth Concerto, one of the Belgian master's best works written in Russia and highly prized by Tchaikovsky. Kreisler accompanied him at the piano, playing by heart. As Ysaÿe described it in his letter:

"It was a great joy to me to play this fine work by my old master and they all admired it. After that we all said good-bye. I was really very touched by these young people. I admire them for their talent and I am deeply grateful for their attitude towards me, whom they call 'notre maître à tous,' without any intention of adding to my years."

Soon after that Ysaÿe went to Russia.

NOTES

[36] The date of this letter is given as January 13 in A. Ysaÿe, *Ysaÿe, Sa vie* . . . and as January 19 in A. Ysaÿe and B. Ratcliffe, *Ysaÿe. His Life* . . .

[37] The German press was somewhat critical of the work but praised highly the performer who, besides the Elgar Concerto, played the Concerto by Leclair. See *Die Musik,* 1912, Heft 9, S. 177, and *Signae* für die Musikalische Welt, 1912, Nr. 2, S. 40.—*L.G.*

[38] Fritz Kreisler, to whom the Elgar Violin Concerto was dedicated, was its first interpreter (London, November 10, 1910, with the composer conducting).—*L.G.*

Ysaÿe with his Del Gesu violin. This photo was taken in the United States in 1912. Photo courtesy of Leslie Sheppard.

Chapter 5

The Concert Season: 1912-1914

The concert season of 1912-13 and 1913-14 was spent by Eugène Ysaÿe in America. Constant travels, countless appearances and recording sessions were very tiring. Besides, he felt anxious about the future of his family, and his lack of funds for the time when his health failed and he would be unable to continue his career of virtuoso artist. Sometimes he considered settling at home and leading a quieter life,³⁹ but his artistic nature would not let him realize this intention and he could not bring himself to end his active life as interpretative artist.

He had hardly returned to his villa, "La Chanterelle" at Le Zoute, when World War I shattered Europe—the Kaiser's armies invaded neutral Belgium and occupied most of this country (with the exception of certain parts of Flanders). It should be remarked here that the greatest resistance to the overpoweringly strong aggressor was offered at Liège, in Eugène Ysaÿe's native parts. Ysaÿe, the man who loved his country, and the father of three sons who immediately joined the Belgian army, was overwhelmed by the events. He had idealistic views on reality, and he cherished pleasant memories of the years spent in Germany in his youth. He held in high esteem German music and musicians, his friends, and at first was unable to grasp what was happening.

An Ysaÿe portrait autographed by Ysaÿe during his concert tour of the United States (Portland, Oregon), 1913.

"La Chanterelle in Godinne," *Ysaÿe's home from 1900-1911. If these walls could talk, what tales they would have of Ysaÿe, Kreisler, Thibaud, Casals and the likes of them! Photo courtesy of Arazi.*

He wanted to share his people's fate. He wanted to help with the only weapon he was master of, his violin. According to his contemporaries,[40] the great violinist rendered considerable assistance to refugees at Le Zoute. He arranged a concert for their benefit, which took place in the church, because there was no other auditorium. There, to the accompaniment of the organ, Ysaÿe gave a fervent performance of Vitali's *Chaconne*, Beethoven's *Romance* and *Romanza* from Wieniawski's Concerto in D minor. The audience could not restrain their tears and since the curé forbade applauding in the church, a storm of applause broke out as soon as Ysaÿe had stepped out on to the porch. In this way he bade adieu to his compatriots.

The population of the invaded country was panic-stricken and Ysaÿe decided to flee to England with his family. Leaving his

Ysaÿe with his wife Louise in Scotland (1915).

house and its contents, he wrote, in German, under the big portrait of Beethoven in his study:

"This house is the property of an artist who has lived and worked in the cult of Bach, Beethoven and Wagner. Treat it with respect." With many difficulties, the Ysaÿe party reached Dunkirk, where they crossed to England in a fishing boat.

Settling in London, Ysaÿe continued his appearances, giving a number of concerts in aid of Belgian refugees, whom he was always ready to help in every way.

The war, however, restricted his concert tours, but eager to work, Ysaÿe disregarded the dangers on his way and went to the Continent to give four concerts at Madrid.

Ysaÿe, the true artist, did not on his return to London, yield to the temptation to appear at the Coliseum, in spite of a very good contract offered him by the management of that big music hall. He wrote to one of his sons then serving at the front:

"Had I accepted, we could all have lived in luxury, but I feel you will approve my decision. One cannot celebrate Mass on a bar counter. I could not barter away my honor as an artist."

Living far from home, Ysaÿe did his best to practice regularly. At moments of anxiety he sought relaxation in classical music. He studied and revised his cadenzas to the Mozart, Beethoven and Brahms concertos and to Mozart's Chamber Symphony for Violin, Viola and Orchestra. He transcribed for violin Bach's Inventions, some harpsichord pieces by Rameau, and Chopin's waltzes.

That was an attempt on the part of the musician to escape the harrowing reality. Ysaÿe loved life, his people, contemporary art, and did not see a way out from the depressing thoughts torturing many intellectuals and artists at that time. One of them was Emile Verhaeren (1855-1916), the great Belgian poet who also found refuge in England and frequently visited Ysaÿe at his London home. Verhaeren felt very strongly the ordeals of his native country and despite his contradictory views he was able to reflect the sufferings of his people and their heroic struggles in his books *Belgium Soaked in Blood, The Crimson Wings of War* and, particularly, the poem entitled *"The Heroes of Liège."*[41]

In his conversations with Verhaeren, Ysaÿe confessed that he was clutching at the past: "I am assiduously revising some of my early works. I am dusting them and presenting them in a new garb,

An Ysaÿe portrait done in New York (1913).

Queen Elisabeth of the Belgians with Ysaÿe, 1916. Her Highness was a violinist, and an extremely cultured person. Ysaÿe was her friend and her teacher. They often played together.

At the Belgian front during World War I, 1916. From left to right: Eugène Ysaÿe, Maréchal Francet d'Esperey, Prince de Teck, General Rouquerole and Victor Rousseau. Photo compliments of Arazi.

Eugène Ysaÿe tried to join the army during World War I, but he was not accepted. He is shown here with his sons Antoine and Théo. Photo courtesy of Arazi.

A group of musicians meet at the front in 1916. From left to right: Germain Privost, violist; Gerard Hekking, cellist; Ysaÿe; Gabriel Ysaÿe, violinist. Photo courtesy of Arazi. Below: King Albert of Belgium walks behind the lines at the front at Nieuport with Eugène Ysaÿe.

Eugène Ysaÿe with his son, Antoine, whom he is visiting at the front. Photo courtesy of Arazi.

Eugène Ysaÿe with the organist-composer Auguste De-Boeck and Alain Joretle(?) during the war (August, 1914). Photo from Arazi.

without interfering with their style. It is entrancing."[42] But work in his study, far from his audiences, was not enough for Ysaÿe and he welcomed every opportunity of playing before those who needed his art. He was particularly glad to participate in charity concerts—he felt that he was not only satisfying his creative urge but fulfilling his civic duty. In 1916, Queen Elisabeth of the Belgians proposed that he should visit the Belgian front and he willingly agreed to it. He played not only at the Headquarters[43] but also at hospitals and at the front lines.

Not far from the line of fire, during periods of lull in the artillery firing, Eugène Ysaÿe would address the soldiers, valiantly defending their fatherland, in the language of his art, and they understood him very well. He had no intention of playing down to them—he wanted to touch their hearts, to give those who faced death the best and the noblest in music, to encourage and inspire them. "I refuse to think that you here are any less capable of enjoying good music than are those who fill the cafés and restaurants in Brussels, and because I respect and admire you I am going to play you something which is beautiful."[44]

Soaring amid a calm that was unusual under the circumstances, was the noble and expressive melody of the Ballade which precedes the Polonaise by that Belgian master, Vieuxtemps. The hundreds of men remained motionless, avidly absorbing every note of the song Ysaÿe's violin was singing. So it was but natural that after that the artist performed with ardor a Partita by Bach: he felt that the unseen but tangible contact which had been established between him and his listeners would help them to comprehend these profound pages of classical music.

NOTES

[39] When the post of director of the Brussels Conservatoire fell vacant in 1912, Ysaÿe applied for it but the Belgian authorities selected Léon Dubois. Ysaÿe was given the position of "Master of the Royal Chapel" instead.
[40] See the reminiscences of George Alexis on pp. 80-81 of the booklet *Centenaire de la naissance de Eugène Ysaÿe*, Liège, 1958.
[41] The titles are re-translated from the Russian.—*Translator's note.*
[42] Quoted from A. Ysaÿe, *op. cit.*, p. 105.
[43] There, Eugène and Théophile Ysaÿe, the viola players Lionel Tertis and Germain Prevost and the cellist Emile Doehard played chamber music, with Queen Elizabeth (a pupil of Ysaÿe's) as second violin.
[44] Quoted from A. Ysaÿe and B. Ratcliffe, *op. cit.*, p. 126.

A group of musicians visits the area behind the lines. Along with General De Keuninck of the sixth Army is Ysaÿe with Lionel Tertis, the violist, at the extreme right.

Chapter 6

The Latter Years

At the end of 1916 Ysaÿe went once more to America. Although America entered the War soon afterwards, there were still many concerts taking place and Ysaÿe played in New York, Philadelphia, Boston and other cities. The constant strain, the unceasing feeling of tiredness, his hands (now the bowing hand gave him trouble, while previously it had been his left hand) and his longing for home and family preyed on the artist's mind and depressed him. Yet he worked perseveringly, trying to compose and even to write poetry. It was at that time that he composed his poem *Exil* for string orchestra without basses.

His surroundings irked Ysaÿe. He did not fully comprehend the nature of social events. He could not reconcile himself to the Americans abandoning themselves to dancing and other pleasures while thousands of human lives were being destroyed and his own country was languishing under the yoke of the invaders.

The only source of consolation and tranquillity was his art; in it, as he said in a letter to his wife in the summer of 1917, he found strength for resistance, without which all would be lost. It was in art that he drowned his sadness and wrath, it was in it that he found energy for fight and faith in victory.

A painting of Ysaÿe sketched after Goldberg's famous photograph (1917).

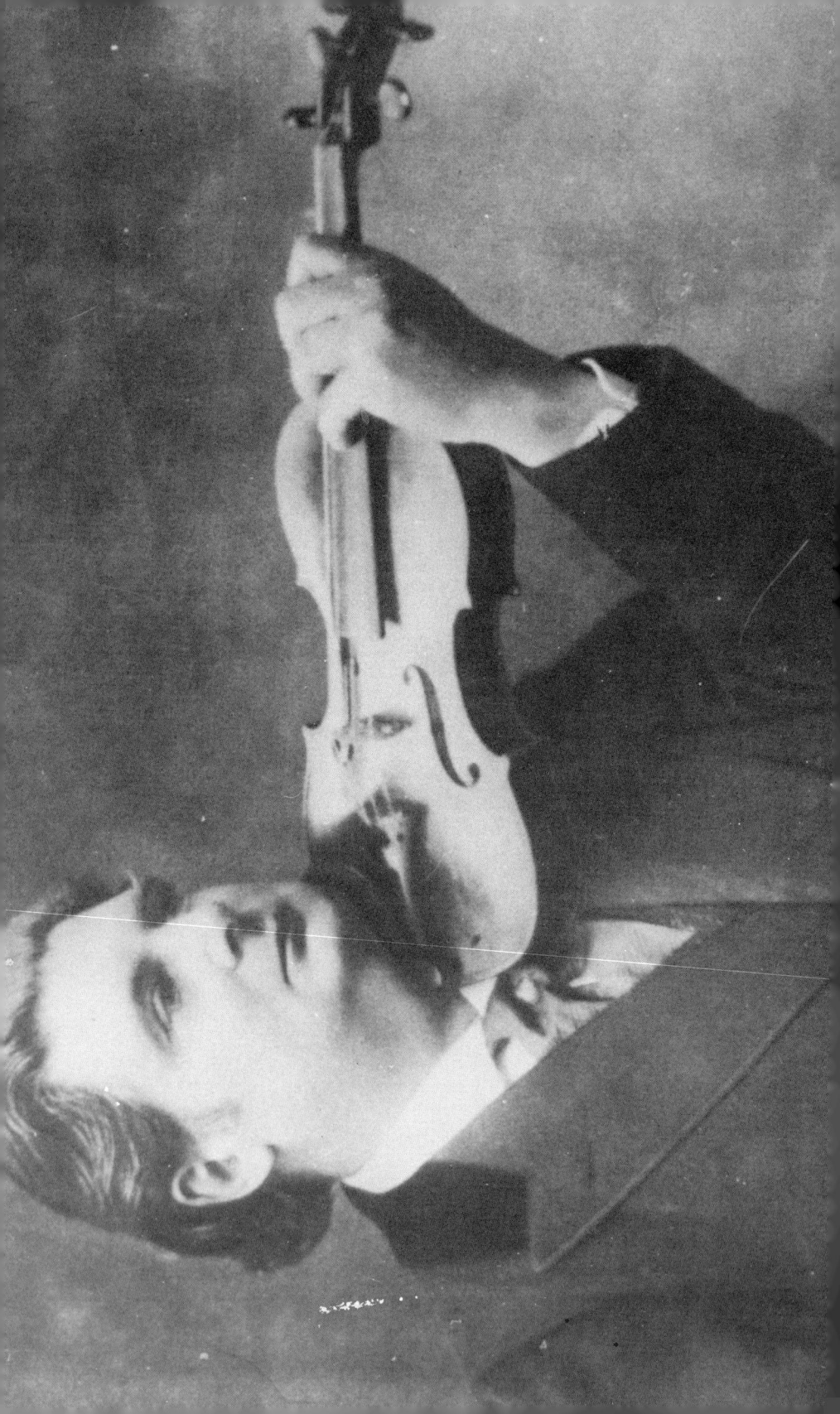

At sixty, Ysaÿe felt that he could no longer continue his career of a touring virtuoso and he accepted the post of conductor of the Cincinnati Symphony Orchestra. Although his health was failing him, he set about his new duties with his wonted vigor. The excellent orchestra acquired an incomparable director, whose artistic principles ensured the success of its symphony concerts.

It should be noted that even here, far from his native country, Ysaÿe never ceased to popularize the music of Belgian and French composers.

He joyously greeted the end of the war. "This indescribable horror, this butchery, this monstrous thing which has obliterated so many lives and has caused such misery, is over. I cannot believe it," he wrote to his wife.

Bound by his contract with the Cincinnati Orchestra, Ysaÿe could not return home until the summer of 1919. He was overjoyed at his reunion with his family and his friends. The provisions of his contract extending over four years, however, made him come back to Cincinnati for the concert seasons, and it was only the summers that he could spend at "La Chanterelle."

The contract expired in 1922 and Eugène Ysaÿe and his wife returned to Belgium for good. For a short period he resumed direction of the Concerts Ysaÿe, but pecuniary difficulties, the loss of old contacts on account of the war, his advanced age and undermined health made him give up the direction of the orchestra which he himself had founded many years before.

He devoted himself to composition, producing two more poems—*Amitié* and *Poème Nocturne*—and some other works. The summit of his composer's and artist's talent became his six Sonatas for Solo Violin, written in 1924 and constituting a valuable contribution to the world violin repertoire.

At the age of sixty-six Eugène Ysaÿe was able not only to create his best and most poetic masterpieces full of romantic fervor and musical revelations, but also to renew his concert tours. "As long as my heart beats I shall go on playing," the old artist said. He appeared in England, Sweden, France, Finland, Switzerland, the Baltic provinces of Russia,[45] Poland (Warsaw, Lodz and Cracow) and, of course, at home, in Belgium.

Ysaÿe, during one of his early American visits, became an idol for female teenagers! Photo courtesy of Leslie Sheppard.

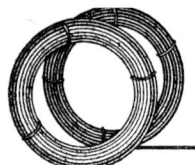
Fiddle Strings

YSAYE'S MASTER CLASS

TUESDAY, October 15, marks an epoch in the history of Cincinnati music schools as on that day Eugene Ysaye will open his master violin class at the Cincinnati Conservatory of Music, thus lending the prestige formerly enjoyed by the great Belgian center of violin playing at Brussels, to this city. Prominent features of the course to be given by Ysaye from October 15 to April 15 will be traditional interpretations of the great works of his teachers Vieuxtemps and Wieniawski, lecture on violin literature and violin-making. Great artists have sat under Ysaye in his master classes abroad and it will be a group of distinguished talents which assembles to greet the master at the Conservatory of Music, October fifteenth.

THE VIOLINISTS' RETREAT

THERE is a certain hotel not far from one of New York's leading concert halls that for some reason or other appeals particularly to musicians. In former seasons it has been frequented greatly by pianists, but this season it seems to be the violinists' retreat, and there if one listened carefully on neighboring floors could be heard the strains of the violinists, Max Rosen, Toscha Seidel and Eddy Brown. In fact, the first named young violin wonder occupied the rooms directly underneath his gifted fellow-artist Seidel, who is a very industrious worker. Confined to his bed by an attack of the prevalent influenza, Max Rosen was forced to listen by the hour to his colleague's practicing. "When I get well," said Max, "I'll get even. I'll hire the room above him and play his whole program over until he cries for help."

THE EARLY LIFE OF YOUNG HEIFETZ

JASCHA HEIFETZ, the young Russian violinist, who first reached this country on September 5th, 1917, and then had phenomenal artistic success wherever he appeared in concert, has figured in press notices almost beyond count, but, rarely, strange to say, have they contained facts about his earlier life.

He was born in Vilna, Russia, almost 19 years ago. He began his study of the violin at the age of three with his father who was a fine violinist. When he was five years old, Heifetz entered the Royal School of Music in his native city, and during the same year he made his first public appearance. When six years old, he played the Mendelssohn Concerto, and two years later he was graduated from the Conservatory. A short time after this, he was taken to Petrograd where after repeated disappointments, he secured a coveted hearing with Leopold Auer, and it is said that this great teacher after hearing him, proclaimed him to be an astonishing genius.

Within the next two years young Heifetz made his formal debut in a recital at Petrograd, and thereby drew to himself the attention of musical Russia. In Odessa alone he played seven times with the Odessa Symphony Orchestra. In 1911 he went on a tour through many cities of Central Europe where he achieved a tremendous success. On this tour he played with orchestras and under such conductors as Safonoff and Nikisch.

At the outbreak of the war Heifetz was not interned in Germany as has sometimes been reported, but was living with his family in Petrograd. Before coming to America he toured Scandinavia and then gave twelve recitals in Petrograd before sold-out houses. As yet he has never played in Great Britain. Crossing Siberia, China and the Pacific en route for New York, Heifetz and his family journeyed two months before reaching San Francisco.

Theodore Spiering, who is an American violinist and conductor, will conduct two concerts given by the Chicago Symphony Orchestra this season. Maeterlinck's "Betrothal" sequel to "Bluebird," with music by Eric DeLamarter will be a noteworthy number on the program. It is to Mr. Spiering's credit that he is becoming more and more prominent as a conductor.

Mayo Wadler at three performances recently featured American compositions. The first of November he played in Hippodrome at a

A rare, numbered lithograph of Ysaÿe, done by Lemaire. This illustration was struck in limited numbers and is considered quite valuable. Courtesy of Marianne Wurlitzer.

On the facing page: a clipping from the Ysaÿe scrapbook made available by Marianne Wurlitzer.

Ysaÿe in the house of the luthier Hell in the French city of

Lille, 26 September, 1926.

Ysaÿe, a close friend of the Wurlitzer family, especially when he conducted the Cincinnati Orchestra, posed for several publicity shots which Wurlitzer used in their advertisements. That made Ysaÿe a "model" as well as a violinist, conductor, cellist, teacher and composer!

A great help to Ysaÿe in his old age was his pupil and friend Jeannette Dincin. After the death of his first wife in 1924, Jeannette Dincin, who was wholly devoted to her master, surrounded him with care and attention, saw to it that he did not overwork himself and spared him every annoyance. Some time afterwards (in 1927) he married her.

Ysaÿe spent his summers at "La Chanterelle" as he used to before the war. Ysaÿe's villa was a place of pilgrimage of his numerous friends, among whom were Pablo Casals, Jacques Thibaud, Alfred Cortot, Joseph Szigeti, Nathan Milstein, Artur Rubinstein and other famous musicians. Often they would take their instruments and make music for the pleasure of it in the informal atmosphere of "La Chanterelle," and at times the old master would play his own compositions to the admiration of his friends and pupils.

Among his particular friends of long standing were the members of the celebrated Cortot-Thibaud-Casals trio. The Belgian violinist spoke of the great cellist, Pablo Casals, with the deepest love and admiration. The two musicians, whose aesthetic prin-

Ysaÿe was loved by most of his colleagues and often concertized with them. This poster advertises a concert with Fritz Kreisler. Kreisler was soloist and Ysaÿe was the conductor of the orchestra.

Jacques Thibaud, left. In the photo below, a younger Thibaud with pianist Harold Bauer. On the facing page, A typical review of Ysaÿe's concerts.

OVATION GIVEN TO LOCAL ORCHESTRA IN THE CAPITAL

Ysaye and His Players Received With Great Enthusiasm.

AUDIENCE ONE OF GREAT DISTINCTION

Roses Tied With Belgian Colors Given to Conductor Ysaye.

(TIMES-STAR SPECIAL DISPATCH)
WASHINGTON, D. C., March 12.—Before an audience of the most distinguished character, the Cincinnati orchestra, led by Eugene Ysaye, at the climax of its present concert tour, achieved a triumph yesterday. The concert was given in the National theater.

The audience was representative of the smartest circles of Washington society, and included Supreme court officials and members of the diplomatic corps. Madame Jusserand, wife of the French ambassador, was in a box with Mrs. Willard Saulsbury, Mrs. James Carroll Frazer, Mrs. Thomas F. Bayard and Miss Sara Lee. The Belgian Ambassador and Baroness de Cartier entertained a company in their box which included Senora De Riano, wife of the Spanish ambassador; Miss Mabel Boardman, formerly of Cincinnati, and Miss Betty Connolly, niece of the baroness. Representative and Mrs. Longworth also entertained a box party, having as their guests Senator Richard P. Ernst of Kentucky; Mrs. Frederic A. Keep, Mrs. Cromwell Brooks and Mrs. Hare Lippencott, who is visiting Mrs. Marshall Field. Former Senator James Phelan of California had with him in his box the counsellor of the Russian embassy, and Mme. De Bach, the charge d'affaires of Sweden, Mr. De Lagerberg, Mrs. Lawrence Townsend, wife of the former United States minister to Belgium, and Mrs. Truxton Beale. Others noted in the audience were Mrs. Thomas Logan and guests, Mrs. Larz Anderson, Mrs. Breckenridge Long, Mrs. James Carroll Frazier, Mr. and Mrs. Henry Price Wright, Mme. Heller and Mrs. Walter Tuckerman.

This was the first time that many of those in the notable audience had seen Ysaye as conductor, although, as the premier musician of his day, they have often been present when he made the masters live again on his violin. But the impression that he made here yesterday, according to the verdict of music-lovers, was not less marked than when he stood alone in the great music halls.

Washington audiences, as may be expected, cosmopolitan as they are in character, are not noted for their warmth, but yesterday was an exception. Time and again the conductor had to acknowledge applause and always, with the generosity that is his characteristic, he made the players stand to share in the recognition with him. The chief composition offered for the concert was that one which, through Ysaye's interpretation, has enchanced the reputation of the Orchestra wherever it has played, viz., the "Marche Heroique" symphony of Saint-Saens. After it had been performed Ysaye was given an ovation, being called back to the stage a number of times. A huge armful of roses, tied with the Belgian colors, in long streamers, was handed over the footlights. M. Ysaye was greatly affected and the flowers had a place on the front of the stage throughout the programme which proceeded to a triumphant close. As the last strain of the "Sylvia Suite" died away there were shouts of "bravo" and the audience seemed loath to leave its seats, while Ysaye was recalled several times to acknowledge the plaudits of the throng. The hope was generally expressed that the orchestra would visit the capitol again next season.

Newspaper criticisms of the concert bespeak admiration of Conductor Ysaye and of the organization itself. The Washington Post this morning says that Mr. Ysaye "directs a splendid organization rich in achievement." The Washington Herald lauds the orchestra for its precision of attack, good phrasing, full tone and exact tempo. It comments on the fact that the audience filed out reluctantly, which is unusual for Washington.

After the concert the orchestra left for Marietta, O., where a concert was scheduled. Ysaye had been overwhelmed with invitations of a social character, but found himself able to accept only that for tea with the Longworths in the morning, and for luncheon at the residence of the Belgian ambassador. The orchestra will arrive in Cincinnati Sunday for the concert in the afternoon in Music Hall.

"... And you could not spot in his playing a single note that was void, that did not breathe life and sincerity."

A Casals' photo autographed to the author.

The entire Ysaÿe family in Le Zoute, 1925.

Casals autographed this photograph for the author. The lady with Casals is his young wife.

Joseph Szigeti, in 1929, was one of Ysaÿe's closest friends. Photo courtesy of Arazi.

Eugène Ysaÿe in Le Zoute. Photo from Arazi.

ciples were very similar, had often appeared together and their playing of the Brahms Concerto for Violin and Cello in 1912 (in Moscow, St. Petersburg and Vienna) was a memorable occasion. "Casals is truly sensitive and profound, a musician in the deepest sense of the word," Ysaÿe used to say. "Not a single detail is neglected, everything is defined with delicacy, knowledge and discrimination. In him action is the direct outcome of thought and is true, vibrant and deeply moving . . . Casals is the greatest interpreter of all that I have ever heard."[46]

On his part Casals cherished the warmest feeling for his older colleague. He said: "The name of Eugène Ysaÿe will always be for us the purest, the most shining artistic ideal."[47]

Casals later recalled a meeting in Paris before the War: after their fatiguing concerts and free at last from their contracts (often exacting) and from their managers (whom they called a band of thieves) Ysaÿe, Kreisler, Enesco, Thibaud and Casals had decided to play for their own pleasure. He said that when they played string quartets "Ysaÿe always liked to play the viola part. And what a great artist he was."[48]

It is noteworthy that one of Eugène Ysaÿe's last appearances as soloist with orchestra was under the direction of Pablo Casals, while the latter was the soloist at the symphonic concert conducted by the Belgian violinist shortly before his death.

These episodes were the last memorable pages in the creative biography of the great Belgian musician and should be discussed at some length.

In 1927, Pablo Casals, an outstanding connoisseur and interpreter of Beethoven's music, organized with his orchestra[49] a music festival in Barcelona to celebrate the centenary of the death of Beethoven. He invited Ysaÿe to take part in it.

By that time, Ysaÿe had almost given up concert appearances. His high demands of himself, his reverence for Beethoven and doubts concerning his own skill (which was not what it used to be before), made him hesitate before consenting. "But do you think I could?" he asked Casals. When the latter answered that he had no doubts whatever, the old master was deeply touched. He pressed the younger man's hand warmly and exclaimed: "As long as the miracle happens!"

Ysaÿe seemed to grow younger. His son wrote to Casals that his

Goodbye, dear Ysaÿe. The final concert in Barcelona,

Casals conducted (1927).

Latvijas Mākslas Aģentura.

Amatnieku biedribas zālē
ceturtdien, 12. februarī 1925. 8 vakarā

vijoļu virtuoza

E. ISAI

koncerts

piedaloties J. du Schastēnam

PROGRAMA

1. Sonate . . . . G Faurè.
   Allegro moderato
   Andante
   Allegro vivace
   Allegro quasi presto.
   (izp. E. Isai un J. du Schastēns).

2. Koncerts G-dur . . . . . Mocarts.
   Allegro
   Adagio
   Rondo allegro
   (izp. E. Isai).

3. a) Adagio . . . . Bachs
   b) Mazurka . . . . J du Schastēns.
   c) Mouvement . . . Debissi.
   (rzp. J. du Schastēns).

4. a) Havanaise . . . Sen-Sanss.
   b) Balade un polonese . Vjetans.
   (izp. E. Isai).

Bechsteina koncertfliģels no P Neldnera noliktavas.

MARGARETES TOIMAN arfas koncerts.
13. februarī, konservatorijā
Nac. op. baletmeistara N. Sergejeva,
baleta studijas I klasiskais baleta,
vakars, 17 februarī, Nac. operā.

Spiestuve D. Apta.

Pablo Casals.

On the 12th of February 1825 Ysaÿe gave a concert in Latvia. This is the program given out in Riga, the capital of Latvia.

Eugène in the shop of the luthier Hell in Lille, 1925. Photo courtesy of Arazi.

father had begun to practice with youthful energy—he played scales slowly by the hour and worked on the Concerto (remember, the artist was nearly seventy!).

Ysaÿe was invited to appear as violinist in the Beethoven Concerto and conductor in the *Eroica* and the Triple Concerto, with Cortot, Thibaud and Casals as the soloists.

On March 19, 1927, Casals, then on tour in Vienna, wrote to Ysaÿe:

"Mon cher Maître et Ami, Your letter gives me great pleasure. A thousand thanks. It is agreed then that you shall conduct the *Eroica* and the Triple Concerto at the first concert on April 19th, and that you shall play the Beethoven Concerto on the 23rd.

"Please set your mind at rest as regards rehearsals. They will take place each afternoon and evening and you shall have as many as you consider necessary.

"I quite agree with you about the Viennese public. There is none better, and I recall our concert here with very great pleasure.[50] People still come and remind me of it and you have no idea of how pleased I am when they do. Age is the glory of the great—do you agree?

Yours ever affectionately,
Pablo Casals."

The two concerts in Barcelona proved veritable triumphs. "There were some unforgettable moments in Ysaÿe's interpretation and the audience was delirious," Casals later recalled. "When he found me afterwards in the artists' room he kneeled down, took my hands and said: 'Resurrection. Resurrection!'[51]—an incredible moment of emotion. Dear Ysaÿe! I went to say good-bye to him next day at the station. Leaning out of the carriage window he was still holding my hands as if he did not want to part with them."[52]

Some time later, Ysaÿe described his impressions of the Orchestra Pablo Casals in a Brussels journal.

He remarked that one had to be present at those concerts, perfect models in every respect, in order to form an idea of the enthusiasm of the Catalan audiences and of their craving for beauty.

"I heard the C minor Symphony conducted by Casals twice. It is thanks to this great artist, to his energy and genius as an interpreter, that Barcelona has become a major musical center.

Ysaÿe sent this photo to friends in 1927.

Thibaud visited his great friend Ysaÿe frequently. This "posed" picture is, perhaps, the most famous of all Ysaÿe photos (1927).

"Casals directs the orchestra he himself has founded with such vigor, such artistry and such a profound understanding of the spirit of Beethoven's music that you sit there deeply moved in an ecstasy of admiration.

"During the festival I had the honor of conducting the *Eroica* Symphony and playing the Beethoven Concerto. I also conducted the Triple Concerto played by that 'Trinity'—Cortot, Thibaud, Casals. That was a friendly union of four comrades-at-arms and I shall never forget the all but frantic enthusiasm of the audience. It was a truly entrancing experience, a moment of such excitement and emotional intensity as rarely happens in life. At the same time it was a glowing lesson of art.

"I should like to tell more about the unforgettable hours spent in Barcelona in that Casals-permeated atmosphere, but I will confine myself to the aphorism: All is possible when the man is there."[53]

This is how Eugène Ysaÿe experienced aesthetic enjoyment at the end of his artistic career, deriving from this experience fresh forces and vigor.

The years that followed were spent in composing and very infrequent concert appearances. His health deteriorated—the diabetes and heart trouble closely associated with it were progressing and he had to economize his strength to the utmost. Nevertheless his illness went so far as to necessitate the amputation of his right foot. But while still bedridden Ysaÿe turned his hand to a long cherished project—writing an opera on the subject of the life of the people. The opera, *Peter the Miner*, dealt with an episode from the miners' strike which he himself had witnessed in his youth.

Although Ysaÿe's social consciousness was to a certain extent circumscribed by his naive idealistic views,[54] his choice of the subject shows the great musician's love for his people and interest in their life.

He worked with abandon and in a very short space of time the opera (or *drame lyrique*) *Pier' li Houyeu* composed in a dialect of Belgium, was completed.

No sooner had Ysaÿe learned to use his artificial leg in 1930 than his ardent desire to renew his artistic career led him to mount the podium to conduct the concerts in Lille and then in Brussels, with Fritz Kreisler as the soloist.

Finally, on November 13, 1930, he conducted an orchestra of

Jacques Thibaud and Alfred Cortot. 1931.

A Alfred Omega, à mon cher ami
Christ Four, bien affectueusement.
E. Yourg
11-1-30

500 during the celebrations of Belgium's hundred years of independence. The program consisted of Schumann's Third (*Rhenish*) Symphony, J. Jongen's *Impressions d'Ardennes* and P. Gilson's *Fantasia on Canadian Folk Themes*. Pablo Casals was the soloist in Lalo's Concerto and in *Méditation* for cello, the fourth poem by Eugène Ysaÿe.

Casals had played as soloist under the direction of Ysaÿe time and again in Brussels and in Cincinnati, but this concert was the last in which the Belgian master was fated to appear. Disregarding the pain in his leg, Ysaÿe stood up as Casals stepped on to the platform and gave the signal for a trumpet fanfare.

Within a few days of that concert in Brussels Ysaÿe had to take to his bed. In the early months of 1931 sorrows came crowding upon him: he lost first his sister Marie and then his daughter Carry. The only consolation was the coming production of his opera in Liège. He even managed to attend a rehearsal.

On the day of the opera's premiere at the Théatre Royal in Liège, on March 4, 1931, Ysaÿe listened to a broadcast of his work while lying in a clinic in Brussels. He thanked the performers and the public by radio while his portrait was projected on the screen in the auditorium amid a storm of applause, expressing the audience's warmest admiration for the work of their esteemed countryman.

On April 25 the opera was brought to Brussels and Ysaÿe was taken on a stretcher to the *La Monnaie* Opera House, where he was placed in a box and so could witness the performance. He was happy at the success of his work.

His health grew worse, but Ysaÿe would not give in. The dying master was full of plans for new works and for the coming centenary of his teacher, Wieniawski.

Thinking of the difficulties which he had to endure in his youth, Eugène Ysaÿe discussed the organization of an international music foundation which would arrange competitions of young musicians in order to help them on their road to the concert stage. He handed this project in to Queen Elisabeth, but the International Ysaÿe

January 11, 1930—an ill Ysaÿe poses with his two grandsons. He died on May 12, 1931.

Trying to regain his strength, Ysaÿe went to the French resort city of St. Tropez. Note the special shoe on his right foot. Photo courtesy of Arazi. (1929).

Carry Ysaÿe (1887-1930), the daughter of Ysaÿe. Her death at the time of his illness took a great toll on the Master's will to live. Photo from Arazi.

Ysaÿe in 1930 recuperating from the amputation of his foot. Photo courtesy of Arazi.

During his illness in his latter years, Ysaÿe was attended (1930) by his former student, Jeannette Dincin. They married (in 1927) shortly before his death in 1931.

This may have been the last time Ysaÿe posed for a portrait. He has a photograph of Queen Elisabeth of Belgium

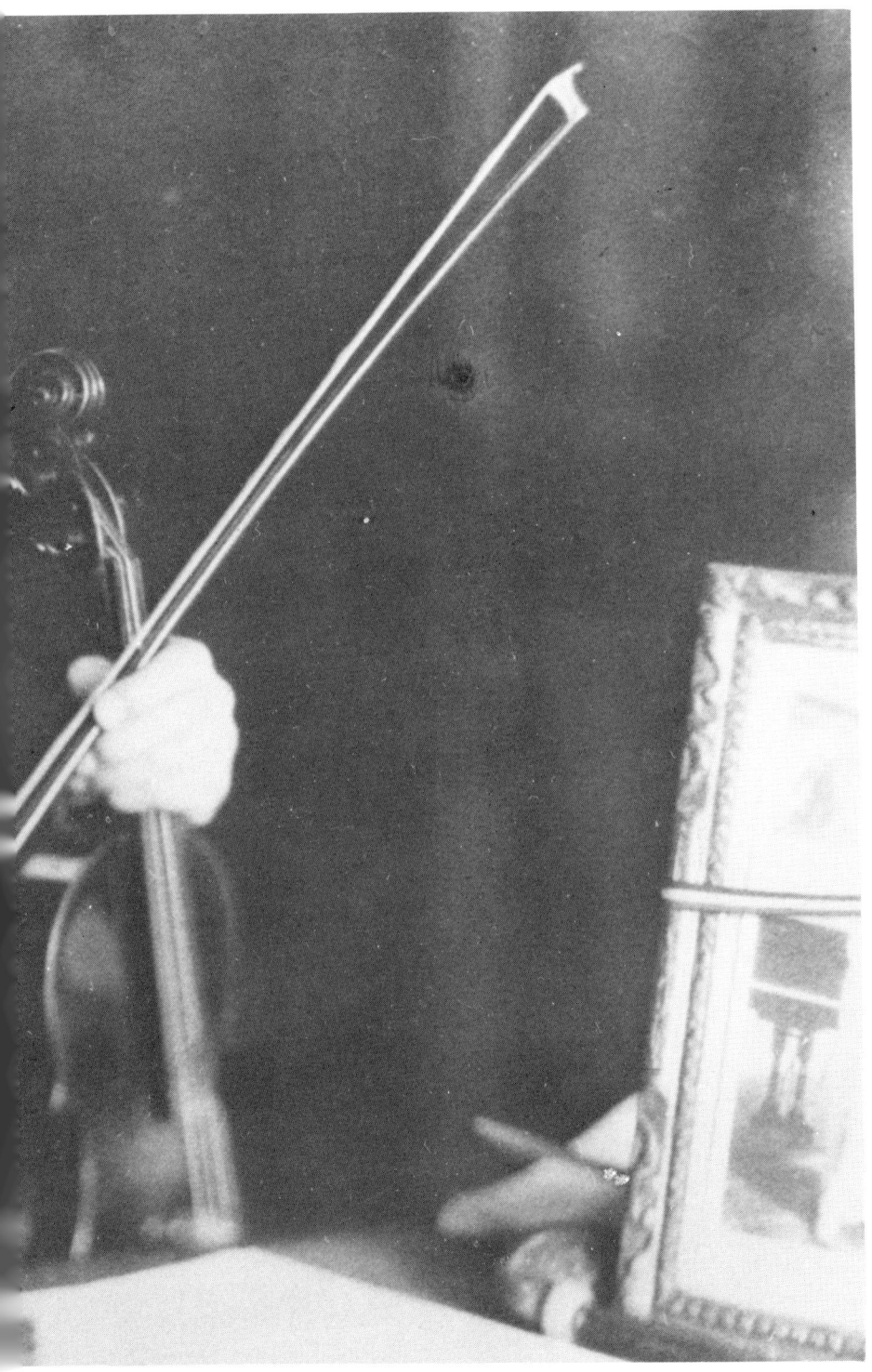

in the right hand corner of this illustration (1930). Photo courtesy of Leslie Sheppard.

Ysaÿe, recuperating from his foot amputation, is visited by

Antoine's sons, Ysaÿe's grandsons.

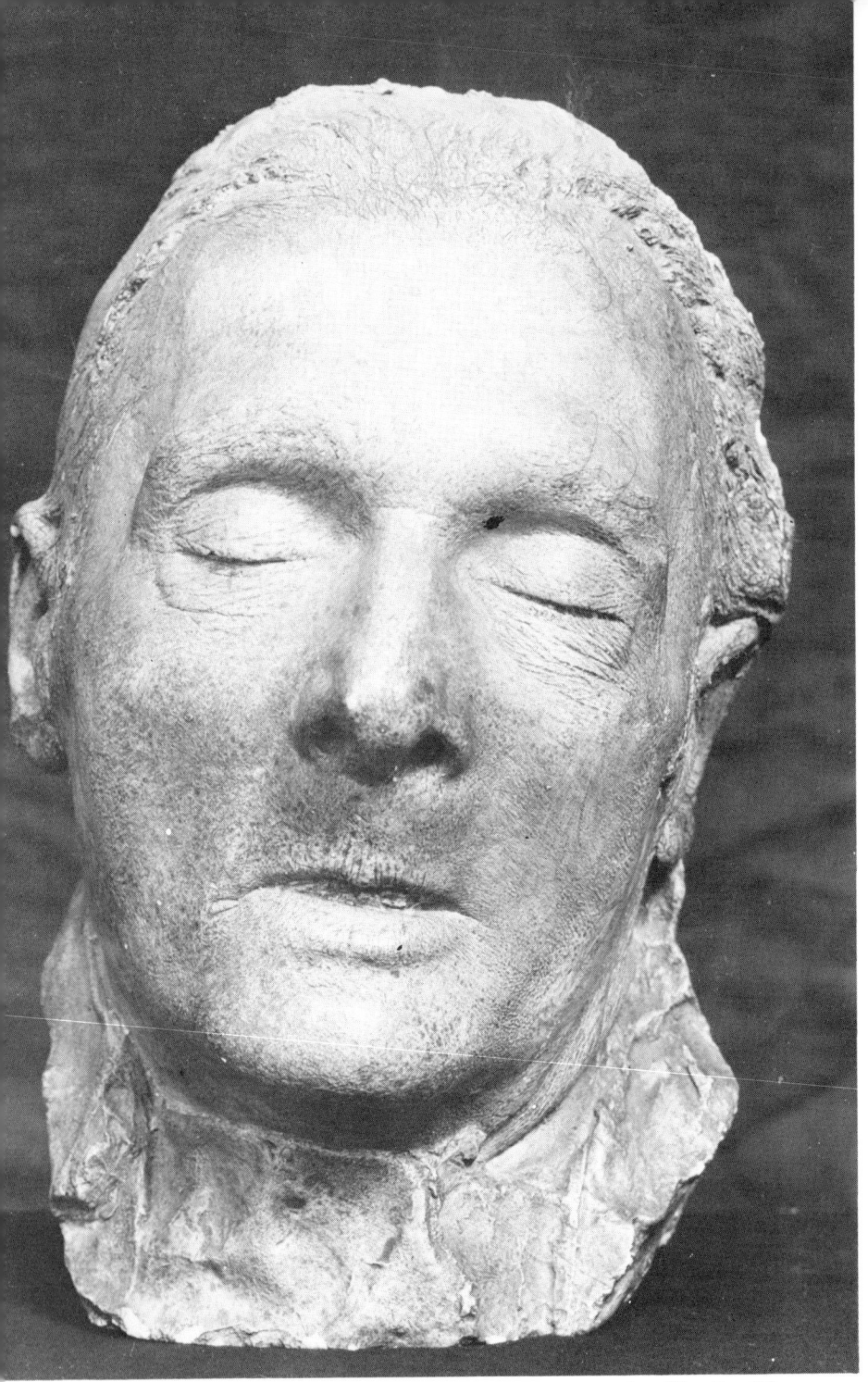

The death mask of Ysaÿe on display at the Ysaÿe Museum of Liege. Arazi photograph.

Competition of Violinists was not held until several years after the death of its founder.

On May 11, a few hours before his death, Ysaÿe heard his Fourth Sonata played in the adjoining room by a young violinist, his devoted admirer.[55] The great Belgian musician, one of the most brilliant exponents of the art of violin-playing at the turn of the century, breathed his last breath on May 12, 1931.

Eugène Ysaÿe was given a State funeral in Brussels, with thousands of people following the coffin. Many prominent musicians, among them Vincent d'Indy, Jacques Thibaud and Joseph Jongen, came to see the great master off on his last journey. His former pupils performed the *Adagio* from his *Poème Elégiaque* to Vincent d'Indy's accompaniment on the organ.

Some time after the funeral Ysaÿe's heart was brought in a small box of exquisite workmanship to Liège, the city where the great artist was born and educated. A monument with the wonderful bas-relief by the Belgian sculptor Constantin Meunier, powerfully presenting the noble profile and the inspired and strong visage of his great countryman, was erected over Ysaÿe's grave.

NOTES

[45] Thus on February 12, 1925, Ysaÿe played in Riga, the Franck Sonata, Mozart's Concerto in G Major, *Havanaise* by Saint-Saëns and Ballade and *Polonaise* by Vieuxtemps.
[46] Quoted from J. Ma. Corredor, *Conversations with Casals*, London, Hutchinson, (1956), p. 10.
[47] A. Ysaÿe, *op. cit.*, p. 252.
[48] J. Ma. Corredor, *op. cit.*, p. 47. Georges Enesco recalled that such meetings for playing chamber music had taken place in 1905. "There were five of us lovers of chamber music," he writes. "Ysaÿe first violin, Thibaud second, Kreisler viola, Casals cello, myself at the piano. We played for the mere pleasure of it. There were a few friends listening to us but actually we played for ourselves."—Andrei Tudor, *Enseco*, Bucharest, 1957, p. 73.
[49] For Pablo Casals and his orchestra, whose activities had such an important educational value for the capital of Catalon, see L. Ginsburg, *Pablo Casals*, 2nd ed., enlarged, Moscow, 1965.
[50] Casals means the concert at which he and Eugène Ysaÿe played the Brahms Double Concerto in 1912.—*L.G.*
[51] It is hard to say what the artist meant by this word, whether his own revival as a soloist or the resurrection of the Beethoven masterpiece in Casals's inspired interpretation.—*L.G.*
[52] Quoted from J. Ma. Corredor, *op. cit.*, p. 85.
[53] *L'Action Musicale*, 1927, 15 juillet.
[54] The opera's main character is a miner's wife who at the cost of her life prevents the explosion of the bomb thrown by her husband.
[55] That was Philip Newman, a pupil of César Thomson. He told us about this episode with great emotion during his visit to Moscow in 1958 as member of the jury at the First International Tchaikovsky Competition.

Eugène Ysaÿe prepared for public viewing after his death

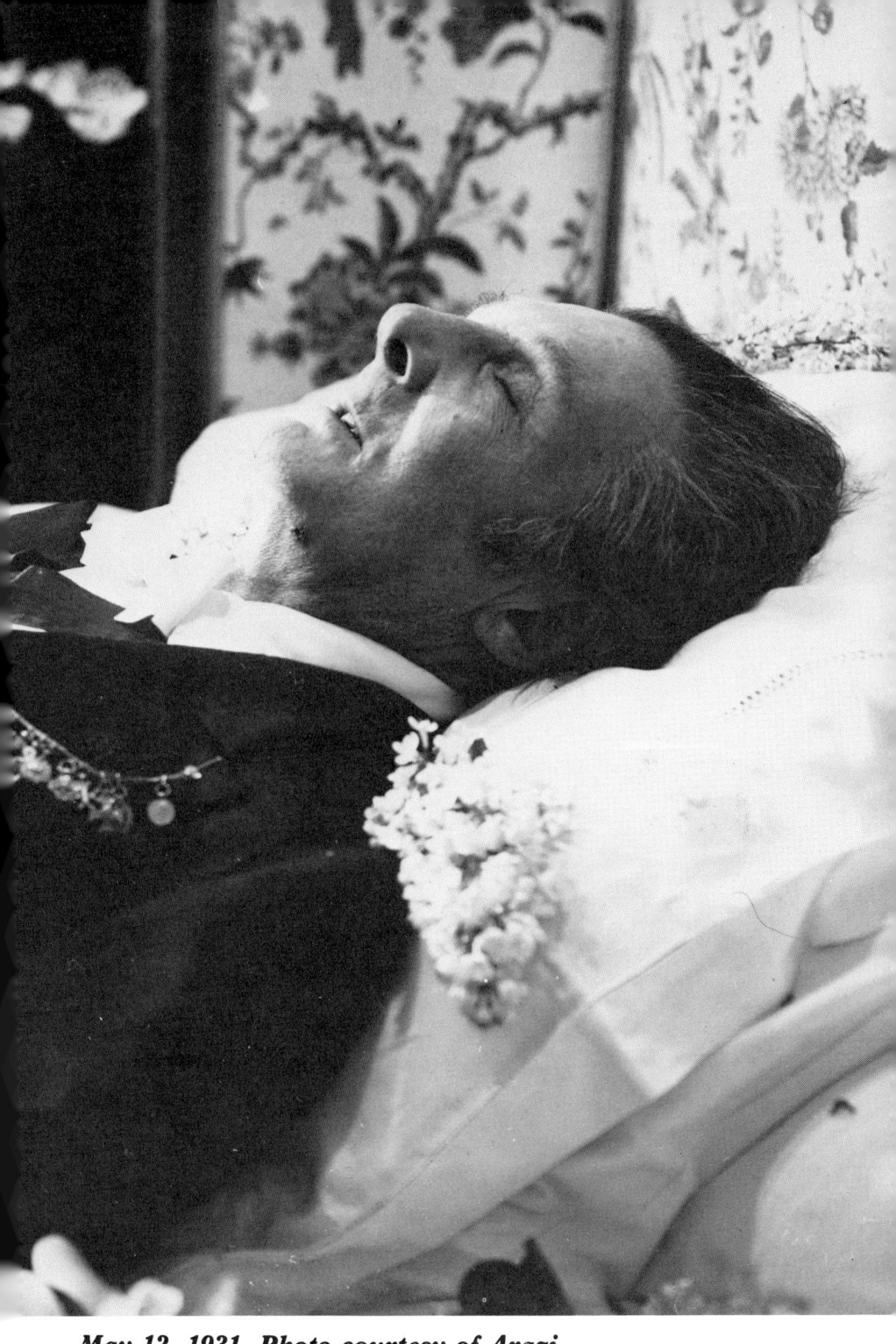

May 12, 1931. Photo courtesy of Arazi.

Ysaye, Romanticist of

Eugen Ysaye, from a Photograph Made During His Conductorship of the Cincinnati Symphony a Decade Ago

BRUSSELS, May 12.—Eugen Ysaye, one of the greatest violinists of his time, died this morning after a lingering illness. Three years ago Mr. Ysaye was forced by severe phlebitis to submit to the amputation of his right leg. Although he recovered from the operation, his health had never been robust since.

Full page spreads showing happier times in Ysaÿe's life

lin, Passes in Brussels

Ysaye on Vacation in the Summer of 1927 at Le Zoute, a Watering Place on the Belgian Coast

opera, "Peter, the Miner" was produced with great success in Liége last March. Queen Elisabeth, who had inspired him to complete the score, attended personally and also arranged a radio broadcast so that he could hear the performance from his bed. It is said that he left several other operatic scores uncompleted.

An Original Player

In the field of violin virtuosos, Ysave

appeared in almost every paper.

The solid silver urn made to hold Ysaÿe's heart. It rests in the Ysaÿe Museum in Liege. Photos of both sides of the urn courtesy of Arazi.

Sketches of Ysaÿe conducting from a chair after his foot was amputated. He refused to play the violin unless he could stand.

Joseph Szigeti.

On the facing page: Ovide Musin appeared on the cover of
The Musical Courier.

The History of the Belgian School of Violin

By Ovide Musin

WHEN we say a School is French, German, Italian or Russian, what is meant by the term? A School means the DISCIPLES of a man of genius, superior knowledge and of new ideas, the value of which he demonstrated and taught to his pupils, who handed down their knowledge to succeeding generations. If the above mentioned Schools exist, it is true that a *Belgian School* exists and has existed from ancient times; and furthermore, that the other Schools were derived from the ancient Masters who went from the Low Countries to Italy, Spain, France, Germany, Austria and even to the Court of Peter the Great of Russia, where they demonstrated their advancement in the Science and art of Composition, Singing, and playing of musical instruments, and where they founded Schools which were the *Source of our Modern Development* irrespective of nationality.

That the artistic generative force of the ancient Belgian Masters was not depleted even to the 19th and 20th centuries is evidenced by the great number of Belgian artists, musicians and teachers throughout the world whose names have added lustre to the ancient School which attained immense renown in the 14th, 15th and 16th centuries. Of our modern School the names of Gretry, Daussoigne Mehul, Francois Prume, Jacques Dupuis, Gevaert, Chas. De Beriot, Leonard, Cesar Frank, Vieuxtemps, Meerts, Radoux, Wery and others of the past generation propagated the Science and Art which produced those who today shine particularly in the realm of the violin. The greatest teachers of the *Modern French* School at Paris were BELGIANS FROM LIEGE. For instance, Lambert Massart of L i e g e (was professor at Paris for forty-seven y e a r s, his most celebrated pupils being Henri Wieniawski, Camilla Urso and Fritz Kreisler), Leonard, Vieuxtemps, Marsick and Remy (present Professor at the Conservatoire National de Paris).

Ysaye was a pupil of the Liege Conservatoire and of Henri Vieuxtemps. He also studied for awhile with Henri Wieniawski at Brussels.

Fritz Kreisler was a pupil of Massart at Paris.

Martin M a r s i c k, Cesar Thomson, Guillaume Remy and myself (Ovide Musin) were pupils of the Conservatoire de Liege and of Leonard.

Jacques Thibaut and Carl Flesch were pupils of Marsick.

Henri Marteau, pupil of Leonard, succeeded to the post of Joachim at Berlin, Germany.

Adolph Betti and Alfred Pochon were pupils of Cesar Thomson.

The catalogue would read as follows:

OVIDE MUSIN

SOME TEACHERS	SOME PUPILS
Charles De Beriot (of Louvain, Belgium)	Henri Vieuxtemps
Auguste Rouma (of Liege)	Henri Leonard
Lambert Massart (of Liege)	Henri Wieniawski, Camilla Urso, Fritz Kreisler
Henri Vieuxtemps (of Verviers, near Liege)	Ysaye, Hubay
Henri Leonard (of Liege)	Martin Marsick, Cesar Thomson, Ovide Musin, Guillaume Remy, Henri Marteau (successor of Joachim at Berlin)
Martin Marsick (of Liege)	Jacques Thibaut, Carl Flesch
Cesar Thomson (of Liege)	Adolf Betti, Alfred Pochon of the celebrated Flonzaley Quartet
Guillaume Remy (of Liege)	Present Professor at the Conservatoire National at Paris

Charles De Beriot, born at Louvain, Belgium, 1802, died in Louvain, 1870, was called the Father of the Modern Belgian School of Violin playing because of a special manner of using the bow, first demonstrated by himself, which gives greater elegance, freedom and continuity of tone. It was said of De Beriot that it was a pleasure simply to hear him tune his violin. His compositions are played the world over, and only an *Artist* can understand his works and play them as they should be played.

The Ancient School

HISTORICAL records among the archives of Rome, Milan, the Escurial, Archives Royal at Madrid, of the crown of Aragon at Barcelona, at Paris, Lille, Ghent, Bruxelles, Liege, Antwerp, Mons, and other cities, establish the fact that *Belgians* (both Wallon and Flemish) were a powerful influence in the development of the Science and Art of Composition, singing and playing of instruments in all the Countries of Europe, also in Scandinavia and Russia; Italy in particular, as its people were more responsive. The Belgians were brought from the Netherlands in great numbers to furnish the music for the Churches and Courts of Popes, Rulers and Princes. Phillippe the Second and Charles the Fifth of Spain, Charles the Ninth of France, Leopold Premier of Austria, The Louis XIV, XV and XVI of France were captivated by the Belgian Choristers.

An Italian historian, Guicciardini, 1523-1589, "in stating his enthusiastic appreciation of the BELGAS did not limit his praise for their talent as instrumentalists and their genius for Composition, but places above all, their *Vocal Art*, which he declared to be renowned and sought after by the Courts of every Christian Prince in Europe." The same historian published a Biography of THIRTY of the principal musicians of his time in Italy who came from Belgium. "When Philippe le Bel (Philip II) arrived at the Iberique Penninsular with his celebrated Choir in which the most famous musicians and singers from the Low Countries predominated, it aroused the most enthusiastic admiration, became promptly a la mode, and the members regarded as beings altogether privileged."

Going further back in musical history, a few names will serve to prove the antiquity of the Belgian School. A Monk named Hucbald, 840, of the Convent of St. Amand, near *Tournay*, Belgium, is called the Father of Primitive or Ancient Harmony. The true founders of the first School of music at Rome (1540) were two musicians from the Netherlands, Arkadelt and Goudimel. From this School came Palestrina, Animuccia, Na-

This article from **The Violinist** *(1917) by Ovide Musin gives some insight into the great place Belgian violinists occupied in the musical panorama.*

nini. Allegri (composer of the celebrated "Miserere") was a pupil of Nanini. This was before the violin as we know it today had appeared, and from one hundred to more than two hundred years before Corelli, Tartini and Viotto were born.

In 1540 appears Jean de Ockegem, born in *Hainaut,* Belgium. One of his pupils was Josquin des Pres., called the Father of Modern Harmony, Chapel Master at the Vatican, Rome. Another illustrious representative of the ancient Belgian School in Italy was Rolland de Lattre (also called Orlando Lasso) born at *Mons,* Belgium, 1520. At 21 he was Director of the Chapel of St. Jean de Latran at Rome. He travelled in France and England, and in 1557 was called to the Court of *Munich,* where he died in 1594.

Franco, called in Belgium Frank, of the Cathedral of Liege—1066—was the inventor of *Modern Rhythm.*

Dumont, born at Liege—1610—was the first to use Thorough-Bass in his compositions.

The Venetian School

THE founder of the Venetian School was Adrien Willaert, born at Bruges, Belgium, in 1480. In 1516 he went to Rome and between the years 1516-1652 he was the Director (Chapel Master) of St. Marc, Venice. His successor and pupil was Cyprien de Rore, born at Malines, Belgium. Ancient records teem with names, dates, places of birth, positions and achievements of Belgian musicians who advanced the Science and Art, founded Schools and left numerous pupils in all the European centers of learning who continued the development from generation to generation through the genius of certain ones. The term School seems not to be clearly understood by individuals who have the idea that to belong to a certain school necessarily means that every pupil is turned out after the same pattern in a mechanical manner. It is true that there is the *Science of Composition* apart from the inspiration. There is the *Science of Technic* and the *Science of Bowing* which must be learned by every one who aspires to something more than superficialty; but although Corelli, Tartini and Viotti owed their knowledge of the Science of the Art to their predecessors of the School at Rome, they were not alike as composers and players, all three retaining their particular individuality. John Sebastian Bach would have found it a difficult matter to give expression to his wonderful genius had he not acquired the knowledge spread before him by the fathers of *Primitive* and *Modern Harmony.* The same with Beethoven and other geniuses. *Purity of Style* is an inheritance left to the modern *Belgian Players and Teachers* by the Classic Masters. They have the traditions from the *Original Sources,* the founders of the schools.

The above brief sketch of a few historical facts taken from authentic records should settle the question of the existence of the BELGIAN SCHOOL in Music from antiquity down to the *predominance of the Belgian School of Violin* since 1827.

PRACTICE, to a large extent, makes the violin player, but reading makes the informed musician. You have probably met the individual who cannot tell the meaning of the commonest musical terms, has no information whatever of the lives of the composers whose works he plays, and could not write the simplest essay on musical history or violin-making. How few violinists there are who can read a dozen notes in the C clef, or tell who composed the operas, Jessonda, Faust, Fidelio or Bohemian Girl!

Not long ago we were surprised to find that right here in Chicago there lives an amateur violinist who never has a bow rehaired, but buys a new one whenever an old one is, as he supposes, worn out. Every six months or so he buys a new five-dollar bow, when any good violin-repairer could fix up the old one better than new for 75 cents.

The Cincinnati Conservatory of Music

TAKES PLEASURE IN ANNOUNCING THAT

EUGENE YSAYE

The "King of Violinists" and Conductor of the Cincinnati Symphony Orchestra
will conduct a **Master Class** in Violin at the Conservatory
beginning October 15, 1918

FOR FURTHER INFORMATION ADDRESS

MISS BERTHA BAUR, Directress   Cincinnati, Ohio

An advertisement for Ysaÿe's master class.

Karl Klein and August Wilhelmj, contemporaries of Ysaÿe.

Eugène Ysaÿe in 1909 at the peak of his career.

Chapter 7

The Style of Ysaÿe: The Performer

E ugène Ysaÿe's artistic personality should be studied in its unity of performer and composer. It cannot be denied that his aesthetic views underwent certain modifications in the course of his life. At the start of his career he experienced the influence of the art of Wieniawski and Vieuxtemps. Then he was strongly attracted to the music of Franck and his followers, but creative searchings which began in Ysaÿe's youth led finally to the development of a markedly individual style all his own. Ysaÿe's art is an original and well-integrated phenomenon. His creative output, predominantly romantic, contains at times life-like realistic imagery.

While speaking of his many-sided musical gifts and noting the artistic value of some of his compositions, we should, nevertheless, accord first place to Ysaÿe's art as an interpreter, for it was this art that for decades used to attract vast audiences in all parts of the world and excite their unbounded admiration. Eugène Ysaÿe was nicknamed "the king of violinists," "the artist of the bow," "the king of the violin," and his concerts were invariably his triumphs.

In what lies the explanation of the tremendous impact of Ysaÿe's playing? What was there in the performance of that great musician that made it so convincing and aesthetically pleasurable?

257

L'Ecole belge de Violon

During the Flanders Festival of 1978, a special day was set aside to celebrate the 120th birthday of Eugène Ysaÿe. His silhouette appeared on the cover. The French title reads: "The Belgian Violin School."

Vecsey and Royalty.
(From the Dresden Anzeiger.)

FRANZ VON VECSEY was invited to the Taschenberg Palace on Wednesday during the violin lesson hour of Prince Friedrich Christian, second son of the King. He played several pieces to his youthful host and was presented with a scarfpin bearing the King's monogram in pearls.

YSAYE

Assisted by JULES DEBEFVE, Pianist.

Season 1904-5.

R. E. JOHNSTON,

Sole and Exclusive Manager
for America and Australia,

St. James Building, NEW YORK CITY.

EMILE LEVY, Traveling Representative.

THIS IS THE ONLY MANAGEMENT THAT HAS
AUTHORITY TO NEGOTIATE
YSAYE ENGAGEMENTS IN AMERICA
AND AUSTRALIA.

"YSAYE" is pronounced as if it were spelled "E-ZI-E."

In 1904-1905 there was a great controversy over who managed Ysaÿe. Johnston eventually went bankrupt.

In the first place, it was the artist's rich gifts; his vivid creative personality. His listeners were captivated by the romantic fervor, poetry, lyricism and improvisatory nature of his interpretation, and they enjoyed the artist's original and perfect mastery of all the expressive potentialities of his instrument.[56]

Eugène Ysaÿe is often spoken of as the last representative of the romantic trend in violin playing, a trend initiated by Paganini, whose exponents—in a greater or less degree—were Joseph Slavik, Henryk Wieniawski, Henri Vieuxtemps, Pablo de Sarasate and some other virtuosi of the past century.

At the same time much in Ysaÿe's playing was determined by realistic principles. "It seems that realism and romanticism occur invariably together in great artists,"[57] wrote the great Russian writer Maxim Gorky, who asserted that this unity of realism and romanticism was capable of lending a peculiar originality and forcefulness to art.

At any rate, the originality of Eugène Ysaÿe's art and its exceptional expressive force were largely due to that combination of romantic and realistic elements. The integrity and meaningfulness of his interpretation, the urge to comprehend the composer's idea fully and objectively, the skill with which the artist, for all his original approach, succeeded in subjecting his technique to the aim of revealing the work's artistic message—these are significant traits in the portrait of this musician. They show that his principles of interpretation were close to our contemporary aesthetic principles of musical performance.

"The artist's first task is to forget himself," Eugène Ysaÿe once said. This precept enables us to oppose the Belgian musician to the numerous virtuosi of the late nineteenth and early twentieth century, who cared very little about penetration into the essence of the work performed and were concerned, first and foremost, with showing their skill to the best advantage, often distorting the composer's idea beyond recognition.

Ysaÿe's art was truthful and sincere, deeply felt and thought out. He used to say that art was the result of perfect harmony between thought and feeling.

His vivid artistic personality, rich imagination, unity of emotion and intellect, subjective and lyrical, and the objective and the notional; his ability to bend his artistic impulses to the logic of the

Pablo de Sarasate.

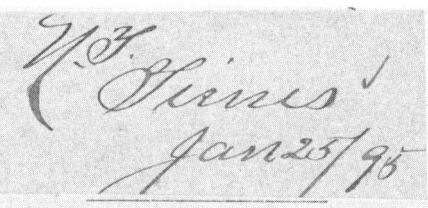

M. Ysaye Plays Once Again.

M. Eugene Ysaÿe, the eminent Belgian violin virtuoso, is now engaged in what Mr. Andrew Johnson of by-gone days called "swinging round the circle," his returning point always being New-York, where attendance at his performances has become one of the devotions of the musical of heart. He gave his third recital yesterday afternoon in the large auditorium of Carnegie Hall, without any perceptible evidence of a diminution in public interest. He was assisted, as heretofore, by M. Aimé Lachaume. The programme consisted of the following numbers: Raff's sonata in E minor, Opus 70, for violin and piano; the first movement of Vieuxtemps's E major violin concerto, a Chopin scherzo for piano, the adagio from Joachim's Hungarian concerto, Walter's prize song, from "Die Meistersinger," and Grieg's sonata in G minor for violin and piano.

For some reason, M. Ysaye's intonation was by no means faultless in the Raff sonata, and it had the misfortune to be thrown against the sharp background of some extremely warm and tender piano playing by M. Lachaume, whose treatment of his share of the sonata was uncommonly good in feeling and in tone quality. In spite of this fact, however, M. Ysaye's graceful reading of the adagio and his clean and vigorous bowing in the scherzo aroused the audience to a mood of approval which continued to the end of the entertainment. A fourth Ysaye recital is announced for Wednesday evening, Feb. 6.

BOSTON POST,
The Representative Democratic Paper
OF NEW ENGLAND.

SUNDAY MORNING, JAN. 27, 1895.

THE SYMPHONY CONCERT.

Mr. Cesar Thomson, violinist, was the soloist at the Symphony concert last evening, his first appearance in this city. His selection was Karl Goldmark's concerto in A minor, an extremely difficult bit of music, but beautifully given by Mr. Thomson. Coming when the Ysaye furore is literally at its height, some comparison was unavoidable, but after the first movement, that was not to the detriment of the soloist of last night, nor could it be said that he wrested any of the well-earned laurels from M. Ysaye. There is a radical difference in the style of the two men. Mr. Thomson lacks, to some extent, Ysaye's force, his powerful tone and tone shading, but he makes up for it by wonderful brilliancy and accuracy of technique and sweetness of tone. After the first movement he seemed to warm to his task with every succeeding note, and as his beautiful work became appreciated by his hearers, they waxed more and more enthusiastic, and at the close of his selection recalled him again and again, until he responded with a brief selection, unaccompanied by the orchestra, and remarkable chiefly for the pearly staccato bowing. Mr. Thomson certainly played himself into great favor, and will be sure of a warm welcome upon his next appearance here.

After the concerto, Smetana's symphonic poem "Sarka" should have been played according to the programme, but M. Paur rose superior to the programme and played Beethoven's overture to Leonore, No. 2, which was down as the last number. When it was finished, the mystified audience hardly knew whether to sit still or get up and go home. Mr. Paur saw the difficulty and hastened to the rescue by starting the symphonic poem, the first time it has been given in Boston. It depicts an adventure of Sarka, the noblest of the mythical Bohemian Amazons, and some of the orchestral effects are almost as startling as the incidents of Sarka's story of love, betrayal, treachery and death.

The audience was unusually large, a double fringe of standing music lovers lining both sides and the rear of the hall.

From the Ysaÿe scrapbook made available by Marianne Wurlitzer.

Chicago
Vanity Fair
Feb 7/95

For the Musical Ear

EUGENE YSAYE

With his heavy, massive features and his mop of black hair combed straight back from his forehead and hanging in a ragged fringe around his collar, Eugene Ysaye is picturesque enough to attract attention anywhere. When his heroic form loomed up on the Auditorium stage at the recent Chicago orchestra concerts he reminded me irresistibly of the pictures of Balzac. The breadth of face and the weight of jaw are Balzac's, and so is the determined indifference and impassiveness of facial expression. For reasons, the wisdom of which appear later on, Mr. Ysaye had insisted upon the erection on the stage of an elevated platform, and some carpenter had evoked from the inner recesses of the Auditorium stage something that looked like a dry-goods box. Standing upon this pedestal Mr. Ysaye's portly form loomed up like the Bartholdi statue of liberty, and added to the suggestion of physical force imparted by his whole appearance.

This impression of a commanding and powerful personality is not entirely borne out, however, and there is something grotesque about the Samsonian gestures with which the gigantic violinist reels and sways while playing. And I must own, also, to a sense of disappointment at the beginning of the Saint-Saëns concerto, in which the sense he communicated was not that of great power but of delicacy and refinement. The real merit of his work first presented itself in the quality of his tone, which is remarkably pure, full, round and flowing, and retains all these qualities even when the performer is going through the most dangerous gymnastics of technique. I do not recall any other player lately heard here whose violin did not in certain florid passages on high notes remind you with painful force that it was a mere mechanical thing of strings and seasoned timber. Ysaye's tone never does this. At times it has almost a vocal quality, and this was preserved not only in the marvelously smooth and facile playing of Bruch's "Scotch Fantasia," but in the mere shreds of tone which occasionally break in on the concerto. With this purity of tone he unites the merit of a technique, which is apparently not to be hindered by any difficulties this side of the extraordinary. He did not repeat some of the feats of magic performed by César Thomson at a previous concert, but whatever he did attempt was done not only in magnificent style but with surprising ease. These are the reasons for rating his skill as a virtuoso less than his talents as an artist, and it is as an artist that he makes his chief appeal. I would rather that he had omitted the habit of synchronous swaying with the orchestra, and in the andante of the concerto he reminded me of an inverted pendulum. But just the same that andante was a beautiful bit of sensuous playing, and must have convinced the audience that whatever he may lack, Ysaye has sentiment and poetry.

The audience broke into a tempest of applause at the close of both the concerto and the fantasia, and there was as much shouting and waving of handkerchiefs as when Paderewski played. I noticed, however, with much comfort, that these same handkerchiefs were perfectly dry, which re-enforces the conviction that Mr. Ysaye is an artist who speaks to the intelligence even more than to the sympathies. That he is an artist, and one of a high order, there can be no question, and his conquest of Auditorium audiences shows that he has impressed the public with the fact. If he will but stay in the vicinity long enough he may receive some of the osculatory adulation which befell Paderewski. He eclipsed every other musical event of the week, and although the rest of the concert afforded excellent specimens of the Chicago Orchestra's work, the audience seemed to be unaware of the existence of anything but the violinist.

From the Ysaÿe scrapbook made available by Marianne Wurlitzer.

YSAYE THE VICTOR

THE GREAT VIOLINIST SCORES THE TRIUMPH OF THE YEAR

One of the Largest Afternoon Audiences Ever Gathered in Chicago Greets His Playing with a Storm of Applause—Chicago Orchestra Also Plays Admirably

The largest audience of the present season, if not the largest ever gathered at an afternoon performance in the Auditorium, filled that great hall yesterday to hear Eugene Ysaye play his violin. The boxes were filled, the seats in every part of the house were filled, and a few hundreds of people who came too late to secure seats stood throughout the concert. Society was there in force. The audience was more than half made up of women, but the number of men present was unusual for a matinee. Club men and business men too were present, as well as musicians, music teachers, clergymen and members of other professional callings. Evidently the spirit of expectancy was high. And it was realized; not one of the vast throng was disappointed or regretted that he had come.

When Mr. Ysaye stepped out upon the platform a moderately vigorous applause told him that he had the good will of his audience. He appeared grateful, and proceeded to show his hearers that they had made no mistake in giving him their welcome.

His first number was Saint-Saens' third violin concerto (in B minor, op. 61), which is in three movements. He played it with feeling and masterly finish. The orchestra, also, was fully equal to its part of the piece, and being in rare sympathy with the soloist, the work of both produced such artistic perfection as is rarely attained anywhere. At the end of the first movement the great throng was beginning to realize something of the wonder of Mr. Ysaye's playing, and demonstrated the fact by generous applause. When the second movement had been given the plaudits were more generous. The violinist had not only satisfied his audience with his art, he had given also some of his personality, had shown his humanity and feeling for humanity.

The audience was becoming more and more attracted, more and more delighted. But it waited until the last sweet notes of the concerto's finale (during which movement every soul remained spell-bound) had floated away into silence to show how completely it had been enthralled by the wizard's bow. When Mr. Ysaye dropped the violin from his shoulder, inclined his head slightly, then turned and grasped Mr. Thomas' hand, the storm broke. And such a storm it was. One in the foyer might have mistaken the tumult for a great political meeting. Everybody in orchestra and audience applauded. "Bravo, bravo," was heard from all sides. Women stood up in their seats; and the pit of the house was a sea of waving handkerchiefs. Mr. Ysaye came from the wings a half-dozen times, bowing all the way out and all the way back, but that wouldn't do. The audience must have more. Finally he consented and played, without accompaniment, a classic bit from Bach. Even after that he was recalled again and again.

* * *

In Bruch's "Scotch Fantasia," which he gave after intermission, Mr. Ysaye displayed, better than before, the fullness of his powers, being more enthusiastic and more forgetful of self. Again there was a storm of applause, again the many recalls and an encore number.

This is the more wonderful because at first sight the man is not attractive. He is large, strong, massive, ungainly in appearance; and gives no hint at all of personal magnetism. But the instant his bow touches the strings one forgets the man in his music. You see the large, square-built, long-haired violinist there drawing the bow back and forth, and working his fingers with lightning-like rapidity, but you do not seem to notice him. You know that you are listening to an artist rather than a virtuoso—an artist of marvelous power, grace and delicacy; and in his clear, limpid tones you float on and on to dreams of wonderful things.

In the brilliant passages Mr. Ysaye is strong and satisfactory but does not develop the leonine power and magnificence one might expect, from a glance at the man, to be the chief characteristic of his playing. It is in the remarkably delicate phrasing and shading, continued throughout every measure of all that he plays, and the depth of feeling and sentiment with which his playing is imbued that the real excellence of his work is found. And herein again is the listener surprised and treated to grace and finish of which he never dreamed. He possesses temperament in a strongly marked degree. From the instant the first note comes singing from his instrument you feel the influence of masterful personality. You realize the presence of great temperamental energy, and know yourself to be at once under the sway of conscious power.

There may be, no doubt there are, greater virtuosi in the world. But there can be but one opinion of Eugene Ysaye as an artist. If he is not, as certain critics and authorities have asserted, absolutely the greatest of living violinists, he is certainly among the very first, and the question of degree is not worth discussing in cases of such towering eminence.

* * *

The rest of the programme (which will be repeated this evening) comprised Mozart's symphony in G minor, Spohr's "Jessonda" overture and Slavonic dances from Dvorák's fourth series. The orchestra played each in admirable style, giving to the beautiful Mozart symphony an almost flawless interpretation.

At next week's orchestra concert the following programme will be given:

Symphony, b flat (B. & H., edition 12)...Haydn
Aria from "Entfuhrung"................Mozart
Overture, "Leonore," No. 3............Beethoven
Concertstück for Piano..............C. Chaminade
"Wotan's Farewell" and) "Walkuere"...
"Magic Fire Scene," { ....Wagner

The soloists will be Max Heinrich, the favorite baritone, and Hans von Schiller, pianist, of this city.

Ysaye.

THE BALTIMORE NEWS.

PUBLISHED BY
THE EVENING NEWS PUBLISHING COMPANY OF BALTIMORE CITY.
Office, No. 201 East Baltimore Street.

CHAS. H. GRASTY,   DOUGLAS H. GORDON,
   President.   Secretary-Treasurer.

SATURDAY EVENING, JAN. 26, 1895.

PADEREWSKI'S RIVAL.

Ysaye, the Violinist, the Latest Matinee Idol.

Ysaye, the violinist, has played in New York and bids fair to rival Paderewski himself in the affections of the matinee girl. At Carnegie Hall Thursday afternoon, where he appeared, the New York Sun says there were nine women to one man, and the enthusiasm began when the violinist had finished the fourth movement of the first number, Raff's "Finale Confuoco," and culminated in a hysterical storm which brough Ysaye out on the stage six times after he had played the last thing on the programme, Greig's "Allegro Guerriero." Ysaye, says the Sun, seems to take the adoration of the fair sex with considerable surprise; not as a matter of right, as "raddy" did. It may be a difference of hair. The pianist, as all the world knows, manipulated his hair, or his valet did, until it stood out like a sunset cloud agitated by the evening breeze. Ysaye's hair is almost in the present style. It is only a little longer than the locks of the smart young men, but he does not part it in the middle as they do. He parts it far down on the left side, and from there it loosely crosses his forehead and dances, as to its ends, when he fiddles.

When the last of the programme had been played, a hundred of the women crowded to the edge of the stage, and leaned there facing the ante-room door, and soulfully longing until their applause brought Ysaye forth. Then they looked as if they were inclined to throw things at him—flowers and ribbons and gloves—as they did at "raddy," but the craze has not quite reached that point yet.

"It will, though," said the man in the lobby. "He's fit to beat Paddy in a walk, but the girls are a little shy yet."

A Sun reporter saw Mr. Ysaye. He found the violinist interested in just one thing, and that seemed a curious thing, too. Ysaye said:

"I am instructor, you know, in the Brussels Conservatory. Now there are always there and coming and going a lot of clever Americans—oh, yes very clever—excellent performers, men with technique and feeling. Well, then, what becomes of them? So! Where do they go, eh? I see in your orchestras here only a lot of baldheaded Dutchmen. Where are those Americans? So! Do they not learn to play as a profession? No! It is strange and too bad. A lot of baldheaded Dutchmen, eh?"

This, and the facing page, from the Ysaÿe scrapbook made available by Marianne Wurlitzer.

Joseph Joachim.

phrase and of the entire work, are qualities which put Ysaÿe in the same rank with such outstanding performers as Joachim, Casals, Enesco, Rachmaninov, Igumnov[59] and Brandukov[60]—to name but a few.

As in the case of these artist-instrumentalists, the originality of Ysaÿe's performing style was determined by his own creative personality and by the national cultural idiosyncrasies. Like these artists, the Belgian musician fully understood the creative nature of the interpretative art. He highly valued the ability of the artist to create visions, to express good and bad, joy and sorrow.

An entry in Ysaÿe's notebook[58] reads: "Without the interpreter the composition is a voice crying in the wilderness . . . The interpretative artist is the life-blood of music."

In another place he wrote: "What would the theater be without the artists who recreate the work of the playwright? What would music be without those who give it life and feeling, who make it known and loved and whose work is thus raised to the highest level of achievement?" Then, speaking of great artists who would be remembered for ages, he mentioned Niccolò Paganini, Anton Rubinstein and the great actors Frédéric Lemaître and Sarah Bernhardt.

The advocates of progressive aesthetic views on interpretative art have always emphasized its creative character and demanded from the artists such interpretation as would reveal the content of the work of art to the full in a truly creative way and with inspiration. This is exactly what Belinsky, Serov, Tchaikovsky, Asafyev and other progressive Russian thinkers insisted upon.

To quote Alexander Serov: "An adequate performance does not mean merely a correct reading of the signs which convey sounds: one must develop in oneself a correct understanding of the musical speech, one must grasp the mystery of musical poetry, accustom oneself to 'reading between the lines' the message which, though unseen, is clear to one's poetic sense."[61]

Progressive artists in other countries, too, have asserted the creative nature of interpretation. In particular, Pablo Casals, Ysaÿe's younger contemporary and friend whose performance was truly creative and inspired, said that the interpretative artist must "bring to life what is written, infuse life, instead of avoiding it with timidity."[62]

After his death, Ysaÿe was featured, along with other artists, in a series of picture postcards. This is one of them.

YSAYE'S ARRIVAL.

SAYE, the Belgian violinist, accompanied by Mrs. Ysaye, are passengers aboard the steamship Kaiser Wilhelm der Grosse, which is expected at this port as we go to press. Mrs. Ysaye will pass the greater part of the winter in New York.

It is said Ysaye has not changed since he was here, only he looks more serious and sedate and his face holds an expression of intense earnestness. Then he was the mellow Bohemian, whose performances were echoes of his Epicurean philosophy, and whose audacious suavity and brilliant virtuosity were irresistible. Now he is the ripe musician, the mature artist, who has a just idea of the seriousness of his mission. It is understood that since Ysaye was here his style has undergone a marked change. It will be interesting to compare his present playing with his performances of five years ago. There can be no doubt that his recent development has been along artistic lines, if the transatlantic music critics are to be believed.

It was arranged to give Ysaye a reception at the Hotel Martin last night.

Next Friday night, in Philadelphia, Ysaye will play for the first time this season in America. He will be the soloist of the concert of the Philadelphia Symphony Orchestra and will perform the Beethoven concerto.

Ysaye will make his first New York appearance this season in Carnegie Hall with the Boston Symphony Orchestra December 8. Later he will give several recitals here. One of these will be a joint recital with d'Albert, and the two artists will unite in a performance of Beethoven's "Kreutzer" sonata.

A 1904 editorial from **The Musical Courier.**

A sketch of Ysaÿe dated 1924. Courtesy of Arazi.

Eugène Ysaÿe possessed a rare gift of penetrating the spirit of the music he was playing. He could bring it to life like none other. The means he employed for this purpose were his astonishingly pure and expressive tone, warm vibration, virtuoso technique that was perfectly natural and spontaneous, exceedingly wide range of dynamics and highly original and poetic rubato.

This last device enabled the artist, for all his rhythmic precision, to overcome the purely metronomic regularity and attain a living declamatory phrasing, which was always noted by his contemporaries.

His rubato was not a matter of chance—it was called forth by the logic of the phrase, while its duration was determined by the artist's feeling, thinking and sense of style, of the spirit, of the work performed. Deeply thought out in the course of preliminary work and brought in conformity with the musical phrase, Ysaÿe's rubato during the performance was the result of his artistic intuition and inspiration of the moment. It was simple and natural and usually it did not go beyond a musical phrase and contained no hint at premeditated effect.

"You must phrase as you breathe," Eugène Ysaÿe used to say. These words are quoted in the recollections of Emile Jaques Dalcroze (1865-1950),[63] the well-known Swiss musician and pedagogue, the author of the system of eurhythmics, who was also a composer and dedicated to Ysaÿe one of his violin concertos. He was Ysaÿe's accompanist on some of the violinist's concert tours and for that reason his recollections are of special value.

"Ysaÿe placed great demands on his accompanists," Jaques-Dalcroze wrote. "There must be an interpenetration of two temperaments, mutual sacrifices, carefully distributed rubato, efforts to achieve uniform sonority and the utmost respect for the phrasing and dynamics indicated by the composer. He hated all kinds of exaggeration and over-sensuous interpretation and paid particular attention to nuances and regular accents."

The plasticity and finish of Ysaÿe's phrasing resulted in his rubato being usually compensated for in the following bars. Hence his demand that his partner at the piano should play rhythmically, thus "balancing his own flights of fancy."

Sir Henry Wood (1869-1944), the well-known English conductor, recalled with pleasure his rehearsals and concerts with Ysaÿe in 1899. He wrote:

"I learned more in these early years from this great man than from all the others put together . . . What impressed me more than anything was his marvellous singing quality and perfect rubato." Noting that many performers had an uncertain rubato that left the conductor hanging in midair, as it were, he said that this never happened with Ysaÿe. The conductor always knew what Ysaÿe intended doing and followed him naturally. His rubato was such that "if he borrowed he faithfully paid back within four bars. It was an absolute inspiration to accompany him."[64]

As Ysaÿe said, "Observing the markings is not all—one must do it well. And sometimes one should even disregard them." In this way he understood the freedom and predeterminedness of the interpreter artist's creativity.

In Ysaÿe's opinion, complete freedom was attained through a deep penetration into the essence of the piece performed, after a

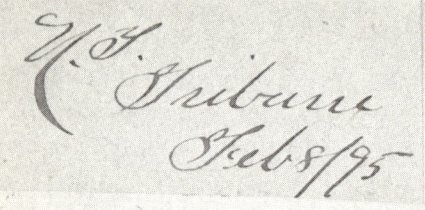

N.Y. Tribune Feb 8/95

BOSTON SYMPHONY ORCHESTRA.

The Boston Symphony Orchestra could measure last evening the high esteem in which it is held by the musical people of this city from the size of the audience that gathered to hear its fourth concert in the Metropolitan Opera House. That so many of its friends braved the storm and submitted to the inconveniences of interrupted traffic was a compliment not to be lightly weighed; the more that the programme in itself was not one that could attract by reason of its novelty. Both Beethoven's eighth symphony and Dvořák's Carnival overture had been heard here lately, and Mr. Paur's reading of the symphony could scarcely arouse to enthusiasm. It suffered from the anxious overelaboration, the artificiality of phrasing to which the Boston conductor seems to be becoming more and more addicted. The Dvořák overture, on the contrary, was read and played with a splendid spirit and a pulsating energy that could scarcely be surpassed.

The noteworthy feature of the concert was a new concerto for 'cello, by Mr. C. M. Loeffler, one of the distinguished first violins of the orchestra. Previous compositions of his that have been heard here, especially his lovely sextet played by the Kneisel Quartet, have proved him to be a musician of original and delicate fancy and high technical attainment; and while the concerto did not reveal itself as the equal of the best he has done, it has nevertheless many qualities of extraordinary interest. Chief among these is the richness and power of its orchestration; indeed, it is in the general effect of its color and its significance in the depiction of moods that it shines, rather than in the pregnancy and logical development of its themes. Mr. Loeffler has absolved himself, perhaps, from too much responsibility in this respect by the title "fantastic" that he has affixed to his composition. The solo part is a grateful one for the performer, and exploits as well as any concerto can be expected to exploit technical proficiency upon an instrument that lends itself the least of any to such proceedings. It was played by Mr. Schroeder with the power and brilliancy and absolute certainty that his hearers have learned to expect of him. He and Mr. Loeffler were several times compelled to bow their acknowledgments of the enthusiastic applause bestowed upon both the performer and the composition.

Mr. Watkin Mills also contributed two bass airs: "Oh, Ruddier than the Cherry," from Handel's "Acis and Galatea," and Leporello's "Madamina" song from "Don Giovanni." He has a rich and flexible bass voice and sings in a manly and musical, if somewhat dry, style. It would be interesting to know why he elected to brave comparisons by giving the aria from "Don Giovanni" from the very stage where it has been several times heard this winter from the greatest of Leporellos, and with the dramatic surroundings which can alone give it its proper effect.

Chicago Tribune Feb 4/95

WIZARD OF THE BOW.

EUGENE YSAYE TOUCHES THE STRINGS AND PEOPLE APPLAUD.

Belgian Violinist Plays at the Auditorium with Thomas' Orchestra and Proves Himself Most Popular—His Charm Lies in Emotional Quality and Manner of Performance—The Vigor of Manliness Lacking—Succeeds in the Romantic, Not the Classic.

The first appearance in Chicago of Eugene Ysaye, the Belgian violinist, took place yesterday afternoon at the Chicago Orchestra concert in the presence of one of the largest audiences ever assembled in that theater at an afternoon performance. Mr. Ysaye is preeminently a popular violinist. Not in the general acceptance of the term, but in a proper sense. His playing is of a description which commands immediate recognition of the generality through two things—its emotional quality and the manner of its performance. Thoroughly French, his art is exquisite in finish, but not convincing in its meaning. That which is failing is vigor, not the vigor of energy, but the vigor of manliness. His tone is neither large nor vibrant, but delightfully sweet and insinuating. The impression produced in connection with M. Ysaye's imposing proportions is that of a large singer, as so frequently happens, with a small voice charmingly sweet in quality.

M. Ysaye's choice in selecting a platform of unusual height to stand upon was of a wisdom at once apparent. It acted in a measure as a sounding-board and allowed a fuller quality of tone than that which he evinced under less favorable conditions at the rehearsals of the previous day. It is in a smaller hall than the Auditorium that M. Ysaye would be at his best. Stripped of the comedy of manners with which he invests his playing, this would be quite clearly apparent. His expression has the charm of delicacy and is of a sentiment that is sentimental, but not of passionate abandon. Smooth finished and elegant, genuine in the French sense, which is premeditated and self-contemplative rather than spontaneous, his success with the public is assured.

His Weakness and Strength.

In his first number, Saint-Saëns' Concerto No. 3, in B minor, he evidenced at once his weakness and his strength. In his second selection, Bruch's "Scotch Fantasia," he displayed the fullness of his powers. He was both more enthusiastic and more self-forgetful in poise. The work of the orchestra in accompanying the Saint-Saëns' number was eminently greater than the work of the soloist. The shadings and effects were remarkable in gradation and in support to the solo instrument. The Bruch number was equally well done, but in this latter instance the soloist, being more completely acceptable, made the fact less evident through contrast. It is in the romantic and not the classic that M. Ysaye must make his success. The Bach given as encore awakens at least such suspicion most distinctly. Future and fuller acquaintance may reverse this impression, but there was yesterday little to justify other expectations. Three orchestral numbers, Mozart's G minor symphony, Spohr's "Jessonda" overture, which the stage could or might be seen was crowded.

The box holders were:
C. H. McCormick,
George M. Pullman,
Norman Williams,
Marshall Field,
T. B. Blackstone,
Mrs. E. S. Isham,
Mrs. H. J. Willing,
Roswell Miller,
Mrs. H. M. Wilmarth,
Mrs. George Sturges,
W. W. Kimball,
T. R. Lyon,
J. J. Glessner,
John G. McWilliams,
F. H. Peck,
Mrs. Henry Corwith,
Mrs. A. N. Eddy,
Mrs. A. J. Caton,
H. H. Porter,
R. H. McCormick,
O. W. Norton,
Edward Norton,
J. M. W. Jones,
S. E. Gross,
John DeKoven,
C. L. Hutchinson,
A. C. Bartlett,
A. A. Sprague,
E. F. Lawrence.

When Ysaye appeared and mounted his platform before he drew his bow across the strings of his violin he was greeted with a storm of applause. The boxes started it, the people in the orchestra seats followed suit, and the rest of the house did the same.

To watch this artist play is not pleasant. Irresistibly and uncomfortably one feels as if the man was working hard. Probably he was not, but it looked that way. It was much more satisfactory to close one's eyes and listen only. But society did not do that. Instead it focused a thousand lorgnettes and opera glasses on the big man in a long black coat on top of his big box, and kept them fixed upon him steadily.

Divinities need a lot of applause and coaxing and the Ysaye proved himself as greedy of tribute as ever Patti herself. And when at length he condescended to mount the long flight of steps to his pedestal society was so delighted that it not only applauded but shouted as though a nation's hero stood before them.

and the Slavonic Dances, fourth series, by Dvorak, made up the complement of the program.

In the saddest passages there is always in Mozart a glimpse of sunny hopefulness. It is the gloom of an April day. The perfect form of the G minor, the contrast of the movements in sequence, and the variation in mood obtained yesterday a memorable expression. It is with the performance of such works, strong in demand upon the finest, most subtle qualities, that the attainments of the orchestra are most impressive. Conductor and orchestra alike were yesterday at their best, and to equal it tonight the performance must be one of the most notable yet given by the organization.

Society Makes a Lion of Him.

Eugene Ysaye also scored a society triumph. Once, and perhaps twice, only before has society crushed into the great house and filled it to the last limits of its capacity at an afternoon performance. Patti did it and perhaps so did Melba. Yet Ysaye is not a handsome man. He is ungainly looking, big, too stout to be graceful, with a mass of long, smooth, black hair, an irregular face, and a supreme disdain of all mortals save himself.

As one looked along the double row of boxes it was hard to believe this was an afternoon performance. Of course there was a predominance of women, that is to be expected at a matinée, but the faces of well-known club men were to be seen in great numbers. The boxes could not begin to hold the throng that seemed determined to make the Ysaye a fad, and it filled the great orchestra and balconies and then flowed over. There was a line six deep at the back of the seats in the foyer, big marble staircases to the balcony were filled with women, fashionable women who came too late for seats, every point from

Both pages, from the Ysaÿe scrapbook made available by Marianne Wurlitzer.

273

Eugène Ysaÿe. 1908.

long and thoughtful work on the means of its recreation in performance. "One must completely identify oneself with the musical idea and feelings of the work, one must study it long, patiently, intelligently and thoroughly in order to forget the technique necessary for its realization during the performance."[65]

To be able to achieve this, the artist must work ceaselessly, so Ysaÿe wrote in his notebook: "It cannot be realized too clearly that interpretation demands strength and energy and deep reflection in order to give life to a work or a role. What self-questioning, hesitation and groping are necessary before an artist can feel that his interpretation is right and that he has entered into the role he has to perform!"

The famous French violinist Jacques Thibaud, who was a close friend of Ysaÿe, wrote: "It was thanks to him (Eugène Ysaÿe—L.G.) that in the art of violin playing the spirit of freedom was revived; not of anarchism but of a freedom based on the deepest love for art in the broadest sense of the word." [66]

Ysaÿe's style of interpretation combined the subjective and the objective; he knew how to convey the essence of the work performed and do it not in a detached and passionless way but to imbue his performance with his own artistic understanding and creative feeling. The interpretative artist "must be at once subjective and objective, he must be able to penetrate even deeper than the author himself into the aesthetics of the work. It is for him to bring into relief all those evanescent details which the author does not underline or even write, details which do not become apparent when the work is merely read. The interpretative artist is a sculptor whose work may well become permanent, for once a character has been created and has been brought into being by a model interpretation, it becomes a tradition. It remains an example to be followed, and is an integral part of the work itself," wrote Ysaÿe in his notebook.

He went on to recall the great artists who, through their creative interpretation, had given life to musical works, revealing in them traits which were overlooked at merely reading the score and were sometimes not wholly clear even to the composer himself. "Who has not felt, when listening to Chopin's *Funeral March*, played by Rubinstein, or even to the whole Sonata with its finale, which seems to echo through the very silence of the tomb, that this work

Eugène Ysaÿe playing sonatas with his brother Théo.

A Latvian caricature of Ysaÿe.

was only really beautiful when played thus? ... Rubinstein remade it, completed it, bringing to it that which was lacking."

The Beethoven Violin Concerto was to Ysaÿe (who himself was an unsurpassed exponent of it) also inseparably associated with Joachim's masterly interpretation of this work of genius. "It is forty years since the Hungarian master played this composition, little known before his time, and he played it so well that he now seems part of it. It was he, I may say, who showed it to the world as a masterpiece. Without his ideal interpretation the work might have been lost among those compositions which are placed on one side and forgotten. It was a consecration ... Joachim's interpretation was a mirror in which the power of Beethoven's thought was reflected." Joachim made the composer's thoughts his own and in his interpretation he avoided everything that deviated from the truth.

It would be in place to add here that a considerable contribution towards the upbuilding of the progressive tradition in interpreting the Beethoven Concerto was made by Ferdinand Laub (1832-75),[67] Professor of the Moscow Conservatoire since its foundation. Then there were other contemporaries of Joachim. At the same time, Ysaÿe's high opinion of the truthful and artistic interpretation of Beethoven's masterpiece by Joseph Joachim is perfectly justifiable, for his reading has gone down in the history of violinistic art as one essentially creative and in perfect harmony with the style of the music.

A genuine artist who has deeply and thoroughly comprehended the content and spirit of the work played can, in the process of execution, enhance the expressiveness of the work and, without distorting its essence in any way, enrich its imagery, bring it into greater relief and add to its effectiveness. The great Russian actor Mikhail Shchepkin was such an artist. Gogol, who was delighted at Shchepkin's interpretation of the Mayor's role in his *Inspector General*, although the actor had considerably altered this character, wrote: "To play one's role with such perfection, such completeness, to show such understanding in its treatment—well, this is something much more than mere interpretation. This is an act of giving it a second birth, this is creating!"[68]

Marceau of San Francisco took this dramatic portrait of Ysaÿe.

A popular caricature of Ysaÿe and Godowsky which resulted from their concertizing without music. During the piano solo, Ysaÿe took a piece of music from his pocket and read it while he awaited his cue to join in the sonata.

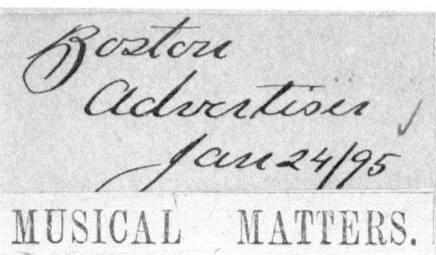

MUSICAL MATTERS.

YSAYE'S SECOND MATINEE IN MUSIC HALL.

Selections from Beethoven, Wagner, Bach and Sarasate Given—Mr. Lachaume and Miss White Support Him—The Apollo Club Gives Its Second Concert of the Season.

The programme of M. Eugene Ysaye's second matinee in Boston was in a measure the reverse of the first, for then a Bach number was the only classical seasoning, while yesterday the giants of the world of melody and melodic expression were ranged at the front with a few moderns as foils. The signs of the earlier day that pointed strongly to a Ysaye craze were still more ominous. Music Hall was crowded and the applause was more rapturous than is usual with a Boston audience. It found a weak spot, too, in the great Belgian violinist's armor, for twice he yielded to encores.

Perhaps the first thing that affects the hearer of Ysaye, after the absorption of the music itself, is the comprehension that the violinist has a tremendous reserve force of nervous energy and artistic expression, or, perhaps, rather for the latter, tutored passion. He never slights, his technique justifies the critic's unvarying phrase—faultless; he has time and rhythm, the last grand; and his shading is truly admirable; but there is noticeable this trait, which is perhaps more of the man than of the artist, the trait of repression, which, however, never renders his subject colorless. Truly he can be tastefully emotional in tense passages and unemotional to a very respectable degree in phrases that demand passion.

The Kreutzer Sonata led the programme, and he approached the first movement—the allegro—with the kind of shyness that is bold. First it was only the precision that one liked. The artist had not emerged. For many bars there was an austerity that the violinist struggled against. The entrance of the ever recurring plaintive phase was a debut that was almost insipid, but the recurrence had all the wonderful shading, and with this the violin sang until the end.

To better perceive what this repression means it is only necessary to hear him play the Wilhelmj paraphrases of Wagner's Parsifal and Siegfried idyll. Into this he threw himself with a robust fervor that the psychologically unsympathetic Kreutzer Sonata did not demand. If these harmonies are not of the kind the player most loves, the audience was deceived, for with the passing of the vision and Parsifal's soul pictured in the upward flight of the violin, there came a thunderburst of applause.

Bach's sonata in B flat, a short work, contains in the first movement a series of melodious chords of which M. Ysaye worked out in a most exquisite way; and in the second an opportunity for the display of violin virtuosity in prestissimo, of which he made the utmost use. Beethoven's beautifully tender Romance in F, which followed, also showed M. Ysaye at his best, for not less than in the two Wagner pieces did he have opportunity to express the passionate melody within him. The audience refused to let him off without an encore, and this he willingly gave. His last announced selection was Sarasate's Zigeuner Weisen—gypsy airs—weird and yet beautiful. In this he reveled in some excellent muted work and violin pyrotechnics, his pizzicato work being truly wonderful.

Miss Priscilla White rendered several soprano songs pleasingly—the aria, "Lusinghe Piu Care," from Handel's Alessandro, and two pretty French songs, Chanson d'Amour, by Mrs. H. H. A. Beach, and Elle et Moi.

It would be unfair to close without a word of praise for Mr. Aime Lachaume, whose excellent pianoforte work in the Kreutzer Sonata made a perfect ensemble possible. Chopin's scherzo in B flat minor was most admirably performed.

From the Ysaÿe scrapbook made available by Marianne Wurlitzer.

Entitled "Grandeur in serenity," *this photo of the Master was taken by Queen Elisabeth of the Belgians at La Panne, 1916.*

Creative approach to interpretation was characteristic of the best representatives of the Russian school of musical performance. This is what was written by a pupil of Karl Davydov, the outstanding artist who headed the Russian school of cello playing in the latter half of the 1880's:

"Anyone who has heard Davydov's recent interpretation, in 1888, of such pieces as the *Lullaby* by Kuznetsov or the *Cantabile* by Cui will agree with me that it was Davydov, who by his playing had recreated these beautiful pieces, giving them life and breathing a soul into them. None, perhaps not even the composers themselves, had suspected these pieces of containing such beauty, such life as were revealed in Davydov's playing."[69]

Eugène Ysaÿe was just one of the interpretative artists who combined the deepest penetration into the composer's idea with its truthful and convincing realization. Rubinstein's performance of the Chopin Sonata and Joachim's playing of the Beethoven Concerto, should be put side by side with his own readings of the Franck Sonata and the Chausson *Poème*. Ysaÿe spoke of these works by Chopin and Beethoven as unsurpassed models of musical interpretation.

Alexander Serov's statement: "The great secret of great interpreters is their ability to shed by the force of their talent an inner light on the work performed, to illumine it and to enrich it with a world of sensations from their own soul, while remaining highly objective."[70] This statement is wholly applicable to Eugène Ysaÿe.

Ysaÿe defined Joachim's interpretation of the Beethoven Concerto as classical and exemplary, but at the same time he warned performers against a mechanical imitation of his reading. He asserted that one must not confine oneself to mere imitation, no matter how excellent the models. In his own word, on this Concerto, Ysaÿe strove to overcome the influence of Joachim, working long and persistently to find his own truth in keeping with the content and the truth of the Beethoven work. This music is the product of genius in that it allows for different approaches to its interpretation and different methods of revealing its true-to-life musical images.

In his interpretation of the Beethoven Concerto, which he did not dare to offer to the public until he was 32, Ysaÿe emphasized the grand and noble simplicity and lyricism of this work, as is clear from his own notes and the recollections of his contemporaries.

Leopold Auer.

The Belgian violinist's approach cannot, of course, be regarded as the only possible one. Different aspects of Beethoven's music have been differently and always convincingly emphasized by Ferdinand Laub, Henryk Wieniawski, Joseph Joachim, Leopold Auer, Georges Enesco, Fritz Kreisler, Joseph Szigeti, Jascha Heifetz, Yehudi Menuhin, Myron Polyakin and David Oistrakh. The important thing is that, at the close of the past century, Ysaÿe was able to discard both the fashionable showy virtuosity and the pseudo-academic style of playing. In performing the Beethoven Concerto he presented it to his listeners as simple and lucid music of profoundly humanistic content.

The character which should be given to Beethoven's Concerto is that of *grandeur in serenity* ("la grandeur dans la sérénité"), Ysaÿe said. Anything that goes beyond this distorts the work which owes its greatness and beauty to its simplicity. The singing should always be calm, although nuances and warmth are not excluded. The performer should be guided by the work's spirit, but this does not preclude improvisation, which is necessary for a living interpretation. One should always bear in mind that this work is predominantly *lyrical*, that singing—*the reason for the existence of the violin*—is its foundation, and that its whole essence and beauty can be revealed only if the melodic phrases are fully understood. Ysaÿe emphasized the Concerto's overall optimism, joy and lucidity, which are brought into greater relief by the contrasting melody in G minor, full of sadness and ineffable beauty.

According to the Russian critic Nikolai Kashkin, the English conductor Sir Henry Wood, the German violin pedagogue Goby Eberhardt and other authors, Eugène Ysaÿe's playing of the Beethoven Concerto was remarkable for an extraordinary nobility and refinement of style, a penetratingly lyrical phrasing and a beautiful and expressive tone. Some of Ysaÿe's contemporaries, for example, the Austrian violinist and pedagogue Carl Flesch (1873-1944), while acknowledging the unusual power of Ysaÿe's art, expressed a critical attitude towards his interpretation of classical works. Flesch held that Ysaÿe performed the Beethoven Concerto in too subjective a manner, and disapproved of excessive use of rubato in his playing of Bach's Concerto in E Major.

At the same time, even Carl Flesch admitted that in the interpretation of music by contemporary composers who were spiritually close to Ysaÿe, he attained the highest standards of artistry. His

From left to right: Albert Spalding, Fritz Kreisler and Jascha Heifetz attending an affair held at the Bohemians Club in New York. The Bohemians are still active. Photo from **Heifetz** *(Axelrod).*

Myron Polyakin, a great and mysterious Russian violinist who fascinated Heifetz and every other great violinist who heard him. His family still resides in Westchester County, New York, though he returned to Russia and died there.

performance of works by Franck, Saint-Saëns, Lalo, Debussy, Vieuxtemps, Mendelssohn and Bruch was unsurpassed. He wrote: "In the performance at the Salle Pleyel in Paris, in 1892, of the César Franck Sonata, which was still unknown to me, the absolute harmony between work and interpreter will remain as unforgettable as the first performance, at the same time, of Debussy's String Quartet. Ysaÿe stood quite alone then, towering high above all contemporary violinists."[71]

Ysaÿe was not one of those artists who feel equal interest in the works of most varied styles and play everything with the same inspiration (or the same indifference) and the same success. A sincere and partial artist, he had a better understanding of music by the composers who were nearer to him in spirit and period—and here he was an unequalled master of his time.

Nevertheless, his broad cultural horizon enabled Ysaÿe, according to contemporary opinion, to create wonderful models in interpreting masterpieces of world classical music.

The contradictions in the appraisals of Ysaÿe's performances of classical music may be explained by the evolution of his own taste and his searchings for different approaches (Alfred Marchot in particular recalls Ysaÿe's work on variants in the interpretation of the Bach Concerto), and also by differences in the views of his contemporaries. These differences become apparent if we compare the opinions of Carl Flesch and Sir Henry Wood, the latter expressing particular admiration for Ysaÿe's playing of Bach's Concerto in E Major and, most of all, for his rubato, or with J.C. Hadden's opinion, stated in one of his last books that Ysaÿe "has an 'inexpressible something' that takes cold judgement off its feet and leaves criticism captive. There are greater technicians perhaps, but no greater interpreter of certain works, such as the Beethoven Concerto."[72]

Of special interest is the opinion of Georges Enesco (1881-1955), that eminent Rumanian musician, who knew Eugène Ysaÿe intimately. He greatly admired the temperamental and inspired playing of Ysaÿe and prized highly his interpretation of Saint-Saëns' concertos and Franck's Sonata.[73] He wrote later: "Ysaÿe was a giant. His titanic nature manifested itself particularly in music. When he played Bach his manner was perhaps not so strict but was deeply stirring in its profundity and immense emotional power."[74]

VILLE DE VERVIERS

PROGRAMME

DE LA

TRANSLATION DES CENDRES

DE

HENRI VIEUXTEMPS

Dimanche 28 Août

Le Cortège se formera à 2 1/2 heures à la gare, et parcourera les **Rues Tranchée**, de l'Harmonie, du Brou, place Verte (côté sud), pont aux Lions, place du Martyr (côté sud), place du Martyr (côté nord), rue du Collège, des Raines, pont de Sommeleville, place Sommeleville, rue de Limbourg et rue de la Cité.

Le Cortège se formera dans l'ordre suivant:

Un peloton de Gendarmes à Cheval,
La **Société Royale de Chant**.
La **Société Royale l'Emulation**.
Les diverses Sociétés de la ville.
Les délégués des sociétés musicales de l'arrondissement avec leur bannière.
Les délégués des sociétés musicales du royaume.
Les tambours.
L'orchestre qui exécutera la marche funèbre composée par H. Vieuxtemps.
Le char funèbre entouré des élèves de Vieuxtemps.
La famille.
Le Conseil communal.
Les directeurs et professeurs des Conservatoires et Ecoles de musique du royaume.
Les notabilités artistiques et les amis du défunt.
Un piquet de Gendarmes fermera la marche.

VERVIERS, le 24 Août 1881.

Par le Collège:

Le Secrétaire,   Le Bourgmestre,

V. GROULARD.   ORTMANS-HAUZEUR.

Verviers, Imp. J.-B. Depouille.

An announcement of the funeral procession in honor of the death of Henri Vieuxtemps.

Edouard Lalo.

The violinist and violin theoretician Goby Eberhardt (1852-1926), whom we have already mentioned, heard Ysaÿe for the first time while the latter played with the Bilse orchestra, captivating his listeners with his interpretation of works by Saint-Saëns, Wieniawski and Vieuxtemps. He later wrote: "But what a serious musician he (Ysaÿe—*L.G.*) subsequently became! One who could cope with classical music equally well. He who can play Bach with such sense of style and beauty of tone, and Mozart, Beethoven, and Brahms, who can grasp these works in all their profundity, is no longer a mere virtuoso—as some would try to make us believe that Ysaÿe was. For me Ysaÿe remains a great artist."[75]

Eugène Ysaÿe's repertoire was extraordinarily rich and varied. Along with the works of Vieuxtemps, Wieniawski, Saint-Saëns, Lalo, Franck, Fauré, Chausson and Lekeu, it embraced the music of Vivaldi, Locatelli, Bach, Beethoven, Mozart, Mendelssohn, Brahms, Bruch, Tchaikovsky, Glazunov, Rimsky-Korsakov, Cui and his own. Ysaÿe won fame as the interpreter not only of music by contemporary Belgian and French composers but also of concertos by Max Bruch (1838-1920), whom Tchaikovsky called "one of the most prominent composers of the modern German school."[76]

Max Bruch regarded Ysaÿe as the best performer of his music. This is how Goby Eberhardt describes it: "Those who have heard Ysaÿe play Bruch's Concerto in G minor and, especially, his Second, in D minor, will certainly share the composer's view. In performing the *Adagios* from these concertos Ysaÿe played them without a trace of sentimentality—just with warmth, with spirit, with a tone that gripped at your heartstrings, that nearly made you cry. His élan and the irrepressible passion pulsating in the finales produced an overwhelming effect. This was inimitable!"[77]

This powerful impression of Ysaÿe the violinist was felt by his audiences not only when he played the poetic and romantic Bruch concertos. Whatever he performed, he strove to imbue his interpretation with the feelings and thoughts he himself believed. That is why his performance was always convincing, and he gave pleasure even to those of his listeners whose conception of the work differed from his own.

Such was the case, for instance, with the Brahms Concerto

Carl Flesch.

SOME VISITING VIOLINISTS.

AMERICA has been called a paradise for pianists. This is true, yet violin visitors from abroad have ever received great homage. Let the master of the four strings appear and even the great pianist will struggle for his laurels. As a nation we are keenly susceptible to music, and string music being the highest development of art, it makes a greater appeal than piano virtuosity. Indeed, before the advent of Anton Rubinstein piano music in the United States was a matter of passing caprice. Gottschalk's influence was tremendous, but it was his personality, not his music, while Thalberg and Leopold De Meyer left but an evanescent impression. Rubinstein in 1873, Von Bülow in 1875 and Rafael Joseffy in 1879 gave an impetus to piano playing that was incalculable.

The case was much the same with violin playing, sensationalism and virtuosity preceding solid scholarship and classic ideals. Ole Bull was perhaps the first of the European celebrities who visited us and reaped dollars and glory. An emulator of Paganini, he came here in 1844, and during this time he made frequent appearances, and successful ones always. Bull was fantastic in his style, a master of technic—his double notes, arpeggios and flauto effects were astonishingly clear—but he often descended to trickery. His taste was not fine, yet he played our national melodies with such an effect that he remained the favorite of the public, although several masters had taught us the value and beauty of the violinist's art.

Camille Sivori came to America in 1846—a miniature Paganini, indeed a genuine pupil of the great man. He does not seem to have made the same impression as his Belgian rival Henri Vieuxtemps, who visited us twice—the last time in the early seventies. Sivori's style was highly finished, but small, the writer remembering him as an old man in Paris in 1878, a timid, feeble old man, but with a matchless intonation. In Vieuxtemps, a distinct representative of the Belgian school, we got an artist bolder, freer and with quite as much finesse as the Italian. Who of us that remembers his purity of tone, infinite variety of shading, charming, graceful style and abundant technic, will ever forget it? His concertos, his Fantaisie Caprice, his ballade and polonaise are now stock pieces of every ambitious violinist. A half century ago they were startling in their novelty. Eduard Remenyi, the Hungarian, who died last week at San Francisco, first came to America in 1848, but it was not for many years afterward that he made a sensation. His strong point in the early days was his technical facility. Wayward, capricious as a gypsy, he interpreted with passionate intensity the music of Magyar land. In his early youth he was a friend of Liszt, of Brahms and had a dispute with the latter over the authorship of some Hungarian dances, but Remenyi never proved his claim. In his later years the virtuoso grew careless as to intonation, but the fire and originality of his play never quite deserted him.

Of all the violinists who visited America none left so lasting an impression as Henri Wieniawski, the Pole, who came in Rubinstein's company in 1873. His talent was perhaps the greatest since Paganini's, and to a fire and breadth almost superhuman was added a repose and appreciation of the classics that placed him in the first ranks of the masters of the art. Even Wilhelmj in 1879 did not efface the memories of Wieniawski's dashing and magnetic performances. Wilhelmj, a pupil of David, therefore an artistic descendant of Spohr, stood for all that is objective and classic. His tone was big, broad, but not very warm, but in cantabile passages he made his instrument vocal beyond belief. Virile, scholarly and reposeful, Paolo Sarasate represented the opposite pole of an artistic ideal. Feminine, capricious and yet fascinating, his interpretation of the classics is far from satisfactory. In his own transcriptions of Spanish melodies he is unapproachable. His tone is small and sweet. He has paid America two visits, the last in company with Eugen d'Albert.

We cannot find any record of a visit from Miska Hauser, the Hungarian virtuoso, yet we believe him to have visited America over a quarter of a century ago.

Emil Sauret, a representative of the extreme Gallic school, is always a welcome apparition on our concert platform. Elegance rather than robustness and a faultless technic are his distinguishing characteristics. The same may be said of Marsick, except that the Parisian has not Sauret's breadth. Sauret has visited us two or three times, marrying Teresa Carreño when he first came here. Joseph White, a Cuban creole virtuoso, made a brief tour twenty-five years ago. He is also French in his school. A gifted lad of brilliant promise was Maurice Dengremont, who soon burnt himself up in the flame of fast living. He had a genius for violin playing that young Kreisler or Hubermann never possessed. Ovide Musin is another favorite of the American concert stage. A true exponent of the Belgian school, Musin never allowed mere technical brilliancy to obscure his reverence for the classics. It is good news to learn that he intends revisiting us and for pedagogic purposes.

We have had Ondricek, the Bohemian virtuoso, a player of more power than delicacy; Carl Halir, an ultra-representative of the German school; Gregorowitsch, finished and graceful, a pupil of Joachim, and last, but by no means least, César Thomson and his wonderful pupil—a master pupil —Eugene Ysaye. Both these Belgians, so different in their styles, yet so masterly, are too fresh in the public's mind to require analysis. Thomson the more intellectual of the pair, Ysaye the more spontaneous, yet a pair not to be easily passed over.

Of the violinists who settled here years ago we may mention Camilla Urso, who came here in 1852, and with Lady Hallé—known to the art world as Norman-Neruda—was considered the greatest female violinist alive. Then there was Theodore Thomas, who came to America in 1848; Leopold Damrosch, a pupil of Ries, who came here in 1871; Jacobsohn, of Chicago, who came here in 1872, and Bernhard Listemann, who settled in Boston in 1870. With the exception of Madame Urso all these artists are either dead or teaching. A new generation has arisen and is as keen after artistic honors as the preceding one. Some day we shall write its history, but the above list of visiting violinists will suffice for the present.

An editorial from **The Musical Courier, May 25, 1898.**

which Ysaÿe played for the first time at the age of nearly forty-five. His performance was not the best and the artist himself was dissatisfied with it. According to Irma Saenger-Sethe,[78] a pupil of Ysaÿe's, the only one who came to congratulate the Belgian artist after the concert was Joachim, the outstanding exponent of the Concerto, to whom it was dedicated. He came up to Ysaÿe and embraced him, saying: "You have shown me a perfectly new Concerto. Perhaps it is more the Concerto of Ysaÿe than that of Brahms, but don't worry, it is as beautiful as ever and you should have no doubts in offering your own interpretation."

In spite of Joachim's encouragement, Ysaÿe worked on the Brahms Concerto assiduously for two more years before he ventured once again to play it in public. He performed the Concerto with assurance and inspiration at a Philharmonic concert under the direction of Artur Nikisch in Berlin. His triumph was so great and so out of the ordinary run of Philharmonic concerts that, on the insistent demand of the public, the conductor and the orchestra, Ysaÿe gave as encores the *Chaconne* of Bach, the Mendelssohn Concerto and his own *Caprice d'après l'Etude en forme de Valse de Saint-Saëns*.

Since there are very few gramophone recordings of Ysaÿe's playing, and those mostly of small pieces (made, besides, at the dawn of mechanical sound recording and therefore far from perfect), we cannot, in our desire to reconstruct his art as fully as possible, dispense with citing the general description of Ysaÿe's performance style by that outstanding violin theoretician, Carl Flesch. His characterization can, in a certain measure, be regarded as defining Ysaÿe's place in the history of violinistic art. In speaking of Eugène Ysaÿe, Flesch referred to him as "the most outstanding and individual violinist" of all whom he had heard in all his life.

In his opinion, at the turn of the century "Joachim and Sarasate had formed the two poles of the axis around which the world of the violin had turned." Joachim was "serious, expansive, profound; technique and pure sound were to him only a secondary means . . . towards the sacred artistic aim. The elegant Spaniard, on the other hand . . . , a master of unemotional euphony," was remarkable for the greatest refinement and polish of technical details. "In their old age," Carl Flesch goes on, "neither corresponded in the least to the taste of the time, which yearned for a synthesis between

Pablo de Sarasate.

Philip Newman sent out this double-faced card dated May
12, 1931 to Alberta Bachman in memory of the great Ysaÿe.
The music is Newman's copy of Ysaÿe's sonata to Kreisler.

It celebrates the 100th anniversary of the birth of Ysaÿe 1858-1958.

A bust of Ysaÿe.

On the facing page, the great violinists of the 19th Century.

By permission of SARONY.
YSAŸE.

An old photograph signed by Ysaÿe.

technical perfection and the greatest intensity of expression. In Ysaÿe, this need found its complete fulfillment. His tone was big and noble, capable of modulation to the highest degree and of responding to his impulsion . . . His vibrato was the spontaneous expression of his feelings . . . the incidental, thin-flowing quiver 'only on *expressive* notes;' his portamentos were novel and entrancing, his left-hand agility and intonation of Sarasate-like perfection. Intuitively, he adapted his bowing technique to his expressive needs. There was no kind of bowing that did not show tonal perfection as well as musical feeling. His style of interpretation betrayed the impulsive romantic who was concerned not so much with the printed note-values, the dead letter, as with the spirit that cannot be reproduced graphically. He was master of the imaginative rubato."[79]

Ysaÿe's beautiful and expressive tone was particularly impressive: now powerful and manly and again tender and lyrical, it was invariably pure and singing.

To round off the appraisal of the Belgian artist's playing, we may add the words of Antonin Dvorak, one of the founders of classical Czech music: "Ysaÿe's reminds me of our great Laub. His tone is of tremendous power and incomparable purity."[80]

The recordings of Ysaÿe's playing confirm the enthusiastic opinion of his contemporaries who had heard this inimitable master of the violin. One cannot but admire the noble phrasing, the crystal-clear and touching tone in Wagner's *Albumblatt*. An elegant melodic line and restrained rhythm (Ysaÿe's other recordings, too, are marked by a perfectly original rhythm), a filigree passage work, a purity of intonation in double stops and a heart-warming simplicity of the lyrical episode characterize his interpretation of Vieuxtemps' *Rondino*. His playing of Wieniawski's Mazurkas appeals by his deep penetration into the nature of these charming miniatures, by the contrasting juxtapositions of the clear-cut rhythm in the dance episodes and the poetic improvisation in the lyrical sections, the warm tone and elegant bowing. In Brahms' *Hungarian Dance* Ysaÿe emphasizes the dance rhythm in a perfectly different way, which, along with the incomparable beautiful tone and vividly emotional and temperamental treatment, make this work a veritable masterpiece.

In everything he plays, Ysaÿe appears before us as a sincere and

Eugène Ysaÿe was nicknamed "the king of the violin."

Walter Damrosch, the famous conductor, took the New York orchestra on tour with Ysaÿe as soloist.

SPRING TOUR, 1905.

WALTER DAMROSCH

and the New York Symphony Orchestra in Texas and the Southwest.

YSAŸE as Soloist.

Tour under the Management of R. E. JOHNSTON, St. James Building, New York

EMILE LEVY, Traveling Representative.

YSAYE

By D. J. TEALL

Ysaye, magician! Lift that wonder-working
    bow,
And lightly touch the strings; and so
Call up for me bright fairy vision
Of things beyond mortal comprehension.
A thousand shimmering shapes glide by,
Melt into nothingness, or like a sunset sky
Shift in unceasing beauteous change.
Oh, play but once and I shall count myself
A very king of men, above, beyond
All mortal wants! Ysaye—name
Above censure, beyond praise, surpassing
    fame!

Ysaÿe played so beautifully that he inspired many artists and poets. This poem was published in **The Violinist** *of May, 1914.*

inspired artist who seems to share with the listeners his own emotions and moods, which cannot but reach the very heart of his audience.

As one of his pupils recalled, "The minute Ysaÿe began to play, it was as if he were playing to you—the two of you might have been alone in the hall. He gave so much more than virtuosity, he gave all of himself. He expressed your own feelings for you—maybe he expressed more than you would have dared to own to. Ysaÿe seemed to enter into your life; he became a friend, an intimate friend; he transposed and exalted all you felt. And when you left the hall he still seemed to be playing, still to be with you."[81]

As has already been noted, the elements of romanticism in Ysaÿe's playing, his poetry and improvisation did not interfere with the manifestation of realistic principles in the interpretation of this artist. When Ysaÿe was at his zenith, the powerful impact of his art was due to the depth and truthfulness of his performance, his sincerity and emotionality, the vivid and perfect form in which he realized his intentions, the unity of phrasing and of technical devices, the harmoniousness of the musical whole and of the finely executed details.

NOTES

[56] The overpowering impression Ysaÿe made on his audiences must have been partly due to his imposing appearance, his noble bearing and that unique combination of athletic build and virility with the highly poetic and refined emotions which he conjured up with the aid of his magic violin.

[57] Gorky, M., "O tom, kak ya uchilsya pisat," *Gorky ob iskusstve. Sbornik statei i otryvkov*, ("How I Learned to Write," *Gorky on Art. Collection of Articles and Excerpts*), Moscow-Leningrad, 1940, p. 192.

[59] Konstantin Igumnov (1873-1948), a prominent Russian pianist, Professor of the Moscow Conservatoire; among his pupils were Nikolai Orlov, Lev Oborin and Yakov Flier.

[60] Anatoly Brandukov (1859-1930), Russian cellist, Professor of the Moscow Conservatoire; Tchaikovsky dedicated to him his *pezzo capriccioso* and Rachmaninov, his Sonata for Cello and Piano.

[58] This and the following passages are quoted from A. Ysaÿe and B. Ratcliffe, *op. cit.*

[61] Serov, A.N., *Kriticheskiye statii (Critical Articles)*, Vol. I, Petrograd, 1892, p. 84.

[62] J. Ma. Corredor, *Op. cit.*, p. 183.

[63] Emile Jaques-Dalcroze, "Eugène Ysaÿe. Quelques notes et souvenirs," *La Revue musicale*, No. 188, 1939.

[64] Henry J. Wood, *My Life of Music*, London, 1938, p. 128.

[65] Emile Jaques-Dalcroze, *op. cit.*

[66] "Sarasate, Joachim et Ysaÿe vus par Jacques Thibaud," *Le Monde musicale*, No. 5, 1937, p. 126.

[67] See Ginsburg, L., *Ferdinand Laub*, Moscow, 1951, pp. 13-15.

[68] Gogol, N.V., "Razvyazka Revizora" ("The Denouement of *Inspector General*"), *Sochineniya (Works)*, XV ed., Vol. IV, St. Petersburg, 1900, p. 59.

[69] Gutor, V.P., *K.Y. Davydov kak osnovatel shkoly (Karl Davydov, the Founder of a School)*, prefaced, edited and annotated by L.S. Ginsburg, Moscow-Leningrad, 1950, p. 25.

[70] Serov, A.N., *Kriticheskiye statii (Critical Articles)*, III, St. Petersburg, 1895, pp. 1318-19.

[71] Carl Flesch, *The Memoirs*, London, 1957, p. 80.

[72] Hadden, J.C., *Modern Musicians*, London, 1914, p. 161.

[73] See Bernard Gavoty, *Les souvenirs de Georges Enesco*, Paris, 1955, p. 96.

[74] Andrei Tudor, *Enesco*, Bucharest, 1957, p. 75.

[75] Goby Eberhardt, *Erinnerungen an bedeutenden Männer unserer Epoche*, Lubeck, 1926, S. 70-72.

[76] Tchaikovsky, P., *Muzykalno-kriticheskiye statii (Musico-Critical Articles)*, Moscow, 1953, p. 131.

[77] Goby Eberhardt, *op. cit.*, p. 71.

[78] Her recollections, along with those by some other of Ysaÿe's pupils, are to be found in A. Ysaÿe, *op. cit.*

[79] Carl Flesch, *The Memoirs*, London, 1957, p. 79.

[80] Quoted from Eugen Simunek, *Problemy estetiky hudobnej interpretácie (Problems of the Aesthetics of Musical Interpretation)*, Bratislava, 1959, p. 20.

[81] Quoted from A. Ysaÿe and B Ratcliffe, *op. cit.*, p. 227.

Ysaÿe testing a violin by plucking the strings with his thumb. Jascha Heifetz employs the same technique.

Ysaÿe, proud of his many visits to America, poses with the American flag.

Chapter 8

The Style of Ysaÿe: The Composer

The description of Ysaÿe's artistic personality would not be complete without a brief mention of his compositions, mainly his works for the violin.

Ysaÿe was attracted to composition while still a young man. In speaking of his early works, among which there were six concertos, Ysaÿe himself said that they were without originality and real artistic value (just "imitations of Vieuxtemps"). In trying to produce musical works in which virtuosity should have given place to music, Ysaÿe experienced the influence of Mendelssohn and Schumann. He began to give opus numbers to his works with a set of four genre pieces for violin and piano, written at the age of twenty. The pieces have typically Schumannesque moods and programmatic titles: *Courte Joie, Badinage, Perdue* and *Retrouvée.*

Besides the opera *Pier' li Houyeu,* Ysaÿe is the author of over thirty instrumental (chiefly violin) pieces, some of which have been lost, while others remained unpublished. Many of his miniatures were written under the influence of his masters, Vieuxtemps and Wieniawski, especially the mazurkas and polonaises.

Despite the more or less pronounced influences of his contemporaries, and Belgian composers, Ysaÿe's poems and sonatas are the most original and representative of his compositions.

Ysaÿe rarely gave musical autographs, but he did so as a matter of course on most Russian tours. On the facing page is a souvenir dated 1895. The autograph above, of Bach's **Chaconne** is dated 28 December 1907 in St. Petersburg.

Нотный автограф Э. Изаи в альбоме В. В. Безекирского (1895)

The poem and the sonata for solo violin (which he treated freely, departing from the classical canons of sonata form) attracted Ysaÿe because they put no obstacles to his romantic flights of fancy, affording free play to his creative imagination, and the bent for improvisation so characteristic of his style.

The imagery in Ysaÿe's poems was inspired by the vividly romantic symphonic poems of Liszt. He has written eight poems, the first of which, *Poème élégiaque*, enjoys particular popularity.

"The form of poem has always appealed to me," wrote Ysaÿe. "It is admirably suited for the expression of feeling and is free from the restrictions of the concerto. It can be dramatic or lyrical, for by its very nature it is romantic and impressionistic; it allows for weeping and singing, for depicting light and shadow—it is a refracting prism. It is free, it lays no restrictions on the composer who is able to express feelings and images outside any literary framework.

"I think that the poem marks further progress in my creative output," Ysaÿe went on to write. "It signifies a decisive stage in my experimentation, in my striving for independence, for combining musical interest with virtuosity on a large scale. I mean the true

Franz Liszt in his ripe, old age.

Henri Vieuxtemps in an early lithograph.

Music example No. 1.

virtuosity which has been so flagrantly neglected since, oblivious of the practice of the masters of the past, instrumentalists have been shy of composing, leaving it to those who do not know well all the secrets and devices at the command of professionals."[82]

Like Ysaÿe's other works, his poems, written as they are by an outstanding musician who was at one and the same time a famous artist-performer and a talented and highly original composer, combine both artistic and purely virtuosic merits. His poems are in one movement, although within each of them one easily distinguishes sections differing in character and motion. All of them have programmatic titles. Four poems are written for violin and orchestra or piano—*Poème élégiaque, Scène au Rouet, Chant d'Hiver* and *Extase*; the *Méditation* is intended for cello and orchestra, the poem entitled *Amitié* is for two violins and orchestra, *Poème Nocturne* is for violin, cello and orchestra, and *Exil*, for strings without basses.

As can be seen from Ysaÿe's own words, his programmatic titles were merely a convention and in no way restricted the composer's imagination; sometimes the titles were added after the work had been completed and more than once were changed. These works were indeed based on feelings and images and it is but rarely that elements of tone painting can be discovered in them.

The music of the *Poème élégiaque* in D minor, Op. 12, is for the most part in keeping with its title, although now and again it goes beyond the elegiac mood, reaching high emotional tension and real drama. It is enough to compare the piece's calm and flowing beginning, marked *soutenu et calme* (Music example No. 1), with the climax of its first section where both the texture characterized by sharp accents and agitated syncopated movement and the dynamics reaching *FFF*, transform the musical image into a turbulent and intensely dramatic one (Music example No. 2).

The middle section, *Grave et Lent*, subtitled "Scène funèbre," introduces another vivid contrast. Its solemn and *pathétique* character is emphasized by the measured tread, by harmonic means and by the specific sonority of the violin's G-string tuned a whole tone below.

The lyrical episode undergoes a gradual modification and, after a series of romantic upsurges, leads to the initial theme of the section, which acquires a majestic and vigorous character.

Like Ysaÿe's other poems, this piece is largely improvisatory; melodic expressiveness is combined here with rich and varied rhythms and fresh harmonies. The composer resorts to violinistic virtuosity, his generous use of double stopping, chords and open strings results in luxurious sound effects and he expertly contrasts the instrument's different timbres, producing a colorful sound palette.

If we accept the idea that the *Poème élégiaque* stems from the Franck sources, this daringly conceived and originally executed work of Ysaÿe's has, in its turn, prompted the appearance of a

Music example No. 2.

series of other violin compositions, in the first place, the well-known *Poème* for violin and orchestra by Chausson.

The *Scène au Rouet* in B minor, Op. 13, is a highly poetic work. It is based on an expressive lyrical song heard against a background of a gently buzzing spindle (Music example No. 3). From time to time the solo instrument takes up the descriptive music, but in

Music example No. 3.

general its part is rich in precipitous *legato* passages, light springing bowing, trills and *pizzicati*.

Ysaÿe's third violin poem, the *Chant d'Hiver* in B minor, Op. 15, dedicated to his wife, is characterized by a sad and pensive mood. The poem was inspired, in the composer's own words, by "regret for the happy days of childhood passed on the banks of the Meuse" (Music example No. 4).

The poem entitled *Extase* in A flat Major, Op. 21, dedicated to Mischa Elman, appeals by its sincere passion. At times the passion is restrained, and yet it is clearly felt in the melodic line, the restless "creeping" harmonies and syncopated rhythm. At other moments it breaks through in vividly emotional climaxes (Music example No. 5). The music seems to quiet down somewhat at the very end: the sounds of the muted violin melt away as they climb from the lowest to the uppermost register of the instrument.

The *Méditation* in B minor, Op. 16, Ysaÿe's fifth poem, is scored, as has already been mentioned, for cello and orchestra. Ysaÿe regarded it as one of his best and favorite works. He made preliminary sketches for it as far back as the 1890's, during his concert tours with the young Belgian cellist Jean Gérardy (1877-1929). Later, on the insistence of the French cellist Fernand Pollain

Joseph Hollmann.

Music example No. 4.

Music example No. 5.

Anton Hekking.

Columbia Strings to Play A Rare Belgian Work

By RAYMOND ERICSON

In 1924, Eugene Ysaye, the distinguished Belgian violinist-composer, wrote a piece for solo string quartet and string orchestra called "Harmonies du Soir." The quartet that he headed and that bore his name took part in a private performance the following year for the King and Queen of the Belgians. Since that time it has not been played. Tonight, however, it will be heard in public in what is a world premiere, as part of a concert by Columbia University's String Revival. This ensemble, with Howard Shanet, its founder as director will appear at McMillin Theater, Broadway and 116th Street, at 8. The event is free.

Mr. Shanet, who was chairman of Columbia's music department for six years and last fall was appointed to the new position of director of music performance, says that he has spent his life in search of novelties, looking into the curious, little corners that don't get explored.

"Someone sent me Ruggiero Ricci's recording of the six pieces for solo violin," Mr. Shanet said the other day, "and I found them to be remarkably fine compositions as well as interesting works for the violin. I got in touch with Ysaye's son in Belgium, who is 85 this month, and heard about the 'Harmonies du Soir.' Like so many other odd scores, this one was available from the Fleisher Collection in Philadelphia."

The conductor founded the String Revival, a fully professional group, in 1975 to restore to the repertory the many fine compositions written for the beautiful sonorities of a string orchestra. On each program he tries to present examples of various kinds of music: one by an established old composer, one by an American, one by a composer once well-known and highly regarded but now forgotten, one by a non-American who has not yet developed a reputation here. Tonight these categories will be represented, respectively, by Schubert's Five German Dances, Peter Mennin's Fantasia for Strings, Niels Gade's "Novelletter" and Nicholas Maw's "Life Study II."

Mr. Mennin is, of course, a composer of high repute today as well as president of the Juilliard School, but he wrote his Fantasia when he was a student at the summer school at Tanglewood, an adjunct of the Boston Symphony's Berkshire Festival. Mr. Shanet asked Mr. Mennin if he would mind having it played, since some composers do not like to have their youthful efforts revived. Mr. Mennin replied, "I liked it when I wrote it, and I like it now."

Gade was a 19th-century Danish composer. Not much of his music is heard today except in connection with Royal Danish Ballet productions. Mr. Maw is a young Englishman, whose music is consistently praised by the music critics in his country. Mr. Shanet said, "When I first saw his music, it jumped off the page at me. It uses modern devices, but it has a theatrical element. It has drive and shape. It goes somewhere."

There is one more piece on tonight's program. It is "A Weeping Willow" by Eda Rapoport, an American who died in 1968. In her will she left money to Columbia to insure more performances at the university. There was no stipulation that her music be played, but Mr. Shanet has always felt that it is a nice gesture to do so, and it has become a tradition to include one of her compositions in a String Revival program.

A clipping from **The New York Times,** *1979.*

Pablo Casals.

(1879-1955), a member of the trio whose other members were Eugène Ysaÿe and Raoul Pugno, the composer completed it.

In his youth Ysaÿe studied several instruments besides the violin, and knew the cello very well. He liked this instrument (incidentally, one of his sons studied the cello) and his interest in it was further stimulated by his friendly contacts with many prominent cellists, among them Gérardy, Pollain, Joseph Servais, Joseph Hollmann, André Hekking, Anatoly Brandukov, Jacques Gailliard, Pablo Casals and others.

Besides the romantic fifth poem, Ysaÿe composed for the cello a melodious, songful *Serenade* in A Major, Op. 22, which he dedicated to his son Antoine, and a sonata for solo cello; in his seventh poem the solo parts are those for violin and for cello.[83]

The sixth poem for two violins and orchestra (in A Major, Op. 26) is entitled *Amitié* and dedicated to Theodore Lindenlaub, Ysaÿe's old friend with whom he visited Russia in the early eighties of the past century.

This poem was written in the last period of Ysaÿe's life. Speaking of it, the composer said: "Here the thought is free; it is allowed to wander at will over the whole realm of friendship with its wealth of happy and sweet memories associated with nearly fifty years of friendly relationship, one that is even better and stronger than love, one that, for me and for him to whom the work is dedicated, is permanent."[84]

Ysaÿe dedicated his seventh poem, the *Poème Nocturne* in E Major, Op. 29, for violin and cello with orchestra, to his friends Albert Zimmer, violinist,[85] and Jacques Gailliard, cellist.[86] Ysaÿe was interested in the little cultivated form of concert pieces for violin and cello, exemplified by Vieuxtemps' *Duo Brilliant* (Op. 39), Saint-Saëns' *La Muse et le Poète* (Op. 132) and, finally, the excellent Double Concerto by Brahms. This is what he wrote: "I let the dialogue between the two instruments flow freely. This is an essentially musical song, without any sentimental or descriptive intentions."[87]

To this dialogue Ysaÿe gives the form now of imitative episodes (Music example No. 6) and again of brief statements, with the two voices interrupting one another in agitation. And there are moments when the instruments unite in an emotionally tense duet. Both are treated as perfectly equal partners, the cello enjoying the same importance and presenting the same technical demands as the

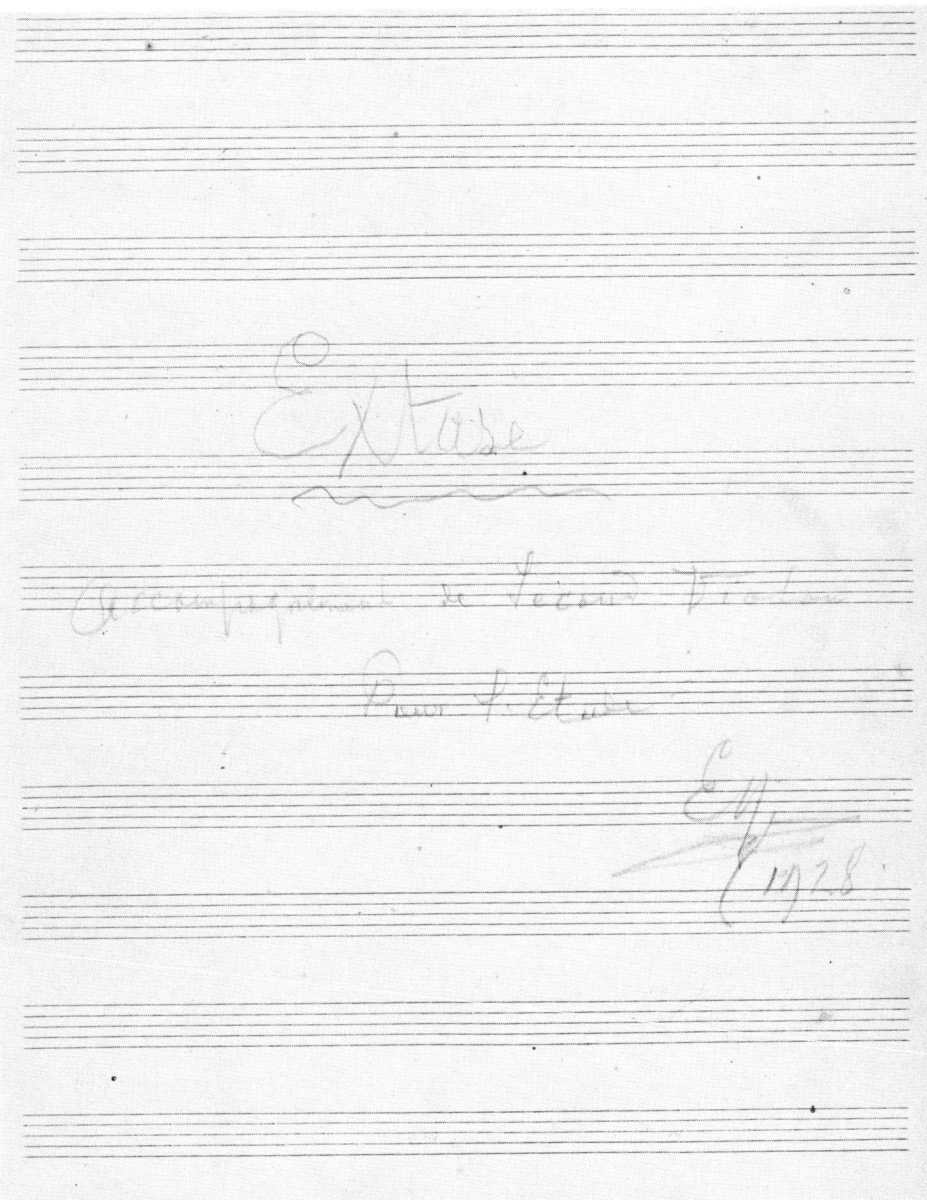

Ysaÿe often wrote violin accompaniments for various pieces, his own as well as those of other composers. As a gift to Josef Gingold, Ysaÿe wrote a second violin part for his Extase. It has never been published. Gingold still has the original and graciously allowed us to engrave the very light autograph done in pencil.

Music example No. 6.

violin. The solo and the orchestral writing is rich and highly varied, at times even excessively complicated. There are double stops, chords, arpeggios in plenty, making for a vivid and full sonority.

Although the work progresses as an uninterrupted whole, here, as in the other poems, separate sections differing in mood can be distinguished.

Then there is the last of the poems, the eighth, entitled *Exil*, Op. 25, for strings without basses. Its score consists of six violin parts and two viola parts. The music is tonally unstable and abounds in chromatic progressions. (It may be considered Wagnerian in harmonization.—Ed.) At the end, after a vivid and dynamic climax, comes the quiet singing of the muted instruments.

Ysaÿe wrote on the MS copy of one of the versions of this poem: "Torment and despair. New York. 1917." He himself conducted the premiere of this poem in Cincinnati shortly after its completion.

Along with some of Ysaÿe's poems, his sonatas for solo violin, Op. 27, occupy a prominent place in the concert repertoire of contemporary violinists.

These six sonatas belong to Ysaÿe's last period and combine high artistic merits with a truly expert utilization of the technical and expressive resources of the solo violin.

"Eugène Ysaÿe's sonatas for solo violin are of exceptional artistic value in the violin repertoire," said David Oistrakh, one of the best contemporary exponents of these works, in speaking to the present author. "All the sonatas are distinguished by the truest inspiration and originality. At the same time, they open up new horizons in the history of violin virtuosity: in them Ysaÿe stands out as the greatest innovator after Paganini, as one who has considerably enriched the technical and expressive potentialities of the instrument, particularly regarding the polyphonic writing. It should be emphasized that his daring enrichment and development of the violin technique in the sonatas has been achieved, not in divorcement from music, but in complete harmony with artistic tasks. Actually, it was in the process of searching for the means to express the musical ideas born of Ysaÿe's creative imagination that the technical devices arose."

Ysaÿe dedicated each of his sonatas to one or another of the world's most famous violinists: Sonata No. 1 (in G minor) is dedicated to the Hungarian violinist Joseph Szigeti; No. 2 (in A minor) to the French violinist Jacques Thibaud; No. 3 (in D minor) to the Rumanian violinist Georges Enesco, No. 4 (in E minor) to the Austrian violinist Fritz Kreisler; No. 5 (in G Major) to the Belgian violinist Mathieu Crickboom, and No. 6 (in E Major) to the Spanish violinist Manuel Quiroga.

Ysaÿe's interest in the form of sonata for solo violin arose undoubtedly under the influence of Bach's great sonatas and partitas, and the Belgian musician never denied it. This is borne out by the number of his sonatas (six), by the keys in which the first and the sixth sonatas are written (G minor and E Major), as well as by the use of such forms as the allemande and saraband. The similarity of

Emanuel Quirogo.

Mathieu Crickboom to whom Ysaÿe dedicated his fifth Sonata and who played second violin in the Ysaÿe Quartet.

Jean Gerardy at age 52.

Ysaÿe had this photograph in his own collection and he marked it as "Enjoying a Havana with Joseph Hollmann." 1903. Courtesy of Arazi.

structure of Bach's First Sonata (*Adagio, Fugue, Siciliana* and *Presto*) and Ysaÿe's No. 1 (*Grave, Fugato, Allegretto poco scherzoso* and *Finale con brio*) should also be noted; with the exception of the third movements written in the relative major, all the movements in the two sonatas are in the main key of G minor. As if all this were not enough, the *Prelude* of Ysaÿe's Sonata No. 2 begins with a two-bar quotation from the *Prelude* from the last of Bach's partitas (Music example No. 7), and the Bach *Prelude* of his sonata "Obsession," meaning, presumably, this motive which gave him no rest.

Music example No. 7.

Ysaÿe as a conductor. This lithograph by Renouard was published in 1907. Courtesy of Arazi.

Antoine Ysaÿe considered this to be his father's favorite photo and he freely sent it to Ysaÿe's admirers with his (Antoine's) autograph.

Notwithstanding these manifestations of admiration for Bach's music, there is no question of imitation or stylization. Ysaÿe's sonatas are essentially original and individual. Even the form as such undergoes considerable modifications at Ysaÿe's hands and is treated freely: we find here, along with the four-movement sonatas (Nos. 1 and 2), a work in three movements (No. 4), one in two movements (No. 5) and even sonatas in one movement (Nos. 3 and 6).

The differences, naturally, apply not only to form but also to content and mood. The No. 1 Sonata is one of the best, with its profoundly meditative *Prelude* followed by the *Fugato*, whose simple and expressive theme recurs in four parts, treated with consummate skill (Music example No. 8). Contrapuntal writing in this

Music example No. 8.

work for an essentially homophonous instrument such as the violin is also present in the development sections and in the *Stretti*. The graceful *Allegretto*, followed by the energetic and strongly marked *Finale*, produces a vivid contrast of mode and mood.

Dedicated to Joseph Szigeti, this Sonata was written in the process of improvisation as it were, under the impression of the Hungarian violinist's performance of a Bach sonata. As Ysaÿe said to his son, "I have found in Szigeti the ability to be at one and the same time a virtuoso and a musician—a combination that is rare nowadays. Szigeti is an artist who is conscious of his high mission which he fulfills like a prophet and you value him as a violinist who has overcome all difficulties and has placed technique at the service of musical expression."[88]

The mood of Sonata No. 2 is somewhat brooding, even somber. This is largely due to the use of the *Dies irae* theme in all of its movements, bearing such programmatic subtitles as "Obsession," "Malinconia," "Danse des ombres" and "Furies." Its first movement is in motoric motion and in its musical texture elements of the Bach theme and of the *Dies irae* recur, presented by means of "hidden part-writing." The second movement, an example of expert contrapuntal writing, is profoundly sorrowful; it closes with the *Dies irae* theme. This is how it begins (Music example No. 9).

Music example No. 9.

The third movement is a *pizzicato* theme with six variations; the Sonata is rounded off with a vigorous and *pathétique* finale. Its middle section presents appealing contrasts between the instrument's natural tone and the *sul ponticello* effect, between *pp* and *FF*.

The one-movement Sonata No. 3, subtitled *Ballade*, is highly expressive and poetic. Its music is declamatory and essentially improvisatory. Beginning with a restrained recitative, the Sonata reaches a vividly emotional climax.

Sonata No. 4 (a set piece in the program of the Eugène Ysaÿe International Competition, Brussels, 1937) falls into three movements—*Allemande, Sarabande,* and *Finale*. The *Allemande* begins with a slow improvisatory introduction followed by a vigorous and impressive section setting the tone of the whole movement (Music example No. 10). Then comes a contemplative

Music example No. 10.

episode and one with a brilliant instance of two-part contrapuntal writing. In the *Sarabande*, which begins with a three-part episode *pizzicato,* a brief theme is repeated throughout the movement (Music example No. 11).[89] At the end of the *Sarabande* this theme

Music example No. 11.

is hidden within the arpeggios. It can also be distinguished in the semi-quavers of the driving *Finale* while in its middle episode the intonations and rhythm of the *Allemande* are repeated. Thus the three movements are closely knit together.

The two movements of Sonata No. 5 bear the subtitles "L'Aurore" and "Danse Rustique," and as a whole this Sonata is the most clearly programmatic and descriptive. Its musical idiom is colorful, in the style of Impressionism.

The first movement is a musical picture of sunrise over the sea—one gets the impression of the stillness preceding the birth of day. Then comes the awakening of nature with the rising of the sun, conveyed by means of the dynamics progressing from *ppp* to *FFF*. The second movement is in ternary form: its first and third sections in dance rhythm (with changing meter 5/4, 7/4, 3/4, 4/4, 6/4) are set off by a slow middle episode, *Moderato amabile*. Music example No. 12 shows the beginning of this movement.

Music example No. 12.

The one-movement Sonata No.6 is a brilliant and vigorous work. Dedicated to a Spanish violinist, its music is associated with Spanish imagery, especially in the *Allegretto poco scherzando* episode, with its *habanera* rhythm (Music example. No. 13).

Ysaÿe's Sonata for solo cello in C minor, Op. 28, was published in 1924, as were his violin sonatas.

After the unsurpassed Six Suites for solo cello by Bach, there appeared Kodaly's Sonata Op. 8, Three Suites Op. 131 by Reger and Sonata Op. 25 by Hindemith. Ysaÿe's Cello Sonata can safely be classed among the best works of this kind. Consisting of four

Music example No. 13.

movements—*Grave, Intermezzo, In modo di recitativo* and *Finale con brio*—the Sonata is closely related to Ysaÿe's violin sonatas both musically and technically. Its first movement is deeply concentrated (Music example No. 14). The expressive *Intermezzo* is full of

Music example No. 14.

grace (Music example No. 15). The *Finale* is rich in polyphonic devices; one of its episodes is a fugato in four parts showing an expert treatment of the instrument's resources.

Music example No. 15.

Music example No. 16 illustrates Ysaÿe's daring use of the cello's virtuoso potentialities.

Among other violin works of Ysaÿe, mention should be made of his two Mazurkas, Op. 10 (in G Major and in A minor) which were published in Moscow. These pieces are in many respects close to some works of Wieniawski (and, to a certain extent, Chopin) and Vieuxtemps. The elegance and lyrical appeal of the Mazurkas have ensured for them a place in the modern violin repertoire. Here is

Music example No. 16.

the beginning of the Mazurka in A minor (Music example No. 17). Ysaÿe's Mazurka Op. 14, subtitled "Lointain passé" (its original title was "Souvenir de Norvège"), is less imitative than the other two.

Music example No. 17.

Then there are such works for violin and orchestra as *Berceuse* Op. 20 and *Les Neiges d'Antan* Op. 23—two short pieces of appealing sincerity and expressiveness (Music example No. 18 is the beginning of *Les Neiges d'Antan*.) The *Divertimento* Op. 24, dedicated to Ysaÿe's son Gabriel, is an improvisatory piece where

Music example No. 18.

virtuoso bowing and fingerboard technique are used with consummate skill; *Fantasie* Op. 32, one of the master's last works, is dedicated to his pupil Jeannette Dincin.

Many of Eugène Ysaÿe's works were brought out posthumously by the Ysaÿe Publishers in Brussels, including the Sonata for two violins written in London during the war (in 1915) and dedicated to Queen Elisabeth of the Belgians, who played the violin. To facilitate the performance of this Sonata, Ysaÿe made a variant for three instruments—two violins and viola. In this latter version the Sonata was performed in London in 1916; in its original version the work was first performed by Yelizaveta Gilels and Leonid Kogan in 1964.

This profound, highly poetic and expertly written Sonata falls into three movements: *Poco lento, Maestoso, Allegretto, Poco lento* and *Finale Allegretto vivo e con fuoco*. This is a vividly colorful and sonorous piece of music, with ample use made of the cantilena and virtuoso technique. The composer reveals here his unique melodic gift, an original harmonic sense and perfect contrapuntal skill.

In his transcriptions and editions of violin literature, too, Eugène Ysaÿe stands out as a creative artist. He has transcribed for the violin the *Caprice d'après l'Etude en Forme de Valse de Saint-Saëns*, a number of Chopin waltzes and some other works. Mention should be made here of *Dix Préludes pour Violon seul. Essai sur le*

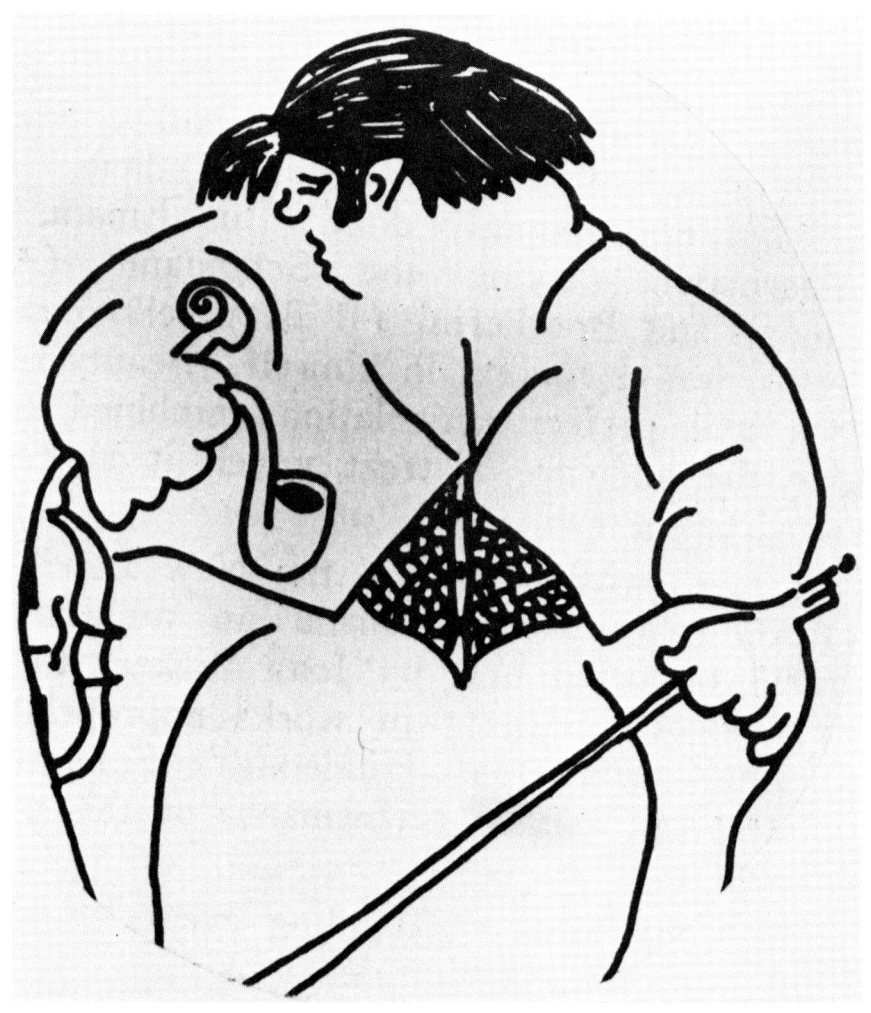

One of the many caricatures of Ysaÿe.

Mécanisme moderne du Violon, dedicated by Ysaÿe to the memory of his teachers Vieuxtemps and Wieniawski. The works were reconstructed from the manuscript by Charles Radoux-Rogier and published (under Henri Koch's editorship) as Opus 35 by the Schott frères, Brussels, in 1952. Ysaÿe's exercises and scales have appeared under the editorship of Joseph Szigeti.

Very valuable are Ysaÿe's cadenzas to Concerto No. 22 by Viotti, Concerto No. 3 by Mozart and the concertos by Beethoven and by Brahms. He has also made excellent editions of some classical violin compositions, among them sonatas by Locatelli, Nardini and

UNICA AUDICION
POR EL
GLORIOSO
VIOLINISTA

EUGENIO YSAYE

TEATRO DE LA COMEDIA

Domingo 10 de Abril de 1927, a las 11 de la mañana

PROGRAMA

I

SONATA en la menor, núm. 4   BEETHOVEN
Presto.
Andante Scherzando, piu allegretto.
Allegro molto.

II

CONCIERTO en la menor, núm. 22   VIOTTI
(Cadencias de EUGENIO YSAYE)
Moderato.
Adagio.
Finale; Agitato assai.

III

"AMISTAD" poema, op. 26 (para dos   EUGENIO YSAYE
violines
MLLE. JANNETTE DINCIN y el autor

IV

"EXTASIS", poema, op. 21   EUGENIO YSAYE
VALS en re menor   CHOPIN-YSAYE
POLONESA en la mayor, núm. 2   WIENIAWSKY

Al piano: TASSO JANNOPOULO

PIANO GAVEAU   DE LA CASA HAZEN

A program of Ysaÿe's concert in Barcelona, Spain. Note that he played a poem **Amistad** *with his student, later to be his wife, Jeannette Dincin. Her name is spelled variously in different lands.*

As a member of his orchestra, I had known him during the years of his conductorship of the Cincinnati Symphony Orchestra and recall the *camaraderie* of his relationship with his musicians.

The spontaneous quality of his art made rehearsals a very irksome thing to him. I remember how, after a few pages of a composition which perhaps did not suit his mood, he would reach toward a hip pocket—the familiar gesture was a sure sign that intermission would follow. A beloved pipe would be taken out and stroked affectionately a few times; then, stepping down from the podium, he would say to the musicians, "We have a smoke, eh?"

A clipping of unknown origin.

Pasquali and concertos by Mozart, Vivaldi and some other composers.

Besides the violin and cello pieces we have mentioned, Ysaÿe wrote *Harmonies du Soir*, Op. 31, a work for solo quartet and string orchestra published (like most of his compositions) by the Editions Ysaÿe in Brussels, and two string trios and a string quintet.

By his violin works Ysaÿe has greatly enriched the technical and expressive media of the instrument, which prompted David Oistrakh to speak of the Belgian violinist and composer as "the greatest innovator after Paganini." He makes an unprecedented and varied use of the violin's timbres, attaining unusually vivid and colorful sound effects, by frequent use of open strings, double stopping, chords (not only four-part but also six- and eight-part), complex polyphonic devices, harmonics, *flautato*, *pizzicato*, highly original passage work, virtuoso bowing and the utilization of scordatura and quarter-tone intervals.

As has been noted earlier, Ysaÿe's daring searchings were determined by his artistic ideas, while his perfect mastery of the instrument's varied technical and expressive potentialities enabled him to achieve the fullest possible realization of his ideas and afforded unlimited scope to his imagination, thoughts and feelings. This is the reason why many of Ysaÿe's compositions strike the listeners as free improvisations. This also accounts for the immense difficulties in interpreting his music.[90]

In many of his works, Ysaÿe displays a highly original musical thinking, a rich creative imagination, poetic gifts and inspiration, embodied in a vivid musical language all his own.

At times this language becomes excessively complicated. This can be explained by Ysaÿe's own creative searchings and experimentations and also by the spirit of the times which manifested itself in different ways in the music of his contemporaries. It is noteworthy that while not escaping impressionistic influences in some of his works (and it was Impressionism that had shaped the personalities of the composers who were his close friends), Ysaÿe denounced modernistic music for its chaos and lack of logic.

We know that Impressionism in music was a reaction to the neoromantic art, the manifestation of French composers' urge to oppose their national traditions to the universal cult of Wagner. This tendency, however, was based on ideologically narrow premises,

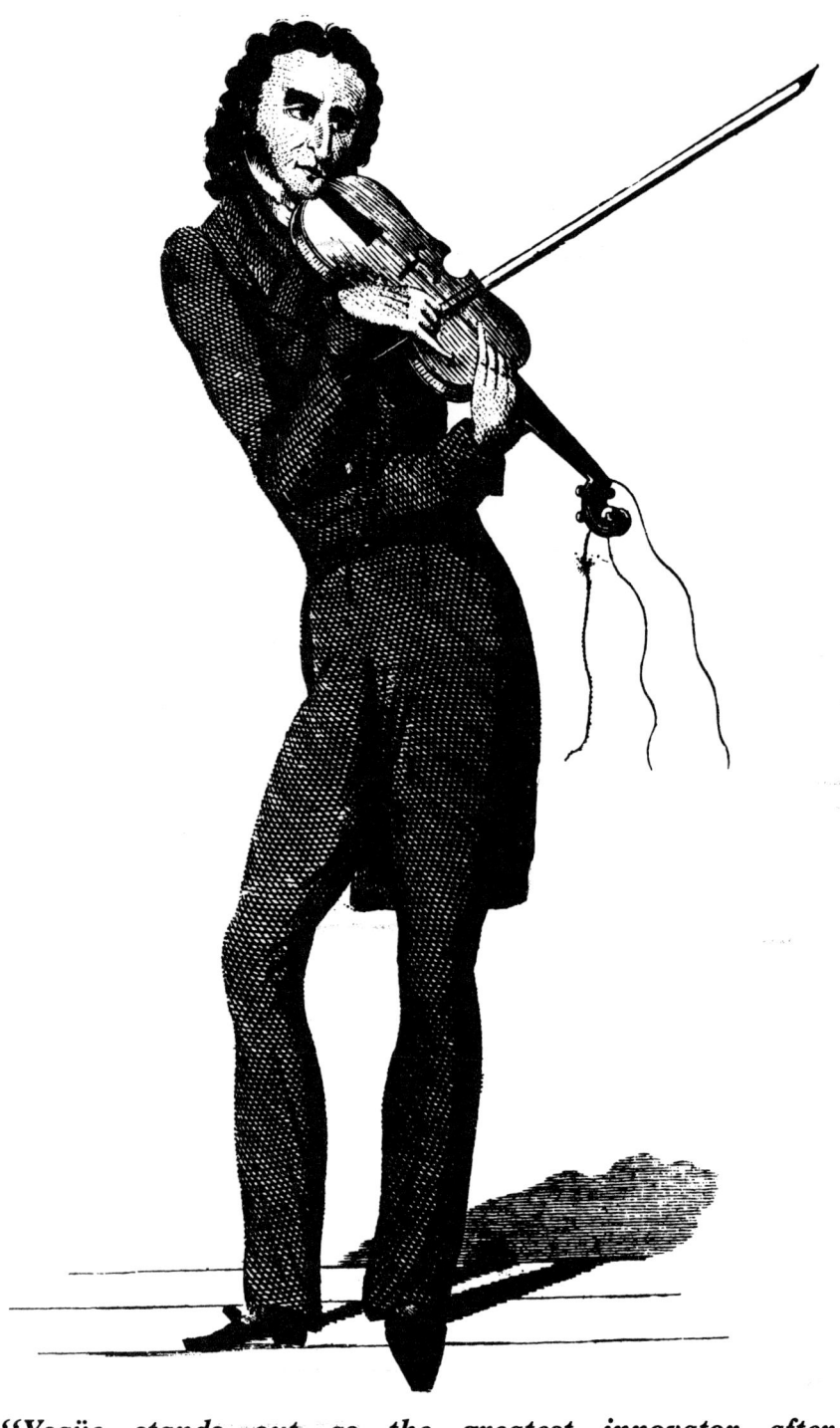

"Ysaÿe stands out as the greatest innovator after Paganini." [Quoted from Oistrakh]

David Oistrakh winner of the first prize at the Ysaÿe Competition of 1937.

not going beyond the fixation of evanescent impressions and moods in music. The most talented representatives of this trend, in the first place Claude Debussy, scored considerable artistic achievements, primarily in expanding musical expressiveness. For all his realist tendencies, Ysaÿe was a romantic artist, and this helped Ysaÿe the composer to overcome the limitations of Impressionism. In many of his works, Ysaÿe created life-like and vivid images characterized by depth of feeling and emotions.

Ysaÿe, the interpretative artist, was an enemy of Philistine narrow-mindedness and fatuous sentimentality. He fought against superficial effects and against all kinds of formalism and indifference in interpretation. This is evident in many of his compositions. The words in which Ivan Sollertinsky defined the new type of the romantic composer are wholly applicable to Ysaÿe. The famous Soviet critic said: "...the composer has at his command all types of weapons in order to fight for the dignity of music against Philistine tastes, against shallow clowning and against mere virtuosity, which has degenerated and became empty formalism."[91]

NOTES

[82] Quoted from A. Ysaÿe, *op. cit.*, pp. 403-404.
[83] Henri Vieuxtemps, Ysaÿe's master, composed not only for his instrument, but wrote also several pieces for cello.
[84] Quoted from A. Ysaÿe, *op. cit.*, p. 413.
[85] Albert Jacques Zimmer (1874-1940), Belgian violinist a pupil of Ysaÿe's, was Professor of the Brussels Conservatoire and headed the celebrated Zimmer Quartet.
[86] Jacques Gailliard (1875-1940), Belgian cellist, a pupil of Joseph Jacob, Professor of the Liège and Brussels Conservatoires member of the Brussels Quartet and later, of the Zimmer Quartet.
[87] Quoted from A. Ysaÿe, *op. cit.*, p. 412.
[88] Quoted from A. Ysaÿe, *op. cit.*, p. 414.
[89] A rare example of this type of writing for solo violin is encountered in the *Passacaglia* by H.I.F. Biber, a 17th-century violinist who was born in Bohemia. In this piece Biber repeats 64 times a theme consisting also of four notes (g, f, $e\text{-}flat$, d).
[90] In speaking of the daring use of technical devices and the development of virtuosity in the works of such violinists as Paganini and Vieuxtemps (and presumably his own) Eugène Ysaÿe emphasized the role such virtuoso works played for the edification of "symphonist composers" as showing what could be performed on the instrument.
[91] Sollertinsky, I., *Muzykalno-istoricheskiye etudy, (Musico-Historical Studies)*, Leningrad, 1956, p. 100.

Joseph Szigeti autographed this photo to the author.

Chapter 9

Russian Music Critics on Ysaÿe's Art

Eugène Ysaÿe's frequent concert appearances in Russia and his creative, friendly contacts with prominent Russian musicians yield interesting material, enabling us to throw additional light on his personality.

It is highly significant that Ysaÿe was encouraged to devote himself to concert activities by that eminent Russian musician, Anton Rubinstein. Ysaÿe cherished a life-long veneration for the great Russian pianist, whom he regarded as his teacher of interpretation. Already in the early 1880's Ysaÿe had many opportunities to play with Rubinstein; in 1883, in-between the concerts, the two artists spent whole days at Rubinstein's playing an enormous number of sonatas for violin and piano. This joint music-making left an indelible imprint on the soul of the young Belgian violinist. Anton Rubinstein's principles of interpretation continued to inspire Eugène Ysaÿe throughout his subsequent artistic life.

While quite a young man, Ysaÿe heard the well-known Russian pianist Anna Yesipova (1851-1914) and played in ensemble with her.

Ysaÿe posed for this photograph in Russia. He was wearing a heavy coat during the winter of 1883 when he gave a memorable concert on January 13 in St. Petersburg.

Within thirty years, beginning with 1882, Ysaÿe appeared in Russia no less than fifteen times, scoring tremendous success in St. Petersburg, Moscow, Orel, Kiev, Kharkov, Odessa, Yelisavetgrad, Riga and other cities.

In August 1882 (between the 3rd and the 27th) Eugène Ysaÿe played eight times at the then famous Pavlovsk Concerts (held at the Kursaal in Pavlovsk, near St. Petersburg) with a very good orchestra directed by Voicech Glavač[92] who was largely responsible for the high artistic level of these concerts.

The Pavlovsk Concerts were given during the summers between 1838 and 1917 near St. Petersburg-Petrograd, and attracted such conductors as Johann Strauss, Benjamin Bilse, Voicech Glavac, Nikolai Galkin, Oskar Nedbal, Alexander Glazunov, Edouard Colonne and other outstanding musicians, Russian and foreign.[93] The programs often featured the best works by Russian and foreign composers and enjoyed a deserved popularity with musicians and music-lovers alike.

Eugène Ysaÿe must have heard about the Pavlovsk Concerts and the enthusiastic Russian public from Benjamin Bilse, in whose orchestra he worked from 1879 to 1882: with his orchestra of 62 Bilse had appeared at Pavlovsk during the summer seasons of 1870 and 1873-75. Already in 1870 the Russian press remarked on the serious trend of Bilse's programs which included Beethoven symphonies, works by Berlioz and Wagner, and also by Russian composers (among them the orchestral pieces *Ivan the Terrible* by Anton Rubinstein, the *Zaporozhye Cossack Dance* by Alexander Serov and some others).[94]

On his first tour of Russia, Ysaÿe played at Pavlovsk, performing the concertos by Wieniawski, Vieuxtemps and Mendelssohn, Vieuxtemps' *Ballade and Polonaise,* Saint-Saëns' *Introduction and Rondo Capriccioso, Hungarian Airs* by Heinrich Ernst and other works, including his own pieces.

Ysaÿe had a serious rival in the person of Konstantin Pushilov, a graduate in 1865, of Wieniawski's class at the St. Petersburg Conservatoire, who was older and was famous for his deep and singing tone and brilliant virtuosity. However, the young guest violinist scored great success at Pavlovsk.

The first press notices, while praising the Belgian violinist, were not free of criticism. One of the critics wrote after Ysaÿe's first con-

Leslie Sheppard, recipient of the Ysaÿe medal and coauthor of Paganini *with Dr. Herbert R. Axelrod. Below, the back of the Ysaÿe medal presented to Mr. Sheppard.*

Ysaÿe portrait taken in Russia. 1912. Compliments of Arazi.

Louis Dupont engraved this medal which was given by Antoine Ysaÿe to special friends. This copy was presented to Leslie Sheppard.

cert: "The young artist is a fairly competent technician, he is full of artistic brio and life and in many respects reminds us of Wieniawski. His playing is full of *chic*, but lacks a deep tone and certain elegance and finish—qualities with which the late Wieniawski was so richly endowed by nature."[95]

Gradually, however, the emotion, sincerity and vivid virtuosity of Ysaÿe's playing won for him more and more admirers.

At his concluding benefit concert on August 27, Ysaÿe played the Mendelssohn Concerto and a number of other pieces. His

Photographed by Dr. Herbert R. Axelrod in Moscow, 1978, this memorial hangs in the Tchaikovsky Conservatory and still honors the great Master.

Oskar Nedbal.

listeners, who had come to love the talented young artist, presented him with a laurel wreath after the first movement of the Concerto. In the words of a critic, the Concerto was performed "so brilliantly, with such deep feeling, such finesse and lucidity as can be expected only of an artist possessing the highest of gifts." In discussing the other pieces in the program of that concert, the critic wrote: "The most enchanting was the *Berceuse* of Radoux, with an astonishingly fine bowing and an incredible singing quality of each note. Meanwhile, in the *Saltarelle carnavalesque*, the work of M. Ysaÿe himself, he aroused our admiration for his daring bowing, purity of intonation and vigor in the most difficult passages."[96]

We learn from the critical review that in the concert "Beethoven's Sonata in C-sharp minor was played by M. Glavac, while the Etude for this Sonata (probably an improvisation—*L.G.*) was played on the violin by M. Ysaÿe." Besides, Ysaÿe performed the solo violin part (with a string quintet) in the *Prelude* from Saint-Saëns' oratorio *The Deluge*.

The next winter season found Ysaÿe once more in Russia. He gave a highly successful concert in St. Petersburg on January 13, 1883. The critic of the *St. Peterburgskiye vedomosti* wrote: "The violinist has a beautiful tone, and excellent technique and a wonderful ability to feel deeply the minutest detail of what he is playing. All that M. Ysaÿe plays he presents with a youthful abandon, and that is why his performance cannot leave his listeners indifferent. Any artificiality in performance is foreign to M. Ysaÿe—with him everything is sincere and emotionally experienced. The works of Vieuxtemps and Saint-Saëns, which he played with great temperament and virtuosity, aroused a long and very enthusiastic ovation."[97]

That tour took Ysaÿe to other Russian cities besides St. Petersburg: in Vilno he gave two concerts and was presented with a valuable Amati violin. His appearances in Riga were eagerly awaited and proved highly successful. He gave four concerts in which he played, with orchestra, the Concertos of Mendelssohn, Wieniawski and Vieuxtemps, Wieniawski's Fantasia on themes

Ysaÿe in Odessa, May 1883.

As popular and great as Ysaÿe was, he never achieved the recognition of Paganini. This sketch, made in 1895, was used in The Musical Courier. *It shows a likeness of Paganini—at the time that Ysaÿe was at his height.*

Anton Rubinstein.

Antoine Ysaÿe sent this photograph of his father to the author in 1960, using the blank backside to write a long message about the publication difficulties with his father's works. Ysaÿe's works were never popular.

from Gounod's *Faust*, and many other works. His appearances in Kiev, Kharkov and Odessa were equally successful.

Ysaÿe gave four concerts in Kiev, delighting his audiences by his performance of classical and modern music. After his first concert, held on April 5, a Kiev newspaper wrote: "In the person of M. Ysaÿe, the violin virtuosos have a rare and precious representative. Apart from his great technique, elegance and the attractive vigor of his playing, M. Ysaÿe possesses in abundance one more highly valuable quality: he is extremely musical and has a fine sense of style. His style of playing puts him between Joachim and Sarasate. In performing pieces of the contemporary repertoire he is very elegant, while in playing the classics his manner becomes serious and simple. Thanks to this versatility, his playing fascinates both the connoisseur and the public. M. Ysaÿe's tone is nobility itself, his strokes of the bow (*Bogenstreiche*) are free and elegant. The program of the concert proved interesting and varied, including classics (Bach, Beethoven) and contemporary composers of most varied schools and trends (Vieuxtemps, Wieniawski, Saint-Saëns, Joachim). . . .The concert was an unqualified success and M. Ysaÿe was recalled countless times."[98]

The program of this concert consisted of Bach's Fugue in G minor, Beethoven's Romance in F Major, Vieuxtemps' Concerto in D minor, Wieniawski's Polonaise No. 2, and some other pieces.

In April and May 1883 Ysaÿe was in Odessa, where he met Anton Rubinstein. They played together for many hours on end, enjoying it very much indeed. Ysaÿe felt a deep respect for the great Russian pianist, who in his turn valued highly the vivid and original talent of the young violinist. Anton Rubinstein used to say that "Of all living violinists only Ysaÿe reminds me of Wieniawski."

Rubinstein singled Ysaÿe out from the multitude of visiting virtuosos who revelled in superficial technique, thoughtless elegance and sentimentality, saying "I like to play with Ysaÿe, that's not *praline.*"[99]

As a momento of their communion, Rubinstein gave Ysaÿe his photograph with the following inscription: "A monsieur Ysaÿe souvenir de Sympathie. Odessa, le *1 avril 1883.* Ant. Rubinstein.*"*[100]

Then Ysaÿe returned to Kiev, where he played the Mendelssohn

Joseph Joachim.

Concerto, which had been performed there a year previously by Joachim and Sarasate. A local critic wrote that, although the Belgian violinist had been surpassed by Joachim in the first movement and by Sarasate in the third, he proved far superior to both in the second movement demanding a singing tone and beautiful phrasing. Especially impressive was Ysaÿe in the works by his masters Wieniawski (*Variations on a Russian Theme, Legend and Polonaise*) and Vieuxtemps (*Rondino*). The critic wrote that in his playing of Wieniawski's music, Ysaÿe displayed "a brio, vigor and brilliance reminding one of Wieniawski himself."[101] In that concert Ysaÿe played his own *Près d'un berceau* and Mazurka.

On May 5, Eugène Ysaÿe gave his farewell concert for the benefit of the Music School of the Kiev Branch of the Russian Music Society. Together with members of the School's staff, including Ottakar Sevĉik, a well-known Czech violinist and teacher, L. Pyatigorovich and L. Alois-Muzykant, Ysaÿe performed Beethoven's Seventh Quartet and Mendelssohn's Trio. His solo numbers were a Bach Fugue, Wieniawski's *Faust* Fantasia, and some other pieces. Pianists V. Puchalski, N. Tutkovsky and G. Khodorovsky participated in the concert.

The *Kievlyanin* critic was not wholly satisfied with Ysaÿe as a quartet player—he considered that the young violinist did not succeed in suppressing his vivid personality and virtuosity in the interest of the ensemble. "But in playing solo M. Ysaÿe surpassed himself. The Bach Fugues, the études for unaccompanied violin, the *Faust* Fantasia were performed superbly, with breath-taking brilliance and brio and, what was especially valuable, each piece was rendered in perfect style: his playing of Bach was remarkable for an earnest simplicity while in performing Wieniawski he displayed unusual brilliance and abandon.[102]

Among the reviews of Ysaÿe's concerts in Odessa (they took place on May 2 and 7) the extensive critique which appeared in the *Odesski vestnik* deserves special mention. The author discussed the first of Ysaÿe's concerts and said that: "M. Ysaÿe captivates and fascinates by the heart-warming quality of his tone and his spirited and profound interpretation. In his hands, the violin becomes a living and animated thing: it sings melodiously, it weeps piteously and moans, it whispers of love, it sighs deeply, it rejoices noisily—in a word, it expresses the minutest shades and tints of feeling.

Ippolitov-Ivanov.

Raphael Hillyer with Ippolitov-Ivanov.

A Russian postcard honoring Ysaÿe

In this lies the power and irresistible appeal of Ysaÿe's playing."[103]

In another review of the same concert, his playing is characterized as "elegant, graceful and at the same time full of force and expression." The critic further says: "The Vieuxtemps' Concerto and Saint-Saëns' *Rondo Capriccioso* were performed faultlessly and evoked a storm of applause, while Ysaÿe played Vieuxtemp's *Legend* just as the composer himself used to play it, that is, with the profoundest feeling and simplicity."[104]

On that tour, Ysaÿe stayed in Russia four months and gave a total of 80 concerts. It was probably in that same year, 1883, that the Moscow publisher Pyotr Jurgenson issued for the first time Ysaÿe's two Mazurkas (in G minor and in A minor), dedicated to S. Weyenberg, the accompanist recommended to him by Anton Rubinstein.

The 1883 tour was the first of many which took place in the 1880's and 1890's and at the beginning of the present century. Ysaÿe liked Russian musicians and the Russian public, and he maintained close creative and friendly ties with many prominent Russian composers, artists and critics. Among them were, besides Anton Rubinstein, Vasily Safonov, Alexander Siloti, Alexander Verzhbilovich, Sergei Rachmaninov, César Cui, Vasily Besekirsky, Anatoly Brandukov, Vasily Andreyev, Nikolai Kashkin, Mikhail Ippolitov-Ivanov, Boris Kamensky, Alexander Goldenweiser, Matvei Pressman, Boris Sibor, Michael Erdenko, and some others.

Eugène Ysaÿe appeared at symphony and chamber concerts sponsored by the Russian Music Society and by the Philharmonic Society in Moscow, at the Siloti Concerts and at his own concerts in different towns and cities. He often took part in charity concerts and in musical events held at private houses.

His growing interest in Russian music, and his sympathy for Russian musicians, as well as his outstanding musicianship and engaging personality, served to strengthen Ysaÿe's friendly relations with Russia, a country in which he won warm and lasting love.

The well-known Russian violinist Vasily Besekirsky (1835 -1919),[105] who was on the staff of the Moscow Philharmonic Music School, used to recall how, on his arrival in Moscow in 1883, young Ysaÿe visited him at his home. There he met several violinists, among them young Karl Grigorovich, a pupil of Besekirsky, who won an international reputation in later years, and spent eight whole hours with them, playing. That must have been the first appearance in Moscow of the young Belgian violinist, of whom little was known at that time.

This is what Vasily Besekirsky wrote: "Ysaÿe played a lot of serious compositions on my violin to my accompaniment on the piano. He struck us as an astonishing virtuoso—and no wonder: he displayed an impeccable technique, a big and beautiful tone and, most important, his playing was full of inspiration. He undoubtedly possessed what is called the *feu sacré*, a rare quality which is not encountered in every one of the famous violinists. Today we can safely ask—is there anyone who does not know Ysaÿe?!"[106]

From that time on, Ysaÿe and Besekirsky became good friends. When the Belgian violinist came to Moscow at the end of 1895, he showed his respect for Besekirsky by writing in the latter's scrapbook[107] a line from his *Prélude du Poème Concertant* accompanied by the following inscription: "Au meilleur Maître de l'école Russe

Dramatic photo of Eugène Ysaÿe, the great Master.

actuelle souvenir de son grand admirateur et jeune ami" ("To the best master of the contemporary Russian school in remembrance of his great admirer and young friend.")[108]

In the period between 1883 and 1895, Ysaÿe made an extensive tour of Russia early in 1885. On January 26, he played Vieuxtemps' Fourth Concerto, under the direction of Anton Rubinstein at the symphony concert of the Russian Music Society in St. Petersburg. (The program of this concert also included Beethoven's Ninth Symphony.)

A St. Petersburg critic thus described the admiration excited by Ysaÿe's performance of this Concerto: "He displayed his astounding technique particularly in the scherzo. Besides, M. Ysaÿe possesses a beautiful tone, he plays with abandon, elegance and consummate musicality—he resembles in some respects Henryk Wieniawski. The public acclaimed the artist with great enthusiasm."[109]

A few days after that, Ysaÿe gave a recital in St. Petersburg.

Already at that time, Ysaÿe showed an interest in Russian music. He did his best to improve his knowledge of it and readily included works by Russian composers in his repertoire.

It would be interesting to quote here Ysaÿe's letters to the Russian composer César Cui,[110] whom he got to know well in St. Petersburg. The first letter, of July 24, 1886, was written in Arlon, Belgium, and reads as follows:

"My dear Colleague, I have just leafed through your wonderful *Berceuse;* it suits me perfectly and I have lost no time in including it into the program of my concert at Nantes on November 5. Have you written an orchestra (or quartet) accompaniment to this heavenly page? If so, be as charming as your music and let me have it, and if not, please make some indications in pencil in the piano part and let me do the rest.

"I await it and should be disappointed at not receiving your kind reply.

Sincerely yours,
Eugène Ysaÿe.

"P.S. Your suite is very good. The *Tarantella* is highly original, but instead of Spanish pieces I should like to play something Russian. I do not know if you are interested to learn that I have just been offered master classes at the Brussels Conservatoire."

César Cui.

The first page of Ysaÿe's letter to Cesar Cui. 1886.

Oil painting of Ysaÿe by von Wolles. 1925.

The *Berceuse* in question is No. 8 of Cui's *Twelve Miniatures*, Op. 20. The suite mentioned in the P.S. is the *Concert Suite* for violin and orchestra (or piano), Op. 25, composed in 1883 and published in 1886. The Suite is dedicated to the celebrated Belgian violinist Martin Marsick (1848-1924). It consists of the following items: *Intermezzo scherzando, Canzonetta* and *Tarantella.*

That Ysaÿe was interested in Cui's music is seen from a second letter written in Brussels on December 23, 1886.

"My dear Colleague and Friend, My wedding, the preparations for it, our marriage journey and honeymoon—all this prevented me from writing to you to tell you that I had received the two scores you sent me.

"Your *Berceuse* is on the program of my first concert in France and I am sure it will prove one of the best items in my other programs as well. If your pen shows its creative power for me, the power of which you know the secret, I shall be very happy, yes, yes, very happy to play everything, no matter how fruitful it may be.

"With a thousand thanks accept the friendly handshake of
Yours devotedly,
Eugène Ysaÿe."

It is a remarkable fact that when, at the age of 32, Ysaÿe decided to play the Beethoven Concerto for the first time in public, he performed it in Russia. We have a review of Ysaÿe's concert given in Riga on March 4, 1890, by the well-known Russian critic Vsevolod Cheshikhin, in which Ysaÿe's playing of the Beethoven Concerto is mentioned. The critic compares Ysaÿe's interpretation with that of Sarasate, "who used to imbue this work of young Beethoven with so much fire and power that he has accustomed the public to an entirely different understanding of this work; at any rate," Cheshikhin went on, "the graceful and tender treatment of Ysaÿe is very interesting."[111]

On March 8 Ysaÿe played in Riga the Mendelssohn Concerto and *Gavotte* and *Prelude* from Bach's E-Major Partita. While praising Ysaÿe's interpretation of the Concerto, the critic reproached him for playing the Bach pieces in a too-fast tempo foreign to their style. He also objected to the artist's indiscriminate choice of repertoire in the rest of his Riga programs.

At the same time, the critic praised "the famous violinist's captivating tone, not very powerful but mellow and beautiful," which could be compared with the human voice and which "astonishes by the unbelievably pure and gentle harmonics."[112]

Eugène Ysaÿe first appeared before the Moscow public at a concert of the Russian Music Society under the direction of Vasily Safonov on November 11, 1895. At that concert the premieres were given of Bedřich Smetana's *Vltava*, the second item from his cycle of symphonic poems entitled *My Country*, and the Interlude before Part III of Sergei Taneyev's operatic trilogy *Oresteia*.

Ysaÿe gave a sensational performance of Saint-Saëns' Third Concerto and Bruch's *Scottish Fantasia*. There is an interesting review by the Russian composer Arseny Koreshchenko (1870-1922), a pupil of Taneyev and Arensky, which appeared in the *Moskovskiye vedomosti*. "To say about the famous violinist M. Eugène Ysaÿe, who appeared at this concert, what is usually said in such cases—that he is an excellent artist with a wonderful, fascinating tone, astonishing technique, outstanding talent and musicianship, that he possesses a facile bow—would be saying but a little part of the whole. To define this whole, no better word can be chosen than inspiration. The public sensed this inspired interpretation by their every nerve and for that reason their enthusiasm knew no bounds. M. Ysaÿe had a tremendous, an immeasurable success."[113]

According to this critic, Ysaÿe's playing of the Saint-Saëns' Concerto was marked by "astonishing elegance" and of Bruch's Fantasia, by "inimitable perfection." On the demands of his enraptured public, the artist played many encores.

To this review of Ysaÿe's Moscow concert, the critique by S. Flerov can be added: "M. Ysaÿe, a Belgian violinist, has shown himself an outstanding and extremely lovable talent. His artistic personality dominates all, and the most conspicuous feature of this personality is lyricism. The artist's lyricism has revealed itself to the full in two works of his choice: the Violin Concerto by Saint-Saëns and the *Scottish Fantasia* by Max Bruch. The *Andantino* from the Concerto, with its dialogue between the violin and the woodwinds, proved enchanting. M. Ysaÿe's talent is characterized by something unusually intimate, songful and tender. These qualities so charm the listeners that they make them disregard the lack of power and plasticity of his tone. It is clear that M. Ysaÿe's is a perfectly original artistic individuality. We must not demand

Max Bruch.

anything of him that is incompatible with its essence."[114]

Thus, already the first Moscow reviewers noted in Ysaÿe's artistic make-up his vivid personality, inspiration and lyricism—qualities that have the greatest appeal for Russian audiences.

Eugène Ysaÿe and his brother Théophile gave the first Moscow performance of the Franck Sonata. Besides, "with a rare musicality and technical perfection" (to quote Koreshchenko) Ysaÿe performed the first movement of Vieuxtemps' Concerto in E Major and "with a unique understanding of their style and spirit"—Bach's *Saraband* and *Gigue*,[115] the paraphrases of Wagner's *Mastersingers of Nuremberg* and *Parsifal*, and other pieces, among them Ysaÿe's own Mazurka. The artist showed an overwhelming brilliance and skill in playing Sarasate's *Zigeunerweisen* and Vieuxtemps' *Souvenirs de Russie*.

On that tour, Ysaÿe also visited St. Petersburg, where he took part in a Symphonic Assembly and a chamber music concert. On the former occasion he played Bach, Saint-Saëns, Wieniawski, Wagner and Sarasate. The program of the chamber concert (on November 19) featured the quartets by d'Indy and Fauré and the first performance in that city of the Franck Sonata (again in partnership with Eugène's brother Théophile). Participating with Ysaÿe in the performance of the quartets were the prominent St. Petersburg artists Boris Kamensky, F. Hildebrandt and Alexander Verzhbilovich.

The St. Petersburg critic Nikolai Findeisen characterized Ysaÿe at the time as "a very good, thoughtful musician who has had a thorough training; the possessor of a beautiful and noble tone, always attentive to every detail of the work performed."[116]

César Cui noted in particular Ysaÿe's excellent taste, which was evident in his choice of repertoire, a trait in common with Anton Rubinstein. Shortly after Ysaÿe's concerts, Cui wrote that a performing artist who had won the audience's respect "must serve his art only, must perform only such music as he considers good and valuable, must educate the public's taste and popularize highly artistic but little known works . . . In his programs Rubinstein has always served only his art, not thinking of the established, hackneyed tastes of the public. That first-rate violinist, M. Ysaÿe who appeared in our country not long ago, has shown us a similar example of a daring and noble independence in his choice of the music he played."[117]

And indeed the programs of Ysaÿe's concerts in Russia show his broad musical horizon and good taste. Even the pieces of Wieniawski and Vieuxtemps, sure hits that they were, soon began to occupy a secondary place in his repertoire. In his Russian programs the leading place belongs to classical pieces of the violin repertoire: Bach (Sonatas and *Chaconne*), the Vitali *Chaconne*, sonatas by Veracini, Handel, Mozart and Beethoven, and concertos by Bach, Vivaldi and Viotti. Several times he performed the concertos of Mozart, Beethoven, Mendelssohn, Brahms, Bruch and Saint-Saëns, and Lalo's *Symphonie espagnole*. He also played the sonatas of Brahms and Strauss. Together with the composer, Ysaÿe performed for the first time Max Reger's suite *Im alten Style* and took part in the premières of d'Indy's and Fauré's Quartets, of Castillon's Quintet and Chausson's *Poéme*[118] and *Concert* for violin, piano and string quartet.

Ysaÿe's chamber music programs included also quartets by Beethoven and Mendelssohn and trios by Beethoven and Tchaikovsky, played in ensemble with Russian musicians.

The bust of Ysaÿe done in marble by Dupont, stands in front of the Conservatoire in Liege. (1934). Courtesy of Arazi.

Works by Russian composers in Ysaÿe's programs deserve special mention. Besides the pieces by Cui, Ysaÿe played Tchaikovsky's *Melancholy Serenade*, Glazunov's *Meditation*, Alexander Taneyev's *Rêverie* and some other works.

Eugène Ysaÿe was in no small measure instrumental in popularizing Russian music abroad and it is noteworthy that his solo repertoire contained the grand violin concertos by Tchaikovsky and Glazunov, Rimsky-Korsakov's *Fantasia on Russian Themes*, and other compositions.

We have mentioned elsewhere that at its concerts, the Ysaÿe String Quartet played Borodin's and Tchaikovsky's quartets while symphonic music of Balakirev, Tchaikovsky, Glazunov and other Russian composers was performed at the Ysaÿe Concerts.

The special concert of Russian music organized by Ysaÿe in 1904 is extra proof of his lively interest in it.

The program of this concert which was held in Brussels on February 14, 1904, consisted of the following works: Glinka, Overture to *Ruslan and Ludmila*, Rachmaninov, Piano Concerto, Op. 18 (first performance in Belgium), Glazunov, Suite *From the Middle Ages*, Op. 79 (first performance in Belgium), Arensky, *Basso ostinato* and *Prelude No. 1* for piano, Liadov, *Etude*, Op. 37, for piano, Rubinstein-Siloti, *Lezghinka*, Taneyev, Overture to *Oresteia* (first time in Belgium), Rimsky-Korsakov, *Russian Easter* Overture.[119]

Alexander Siloti, the soloist at this concert, wrote from Brussels to Sergei Taneyev a few days later (on February 19, 1904): "Dear Sergei Ivanovich, I enclose the program of the Ysaÿe Concerts and the article. The Overture was performed excellently. Ysaÿe asked me to tell you that of the whole program he liked your piece best of all, and his attitude was evident in the way he conducted it. He asked me to send to him the score of your Symphony and I'll do it (if the score is at the Philharmonic), but I think that if you happen to have an extra copy you'd better send it to him yourself."[120]

In another letter, written in Viborg on July 5, 1904, Siloti once again reminded Taneyev of sending the score to Ysaÿe.

The appearance of Glazunov's *From the Middle Ages* on the program of the concert was due to the interest this work had aroused in Ysaÿe when he heard it under the composer's direction at a

The same Dupont bust as it now looks (1979). Photograph by André Humblet of Liege.

Edouard Lalo.

Siloti Concert in St. Petersburg a few months previously. That was the concert (held on November 28, 1903) at which Eugène Ysaÿe performed with the orchestra the concertos by Bach and Bruch.

Speaking of Ysaÿe's concerts in Russia, we shall now quote some reviews by Russian music critics of the early twentieth century. The Belgian artist attracted the attention of such critics as Nikolai Kashkin, Alexander Ossovsky, Nikolai Kochetov, Ivan Lipayev, Julius Engel, Yuri Sakhnovsky and many others.

When, in 1900, Ysaÿe performed Bach's Concerto in E Major and Lalo's *Symphonie espagnole* at the Symphonic Assembly of the Moscow Philharmonic on February 28 (incidentally, on that night the 50th anniversary of the artistic career of Ysaÿe's colleague Vasily Besekirsky was celebrated), the Russian press noted "the noble simplicity and austere style" of his interpretation of Bach's music and "the tempestuous, overwhelming temperament" which he displayed in the Lalo *Symphonie*.[121]

The critic of another Moscow paper called Ysaÿe "a great artist, a musician of genius," noting in particular the combination of "a wonderful tone, an astonishing technique, an unsurpassed musicianship and temperament."[122]

The charity concert on December 2, 1901, was a major musical event, for three outstanding artists—Sergei Rachmaninov, Anatoly Brandukov and Eugène Ysaÿe—participated in it. The program of that concert featured one of Rachmaninov's best works—his splendid Cello Sonata dedicated to Brandukov.

Ysaÿe gave a memorable performance of Vieuxtemps' Fourth Concerto,[123] Beethoven's *Romance* and Saint-Saëns' *Rondo Capriccioso*, with Rachmaninov as his partner at the piano. As Nikolai Kashkin wrote: "M. Ysaÿe held the public captive by his unrivalled playing, which may be said to put him at the head of contemporary violinists, naturally, excepting Joachim, whose fame remains with him to the end of his days. We shall not discuss each of the artist's contributions separately, but the Beethoven *Romance*, for instance, was played just ideally."[124]

It would be interesting to compare this opinion with that of another Moscow critic, Julius Engel, who wrote about the same concert: "He (Ysaÿe—*Ed.*) is one of the best contemporary violinists, perhaps the first. If Joachim is unrivalled in classical music, if Wilhelmj is famous for unique power and volume of tone, then M. Ysaÿe's playing may serve as a wonderful model of noble and gentle grace, fine finish of detail and warmth of interpretation. This, however, should not be understood to mean that M. Ysaÿe is incapable of classical perfection in his style or that his tone lacks power and volume—In these respects, too, he is a remarkable artist, which was evident, among other things, from his impeccable playing of the Beethoven Romance, Fourth Concerto of Vieuxtemps (incidentally, Ysaÿe's violin master) and other pieces. M. Ysaÿe played the scintillatingly virtuoso *Rondo Capriccioso* of Saint-Saëns with special elegance and purely French élan. In any case, he is one of those artists by the grace of God, who captivate the listener's heart from the very first moments and reign there supreme, no matter what they play; for even a poor piece of music after passing through the crucible of truly artistic creativity acquires some undefinable significance and appeal. No wonder that the capacity audience accorded M. Ysaÿe an enthusiastic reception and demanded countless encores."[125]

While fully acknowledging the important role played by an outstanding performer in the life of a musical work and in the impression which it produces on the listeners, we should, however, state that a really poor work ought not to interest a true artist and that the best of interpretations cannot turn bad music into good music. Vissarion Belinsky held that it is impossible to perform good and bad music equally well. "If the character created by the poet is not true to life, not convincing," the famous publicist wrote, "then no matter how brilliantly the actor may play, it is no more than mere histrionics and not art, just make-believe, and not inspiration. If an actor utters with deep feeling a pompous sentence from a poor play, then this is an example of play-acting, of trickery and not feeling, not breathing life into the role, because feeling is always animated by thought, always reasonable, and one can only be animated by truth—and by nothing else."[126]

But then we should further state that Julius Engel's words about "a poor piece of music" that have called forth the above paragraph have no reference to the works of Beethoven, Vieuxtemps and Saint-Saëns listed in the program of Ysaÿe's concert, for they are acknowledged masterpieces of the violin repertoire.

The public at this concert was particularly excited by the playing of Tchaikovsky's Piano Trio by Rachmaninov, Ysaÿe and Bran-

Camille Saint-Saëns.

Sir Henry Heyman (standing) with Camille Saint-Saëns.

dukov. Nikolai Kashkin defined it as excellent while Julius Engel said that it was wonderful and incomparable, remarking, however, that the vivid artistic personalities of the performers prevented them from merging into an organic whole.[127]

From 1903 on, Ysaÿe, then at the peak of his creative powers, became a frequent visitor on Russia's concert platforms and Russian critics were unanimous in extolling the artistic pleasure afforded by Ysaÿe's simple, noble and highly emotional interpretation of Bach and Beethoven.[128] His playing of Bach's Sonata in F minor (jointly with Siloti), Concerto in E Major and Double Concerto in D minor (with Kamensky) and the famous *Aria*, and of the Beethoven Concerto delighted his audiences and aroused storms of applause. To quote a Moscow critic: "The public highly appreciated the artist who has come in order not only to garner laurels but also to promote the progress of art . . . There is not the slightest attempt at superficial effect. Simplicity and the summit of artistry—these are M. Ysaÿe's aim, but then what an astonishingly powerful and rich tone, what expression, what daring and vividness in the performance, what irresistible temperament—and all this within the framework of artistry imbued with genius. You witness him making his listeners live his life and think his thoughts."[129]

A critic of the *S. Peterburgskiye vedomosti* emphasized in particular the "heartwarming simplicity and classical nobility" in Ysaÿe's interpretation of Bach.[130]

As time went on, the critics began to speak of the power and volume of Ysaÿe's tone which, probably, he had lacked earlier. Speaking in the highest of terms of the artistic merits of Ysaÿe's playing, a contemporary critic wrote: "He is a real giant captivating you from the first note of his powerful and rich tone, bidding you listen to everything that was the life of great Bach, a Bach we have not heard since the time of Anton Rubinstein, who alone spoke on his behalf in the language of an artist and a poet."[131]

Ysaÿe demonstrated his versatile talent and impeccable sense of style by playing in that same year the concertos by Mendelssohn and Bruch ("Everything was there—warmth, technique, cantilena, powerful expression and the fullest understanding," wrote Ivan Lipayev[132]), pieces by Vieuxtemps and Saint-Saëns, and also by Tchaikovsky, Glazunov and Alexander Taneyev.

The Russian artist Valentin Serov sketched Ysaÿe in 1903.

It was in 1903 that the well-known Russian artist Valentin Serov (1865-1911) drew that forceful portrait of Ysaÿe playing. In the realistically-depicted image of the Belgian musician, one senses concentration, inspiration and artistry.

Academician Igor Grabar regarded this drawing as one of Serov's best, classing it along with his portraits of Nikolai Rimsky-Korsakov, Konstantin Balmont, Vasily Kachalov, Konstantin Stanislavsky, Anton Chekhov, Ivan Moskvin, Mikhail Botkin and Wanda Landowska. Grabar wrote about that period of Serov's evolution that "He was so much taken by searchings for character that often after setting off to paint a portrait in oils he would content himself with a crayon drawing, finding it sufficient to satisfy the interest excited by his model. These drawings were, naturally, not mere sketches—in many cases they were more important than some of his large canvases, and Serov gradually developed his own style of portrait drawing. One hesitates to call certain portraits of this kind 'drawings,' because they are technically very complex and are thoroughly executed. But there also are such that, although not 'thoroughly executed,' are nevertheless excellent portaits."[133]

The Belgian violinist's art and expressive image inspired Serov's drawing, a portrait of the type just described and one more proof of Eugène Ysaÿe's numerous Russian contacts.

Ysaÿe was scheduled to come to Russia next in 1905, but the project fell through owing to the revolutionary events. (Of several foreign artists invited to participate in the Siloti Concerts only Pablo Casals managed to come to St. Petersburg, where he appeared on November 5, 1905.) Ysaÿe was to play at the Siloti Concert on December 10, 1905. As far as one can judge from the letter of Glazunov's mother to Nikolai Rimsky-Korsakov, dated June 25, 1905, Ysaÿe intended to play at that concert the Glazunov Concerto completed shortly before.[134] The letter says: "Ysaÿe will play Alexander's Concerto at Siloti's. [135]

After his Violin Concerto had been first performed (from the manuscript) by Leopold Auer under the composer's direction in St. Petersburg on February 19, 1905, Glazunov was eager to hear it played by the famous Belgian violinist. This is clear from the letter he wrote to F.I. Gruss, manager of the Mitrofan Belaiev music publishing firm, on July 3, 1905, in which the composer said that he was sending the piano score of his Concerto to be engraved in

Jan Kubelik, a first-rate virtuoso surpassed by Ysaÿe.

Leipzig and urged the manager to expedite the engraving so as to send one of the first proof sheets "the moment they are ready . . . from Leipzig to Eugène Ysaÿe in Brussels."[136]

Although the planned appearance of Ysaÿe in St. Petersburg did not take place, the Russian composer's excellent Concerto was subsequently firmly established in the repertoire of Ysaÿe and of other prominent violinists.

A number of Russian critics make a point of remarking on the beautiful "singing" of Ysaÿe's violin. "And you should hear his violin sing!" cried one of the critics. "Pablo de Sarasate's violin used to, in its time, sing enchantingly, but that was the sound of coloratura soprano, beautiful indeed, but expressing little feeling. M. Ysaÿe's tone, always ineffably pure, foreign to that 'scraping' quality characteristic of the violin, is beautiful both in *piano* and in *forte*. It always flows freely and reflects the minutest shadings of the musical expression."[137]

There are countless references in the Russian press to Ysaÿe's brilliant technique spoken of as "singing technique."

What attracted the Russian public most was Ysaÿe's ability to place his impeccable technique and beautiful tone at the service of the artistic truth. They were captivated by his sincere and inspired interpretation, in which the artist's subjective attitude to the work played combined with the objective presentation of its idea. In this respect Ysaÿe by far surpassed many of his contemporaries.

Nikolai Kashkin wrote after one of Ysaÿe's concerts in 1906: "Two main tendencies may be observed among virtuosi of all types, one where the virtuosi regard music mainly as a means for displaying their skill in the handling of an instrument and making the best use of its effects so as to attract the attention of their listeners, regardless of the artistic value of the works performed; and in violin playing this unadulterated virtuosity is represented, for example, by M. Kubelik,[138] who sometimes plays pieces devoid of any musical merit, which appeal to masses of his listeners. For the virtuosi belonging to the other trend their virtuosity is merely a means for the best possible realization of musical works of a loftier order. In violin playing such virtuosi were, for instance, the late Laub and the Dean of living violinists, Joachim." Kashkin went on to say: "M. Ysaÿe for whom his staggering technique is a means for achieving the highest artistic aims,

Pablo de Sarasate dated this photograph 13 January 1891.

should be classed with the second group. M. Ysaÿe is a great artistic personality who leaves his stamp on any work he plays although he most scrupulously observes the composer's indications. The artist's personality reveals itself in the point of view from which he treats this or that composer."[139]

By way of example, Kashkin cites Ysaÿe's performance of the Beethoven Concerto on December 12, of which he says that "Ysaÿe seemed to lose himself in an awesome contemplation, and his playing was stamped with a majestic calm imbued with a deep and sincere feeling."

After attending the symphonic concert in St. Petersburg under the direction of Siloti, in December 1906, at which Ysaÿe played the concertos of Mozart and Beethoven, and also Bach's Double Concerto (with Boris Kamensky), César Cui wrote to Maria Kerzina[140] in a letter dated December 18, 1906: "The other day I heard two famous artists—Hofmann[141] and Ysaÿe, and was greatly impressed by the latter."[142]

Another St. Petersburg critic wrote that thanks to his astonishingly harmonious technique, perfect interpretation, exalted and finely rounded-off, "Ysaÿe far surpasses even such first-rate virtuosos of the violin as Kubelik and Sarasate, to say nothing of Hubermann and Pechnikov. At present he is the *first* artist of the violin, just as Anton Rubinstein was the first artist of the piano a quarter of a century ago."[143]

Alexander Ossovsky has left a vividly graphic record of his impressions from Ysaÿe's concerts in St. Petersburg at the time. Ossovsky notes the force of the artist's personality and his dedication to exalted art free from drawing-room prettiness and empty virtuosity. He goes on to say in his extremely informative article: "In the history of modern virtuoso art of the violin where even the best-known names are allotted a few pages or even a few lines, Eugène Ysaÿe alone occupies a whole chapter full of beauty and meaning . . . Born a true musician and not merely a virtuoso, he has endowed his violin with the mind and spirit of contemporary music while his overwhelming technique has served him only as a sure foundation for that which is of the greatest importance in art—for artistic creation . . . The very appearance on the platform of that giant of a man casts a spell on the audience. His big head, his bulk, his imposing figure, his body, sturdy and full of youthful

Hans von Bülow.

vigor in spite of his 48 years . . . His gestures are those of a strong man who is sure of himself, their spontaneity reveals his sanguine temperament. Were I a painter, I would be tempted to depict the artist's figure, trying to catch its typicalness.

"The first stroke of the bow—and the audience is completely swayed by Eugène Ysaÿe's spiritual power. His artistic personality is simply irresistible. Of the two imaginable types of performers, artists of temperament and artists of style, Eugène Ysaÿe certainly belongs to the former. He played classical concertos by Bach, Mozart, Beethoven and also chamber music[144]—the quartets of Mendelssohn and Beethoven and Suite by Reger and, finally, to appease the pleasure-seeking crowd, he tossed off a few spectacular baubles of Saint-Saëns.[145] But no matter what he played, Eugène Ysaÿe was always himself. Some would say that it is a fault. But I should retort by reminding them of Rubinstein. If Hans von Bülow played Mozart as Mozart and Brahms as Brahms, the performer's personality manifesting itself in this superhuman objectivity, in cool and sharp as steel analysis, this did not make Bülow better than Rubinstein. Neither is Joachim better than Ysaÿe today . . . Eugène Ysaÿe's unique artistic individuality is based first of all on his original technical devices. A Belgian by extraction and training, he belongs to the famous Belgian school of violin playing, of which he is an illustrious representative. The harmonious combination of rare virtuoso qualities puts Eugène Ysaÿe beyond comparison as a technician. But it is not virtuosity that counts . . ."

Remarking that Eugène Ysaÿe militated against music "brought up in the atmosphere of drawing-rooms and expressing a light-hearted and negligent attitude to art," Ossovsky went on saying: "For him art and the exalted are synonymous. Art is a sacred mission and therefore demands a serious attitude and dedication in its service. Ysaÿe worships beauty and reaches the summit of ecstasy in his adoration. And at the moments of exaltation, Ysaÿe's passionate temperament is in its element and the artist's playing attains the heights of majestic pathos.

"Do you remember the figure of Apollo in Raphael's *Triumph of Poetry?* Apollo is depicted playing the viol. His face is grave and transported with holy fervor. His gaze is directed heavenwards where, in the blue spaces, he beholds the prototypes of the

Rosen's modern conception of Ysaÿe.

melodies which he creates, thither his heart is wafting its flight . . . This is a fit allegory of Ysaÿe's art. When, in the middle episode of the Rondo from Beethoven's Concerto, there flowed from under Ysaÿe's bow the tender and mellifluous sounds of the songful melody, touchingly pure like a young maiden, the artist's uplifted eyes reflected the same sunlit azure skies that presented themselves to Apollo's gaze in the Raphael picture. His head thrown back, his heart overflowing with rapture, the artist drank in the sounds to which he was giving birth and seemed to ascend on them to the sacred precincts of eternity . . . And you could not spot in his playing a single note that was void, that did not breathe life and sincerity.

"Victor Hugo's precept 'Mêlez toute votre âme à la création'[146] has found a new realization in Eugène Ysaÿe. It is quite natural that one recalls Hugo, for this majestic flight heavenward, that the exalted feeling in the famous virtuoso's playing is akin to those of the French poet. And there is the same ecstasy attaining the height of *pathos* in their worship of beauty. "That is the spirit of French Romanticism."[147]

Alexander Ossovsky was perfectly justified in speaking of romanticism in Ysaÿe's art. At the same time Nikolai Kashkin, too, was right when he said: "The general style of his performance suggests counting M. Ysaÿe among representatives of the classical school. There are moments of passionate expressiveness in his playing, but they do not stand off strongly out of the overall harmonious plan and singleness of purpose characteristic of his treatment of every work of music, past or present. At any rate, he shows a leaning towards musical classics. Among those who perform this music, our excellent artist occupies at present, to our mind, the first place, although he is such a perfect virtuoso that he feels at home in any style, any kind of music."[148]

The critic quite rightly makes a point of Ysaÿe's ability to identify himself with music of different styles. It should, however, not be assumed that the Russian press found nothing to criticize in Ysaÿe's playing. None other than Kashkin, while speaking with approval of the Belgian artist's introducing to the public Mozart's violin compositions (which were rarely played at the time), noted that "for all the merits of his performance, in the Mozart Concerto M. Ysaÿe seemed to lack that spontaneity and simplicity which are

the hallmark of all instrumental music by that greatest of eighteenth-century composers."[149]

Ysaÿe was also reproached (particularly during his first tours of Russia) with a too-free interpretation of Bach's music. Such reproaches, both in Russia and elsewhere, were an exception and were usually made by critics who held a one-sided view of Bach and were incapable of appreciating Ysaÿe's full-blooded approach, which revealed in Bach's music its profoundly human essence and emotions. The author of the article about the Third Siloti Chamber Concert on December 5, 1907, which appeared in the *Russian Musical Gazette*, retorted, speaking of Ysaÿe's performance, that "The pedants who believe that they know 'their' Bach inside out might find Ysaÿe's interpretation of the *Chaconne* too fanciful, unusually free, they might be nonplussed at the wealth of live beauty, at those rainbow colors in a work of music which they would like to hear as morbidly plain (calling this plainness 'austerity'). But beauty is life and talent—and life-giving power. Ysaÿe turned the *Chaconne* into a symphony played on four strings, an astonishingly sonorous and profound poem, breathtaking in its variety of moods, characters, eloquence, richness of shadings and stylistic perfection." The critic further spoke of "a freely flowing powerful wave of sheer beauty emerging from under the bow of that great wizard of the violin."[150]

Another critical article in the *Russian Musical Gazette* described Ysaÿe's acute sense of style and his gift for bringing music by the great classical composers nearer to the listeners, for making it stir the hearts of twentieth-century audiences. That was a review of the Sixth Siloti Concert which took place on December 16, 1906, and at which Ysaÿe performed Mozart's Concerto in D Major, Beethoven's Concerto and, together with Boris Kamensky, Bach's Double Concerto (other items on the program were Glazunov's *Solemn Overture* and two pieces by Sibelius performed under the composer's baton). The article ran: "Ysaÿe brought with him. . .Bach, Mozart and Beethoven, all the three full of life and perfectly authentic. This produced a rare impression, one that will remain unforgettable. Ysaÿe does not play the violin—he creates

Ysaÿe at age 45.

Ysaÿe inscribed this photograph to his Russian accompanist, Alexander Goldenweiser. The inscription reads: "A souvenir of the performance of 3 Sonatas with the precious assistance of Goldenweiser. With friendly admiration. E. Ysaÿe. Moscow, 2 February 1910."

music so that the melodies almost a hundred years old are born anew under his all-powerful bow, fresh, spontaneous and so convincing in their sincere expressiveness that they seem to have been created on the spot. For his art, for his heart-warming enthusiasm there is no 'past,' everything is a living 'present,' and so instead of the usual tale with its 'once upon a time there were men called Bach, Mozart and Beethoven' we heard from the platform Bach, Mozart and Beethoven, alive and addressing us in their very persons."[151]

Much praise was lavished on Ysaÿe's performance of Viotti's Concerto No. 22.[152] Even the Moscow critic B. M. Popov, who signed his articles "Mizgir" and thought, on hearing Ysaÿe play in December 1907, that there was "something cold and diamond-like" in Ysaÿe's playing, wrote that in the *Adagio* from Viotti's Concerto, Ysaÿe had wholly captivated his audience. "His violin sings in a powerful and beautiful tone, captivating everybody by the entrancing nuances of its speech."[153] Nikolai Kochetov and Nikolai Kashkin concurred in this opinion. After hearing Ysaÿe perform this concerto at the Second Symphonic Assembly of the Moscow Philharmonic, Nikolai Kashkin wrote: "Nobody plays Viotti's concertos nowadays, because for today's violinists this task seems too simple and they see nothing in these works to display their virtuosity on. But M. Ysaÿe's greatest merit is not superficial brilliance but an incomparable wealth of feeling and expression, which has enabled him in this very simplicity to scale the peaks of virtuoso inspiration. At any rate, for us the *Adagio* from Viotti's Concerto proved a peerless experience, something not to be expected—nor heard—of any other violinist. Although we admired M. Ysaÿe in former years," Kashkin concluded his review, "we must admit that now he has risen still higher in our opinion and, indeed, his talent seems to grow ever stronger, broader and deeper."[154]

The competent critic's words are one more evidence of the fact that those years were the climax of Eugène Ysaÿe's artistic achievements. Although on his subsequent visits Ysaÿe still remained a great artist, in some of the Russian critics' reviews we encounter statements to the effect that his artistry had somewhat diminished, and that there were elements of thoughtlessness and coldness in his playing.[155] Of course, some of these statements are

The Ysaÿe Museum in Liege has this small bronze statuette of Ysaÿe. Commissioned in 1927 to LaMonaca. Arazi photo.

purely personal opinions of this or that critic, yet it should be borne in mind that at that time (1910-12) Eugène Ysaÿe's health had been undermined by his intensive activities of a touring virtuoso. The diabetes had grown more acute, his heart was out of order and he was especially worried at the state of his hands, which could not but affect his playing now and again. Nevertheless, there could have been merely accidental lapses and temporary weaknesses along with which the venerable artist had instances of inspired, truly creative interpretation, displaying indisputable mastery. This is further borne out by the reviews in the Russian press of 1910 and 1912, as well as by the reminiscences of our musicians belonging to the older generation.

Here is an excerpt from Julius Engel's review of the concert held in Moscow on January 16, 1910, at which Ysaÿe performed under the direction of Emil Cooper the Vivaldi and Bach concertos: "The soloist at this concert was Eugène Ysaÿe, probably the best of contemporary violinists, the king of violinists, just as Casals is the king of cellists. Everything in Ysaÿe's interpretation is refined, inspired and perfect; everything is mature, bearing the imprint of that noble and tender grace of which he alone is the master. The artist's technique is astounding, but the virtuoso element in his playing is thrust to the background while the foreground is occupied by the pure musical idea whose realization the artist endows with ineffable charm by the power of his talent while always remaining behind the scenes, as it were."[156]

Nikolai Kashkin, Grigory Prokofiev and other Moscow critics also spoke of Ysaÿe in very high terms.[157]

The extraordinary concert of chamber music of the Russian Music Society, which followed shortly after that and in which Ysaÿe's partner at the piano was a well-known Moscow pianist, Alexander Goldenweiser, aroused considerable interest.

The program of this concert, held at the Large Hall of the Conservatoire on January 19, featured the following Sonatas: Mozart (in D Major), Brahms (in D minor) and Franck (in A Major), as well as Handel's *Aria* and Wagner's *Albumblatt*. Vladimir Derzhanovsky wrote in the *Russkiye vedomosti:* "Ysaÿe is one of the few first-rate violinists who are equally good as soloists and in ensembles. Of course, even artists of genius attain a perfect ensemble only after a long time of playing together . . . But even an impromptu ensemble, in which Ysaÿe took part yesterday with Alexander Goldenweiser, can afford a rare enjoyment. The ability to thrust virtuosity into the background and give place of honor to the pure musical idea, so characteristic of Ysaÿe, is even more valuable in chamber music than in anything else. As for the way in which the artist realizes this idea, the way he can recreate its various meanings and styles in Mozart, Brahms and Franck—particularly in Franck—words fail me to describe it . . . M. Goldenweiser, who was at his best this time, proved a worthy partner of Ysaÿe."[158]

The success was tremendous and Ysaÿe had to give as encores Saint-Saëns' *Rondo Capriccioso* and Vieuxtemps' *Polonaise and Rondino,* once more demonstrating that he was master of both chamber and virtuoso music.

Professor Goldenweiser has kindly allowed the present author to quote from his reminiscences of Eugène Ysaÿe—one more source of vivid descriptions of that artist and human being.

"In the 1890's and early 1900's the famous Belgian violinist Eugène Ysaÿe used to visit Moscow often. I had many opportunities to hear him and once I was his partner at the piano. I have heard Ysaÿe play several concertos with orchestra—Bach's in E Major, Mozart's in G Major, Beethoven's, Mendelssohn's, Bruch's in G minor, Saint-Saëns' in B minor, and a few more, as well as many shorter works.

"Ysaÿe's playing left an unforgettable impression. He was a violinist with an exceptionally bright tone of a beautiful quality and with impeccable virtuosity. His supreme mastery of the bow was a distinguishing feature of his technique: he changed his bow in cantilena in a way that made you think he had an endless bow, you never felt when the change took place.

"He might have lacked chaste simplicity in playing classical music but he was inimitable in performing the Romanticists. In a word, he was one of the greatest violinists I have ever heard.

"On invitation from the Russian Music Society, Ysaÿe gave a sonata concert with me at the Large Hall of the Conservatoire on January 19, 1910. We played three sonatas: Mozart's in D Major, Brahms' in D minor and the Franck Sonata in A Major dedicated to Ysaÿe. The day before the concert we agreed to meet at Sibor's in the morning for rehearsal—Ysaÿe and Sibor had often met

A sketch of Ysaÿe.

Gabriel Fauré.

abroad and knew each other well. After the rehearsal Sibor treated us to the traditional *blini* (pancakes) because it happened to be the Russian carnival.

"We did not waste the time rehearsing: Ysaÿe saw that he had an experienced musician to deal with and was eager to have stopped playing and start discussing the pancakes. The meal passed in a merry atmosphere and after it Ysaÿe said that he liked playing the cello and suggested we should play a trio. Sibor chose Arensky's Piano Trio, a piece of considerable virtuosity, and we played it with Sibor taking the violin, Ysaÿe the cello and myself at the piano. Ysaÿe acquitted himself with credit, playing at sight this difficult work without any mishaps, if not actually with brilliance. He enjoyed himself vastly.

"That night during the concert I fully understood what a wonderful artist I had as a partner. He played the beautiful Franck Sonata especially well, with real inspiration.

"I shall never forget the satisfaction this encounter gave me, that was one of the most interesting artistic experiences of my life."

During that visit to Russia, Ysaÿe appeared together with Gabriel Fauré[159] in Moscow and with Alexander Siloti in St. Petersburg, playing with the latter sonatas by Bach and Lekeu, and the Chausson *Poème*, and with the organist Jacques Handschin, Vitali's *Chaconne*.

In describing the chamber music concert of Siloti, dedicated to "the greatest instrumentalists of our time, Ysaÿe the violinist and Casals the cellist," a St. Petersburg critic wrote: "Ysaÿe 'created' before us the Chausson *Poème*, a Bach sonata (in F Major) and a sonata by a French modernist Lekeu, which, under the artist's magic bow, seemed to take on a certain clarity and lucidity of idea—qualities which the composer must have been avoiding in the process of writing this sonata."[160]

The curious thing about this opinion (which emphasizes Ysaÿe's creative approach to performance, and his striving to overcome the modernistic features of Lekeu's Sonata) is that it was expressed by Vyacheslav Karatygin, who is known to have repeatedly advocated formalistic views in his theoretical writings.

On that tour in January 1910, Ysaÿe also played the concertos of Vivaldi, Viotti, Mendelssohn and Brahms.

November of that year found Ysaÿe in Russia once more, this

№ 854.

Московское Филармоническое Общество.

Въ Субботу, 8-го Декабря,

въ большомъ залѣ

Россійскаго Благороднаго Собранія

ПЕРВОЕ СИМФОНИЧЕСКОЕ СОБРАНІЕ,

подъ управленіемъ **К. Панцнеръ**, съ участіемъ **Э. Изаи.**

ПРОГРАММА.

Отдѣленіе 1-е.

1. *Бетховенъ* (1770—1827). Симфонія № 3 (Героическая) Es-dur.
 a) Allegro con brio.
 b) Marcia funebre. Adagio assai.
 c) Scherzo. Allegro vivace.
 d) Finale. Allegro molto.

2. *Э. Моора*. Концертъ для скрипки (въ 1-й разъ).
 a) Allegro moderato.
 b) Scherzo vivace.
 c) Adagio.
 d) Finale. Allegro ma non troppo.

Исп. **Э. Изаи.**

Антрактъ **20** минутъ.

This and the facing page is the program for Ysaÿe's concert of 8 December, 1907 in Moscow. The orchestra was conducted by K. Pantsner.

Отдѣленіе 2-е.

3. *Листъ* (1811—1886). „Прелюдіи", симфоническая поэма.
4. *Брухъ*. „Фантазія" на шотландскія мелодіи.
        a) Introduction—grave.
        b) Adagio cantabile.
        c) Allegro.
        d) Andante. Sostenuto.
        e) Finale. Allegro guerriero.
        Исп. Э. Изаи.

Начало въ 8½ час. веч.

Рояль фабрики **Беккера** изъ магазина **Циммермана**.

    Второе симфоническое собраніе имѣетъ быть во Вторникъ, 11-го Декабря, подъ управленіемъ К. Панцнеръ, съ участіемъ Э. Изаи.
    Программа: *Чайковскій*—Симфонія № 5. *Вагнеръ* Увертюра къ оп. „Мейстерзингеры". *Віотти*—Концертъ для скрипки № 22. *Сенъ-Сансъ*—Концертъ для скрипки.

Правленіе Общества покорнѣйше проситъ:

    1. Лицъ, находящихся на хорахъ, не класть биноклей на барьеръ.
    2. Во время исполненія музыкальныхъ номеровъ не входить и не выходить изъ зала и громко не разговаривать.
    3. Не занимать мѣстъ въ залѣ биноклями, вѣерами, платками и другими вещами.
    4. Предъявлять свои билеты при входѣ въ залъ; безъ билетовъ входъ ни въ какомъ случаѣ не допускается.

На основаніи ВЫСОЧАЙШЕ утвержденнаго 5 мая 1892 года мнѣнія Государственнаго Совѣта и утвержденныхъ 20 августа 1892 года правилъ и изъ исчисляющихся съ публичныхъ зрѣлищъ и увеселеній, съ totальныхъ билетовъ взимается сборъ, означенный цифрами сверхъ цѣны билета на обратной сторонѣ.

Печ. разр. 5 декабря 1907 г. И. д. Моск. Град. Полковникъ **Климовичъ**.

Тип. Императорскихъ Московскихъ Театровъ (Т-во Скоропеч. А. А. Левенсонъ).

Raoul Pugno.

time with his old friend and partner Raoul Pugno. They played the sonatas of Veracini, Beethoven, Franck, Lazzari and Strauss, and some other pieces.

The Russian press wrote of the great artistic pleasure afforded by the wonderful duo Ysaÿe-Pugno; in describing their performance of sonatas for violin and piano, a critic remarked on "the astonishing spiritual unity between the pianist and the violinist."[161]

At symphony assemblies Ysaÿe played the concertos of Mendelssohn and Bruch.

It may be deduced from the press notices[162] that the concerts in St. Petersburg were more successful than in Moscow. Nevertheless, in spite of certain critical remarks in the Moscow press, even there Ysaÿe was appreciated as an outstanding artist of his time.

The Moscow public was particularly interested in the "popular chamber music matinee" dedicated to Beethoven, which took place on November 21. Its program featured Piano Trio Op. 70 in D Major, the Kreutzer Sonata, the two Romances and Piano Sonata Op. 27, No. 2. The Trio was performed by Ysaÿe, Pugno and Brandukov (who also appeared with Ysaÿe and Pugno in Saint-Saëns' Trio on another occasion). As an encore, Ysaÿe gave a brilliant rendition of the Bach *Chaconne.*

Ysaÿe was uncommonly busy on his last tour of Russia in January 1912: in the course of twenty days he gave nine concerts in Moscow and St. Petersburg.

At the end of 1911, Ysaÿe appeared in Warsaw twice, playing on one occasion Bach's Double Concerto with his son Gabriel. While noting that Ysaÿe's playing was in some respects inferior to that of Fritz Kreisler, then at the peak of his powers, a critic wrote: "True, Ysaÿe's mellow, 'velvety,' tone has so far not been surpassed by Kreisler. The tremendous concentrated musiciansnip of the Belgian master still produces a deep impression in such pieces as the Beethoven Concerto, that work of genius."[163]

On January 7, 1912, Ysaÿe appeared in St. Petersburg in a concert for the benefit of the Society of Friends of Chamber Music, performing the Beethoven Concerto and Saint-Saëns' *Rondo Capriccioso.*

Siloti, Ysaÿe and Casals joined forces for the chamber concerts

Большой залъ Россійскаго Благороднаго Собранія.

№ 555.

Въ Воскресенье, 21-го Ноября,

ПРОЩАЛЬНОЕ

ОБЩЕДОСТУПНОЕ КАМЕРНОЕ УТРО

гг. Э. ИЗАИ и Р. ПЮНЬО,

СЪ УЧАСТІЕМЪ

А. БРАНДУКОВА

ПОСВЯЩЕННОЕ ПАМЯТИ **БЕТХОВЕНА.**

Начало въ 2 часа дня.

Ysaÿe's 21 November 1910 program. It proclaims: "On Sunday, 21st of November, Farewell, Popular Chamber Music Morning, E. Ysaÿe and R. Pugno with Brandukov in commemoration of Beethoven. Begins at 2:00 P.M."

Gerardy and Pugno.

Jan Kubelik, "the precise motoric technician."

held in Moscow on January 9 and 16 and in St. Petersburg on January 19. They played the Piano Trios by Beethoven (Op. 70 in D Major), Mendelssohn (Op. 49), Brahms (Op. 8) and Tchaikovsky.

It was hardly possible to speak of a real ensemble in those instances (indeed, some newspapers remarked on its absence[164]). Nevertheless even a chance combination of those outstanding musicians could not but afford the listeners immense pleasure. Georges Conus, a Moscow composer and critic, former pupil of Taneyev, defined the concert of January 9 as "a feast of music," particularly praising the playing of the scherzos in the Mendelssohn and the Brahms trios.[165] He noted that the performers gave a brilliant rendition of the Tchaikovsky Trio on January 16, saying that "the mellow, singing tone characteristic of the three artists was especially in place here;" another critic wrote that "this time, too, one could not say that the ensemble was perfect."[166] We may assume that each member of the trio was too vivid an artistic personality to blend in a unified ensemble without previous rehearsals.

The solo appearances of Ysaÿe and Casals were immensely successful (Ysaÿe played in the chamber concerts just referred to as the Bach *Chaconne*, doing pieces by Saint-Saëns and other composers).

On January 14, Ysaÿe performed Mozart's Concerto in G Major and the Beethoven Concerto with an orchestra directed by Rachmaninov.

In his review of this concert, Grigory Prokofiev wrote that the *Adagio* from Mozart's Concerto had sounded particularly well and noted Ysaÿe's inspired performance of the second and third movements from the Beethoven Concerto.[167] Another critic writing about this concert also had the highest praise for Ysaÿe.[168]

Next was the concert in St. Petersburg on January 21, after which Ysaÿe appeared in Moscow on January 24, playing on both occasions the Double Concerto by Brahms together with Casals (under the direction of Albert Coates in St. Petersburg and of Alexander Siloti in Moscow). In St. Petersburg, Ysaÿe played a Vivaldi concerto with the organist Jacques Handschin and, with Boris Sibor, Bach's Concerto for two violins.

A Moscow newspaper wrote that in the Bach Concerto, "the

great artists Casals and Ysaÿe displayed their talents in all their breadth and depth, the Concerto being performed with a wonderful ensemble."[169] Another reviewer emphasized the wonderful sense of ensemble shown by Casals and Ysaÿe and their dedication to the noble and austere music of Brahms.[170]

Some critics stated that, compared with Casals, Ysaÿe's playing seemed less vivid and masterly. We should remember that by that time the Belgian violinist's art had passed its zenith while the Spanish cellist, who was younger by eighteen years was at the peak of his inspired artistry.

In speaking of the Bach Double Concerto, the critics noted the similarity of conception and style of the two violinists,[167]one of them adding that Boris Sibor, who appeared with Ysaÿe, "proved himself a partner worthy of the famous Belgian violinist, at least in works by classical composers."[172]

On his previous visit, Ysaÿe had already spoken well of Sibor, calling him "an artist of high merits and profound knowledge." These words are found in Ysaÿe's "Preface" (dated November 30, 1910) to the *Technical Exercises for the Violin* by Boris Sibor, which were brought out by Pyotr Jurgenson in Moscow in 1911.[173]

Boris Sibor (1880-1961) graduated from Leopold Auer's violin class at the St. Petersburg Conservatoire in 1901 and at the time of Ysaÿe's visits was known for an excellent performer (he was the first to play Sergei Taneyev's Concert Suite for violin and orchestra). In 1904, he was appointed professor of violin at the Moscow Philharmonic Music School and soloist of the Bolshoi Theater orchestra.[174]

Professor Sibor told the present author: "I have heard many of the world's famous violinists—the brilliant and elegant Pablo de Sarasate, the precise motoric technician Jan Kubelik, and Eugène Ysaÿe, who as a musician and artist was head and shoulders above the two virtuosos. Ysaÿe had a noble, full tone, an astonishingly logical and convincing phrasing. His playing of the Saint-Saëns' Concerto was an unforgettable experience, he played Vieuxtemps' *Ballade and Polonaise* as none other, then Saint-Saëns' *Rondo Capriccioso*, Lalo's *Symphonie espagnole*, and many other pieces . . .

"Ysaÿe had an imposing presence—tall, big, with a manly and characteristic head and a noble bearing. His big violin (a Guarnerius) seemed tiny in his big hands.

Pablo de Sarasate, "the brilliant and elegant."

Dmitri Shostakovich.

Jacques Thibaud sitting next to Ysaÿe, with Leo Strokov in the back.

Ysaÿe's famous letter to Leo Strokoff (Strokov) written from Paris in June, 1926.

"I had the happiness of playing in public a Bach concerto with Ysaÿe. We rehearsed conscientiously, striving for a unified approach and perfect ensemble. Ysaÿe was a severe taskmaster; we worked assiduously, but the work was truly creative and afforded a true aesthetic pleasure. Ysaÿe knew how to work and how to enjoy himself, he liked good food, laughing and joking. He had refined tastes both in art and in life, a wide range of interests and a high culture. I had occasions to converse with him not only about the art of interpretation, but also about pedagogy—he was interested in my *Exercises*. In this sphere, too, Ysaÿe expressed views that were in advance of his time."

On his visits to Russia, Ysaÿe appeared not only in public but also at the homes of musicians and music lovers. There, too, he played with the same ardor and inspiration as on the concert platform. On such occasions he liked particularly to play chamber music. From the recollections of Adolph Metz, a noted violinist,[175] we knew that he had played quartets with Ysaÿe in Moscow, with the viola and the cello parts taken by the well-known Moscow musicians N.K. Avyerino and O.F. Asperger. Ysaÿe enjoyed himself at such sessions immensely and his enthusiasm was infectious, so that once they played until five in the morning.

And now we shall speak of Ysaÿe's last appearance in Moscow on January 26, 1912, at the farewell concert of Mme. Wieniawska and Eugène Ysaÿe, with M. A. Bichter as the accompanist.[176]

Ysaÿe played a Handel sonata and Vieuxtemps' Fourth Concerto with an inspiration and artistry that brought back to his listeners his art at its best. Georges Conus, who enjoyed the reputation of a serious musician, spoke of that concert as Ysaÿe's triumph: "Ysaÿe played all the items on the program (besides solo pieces he played in ensemble with the singer Mme. Wieniawska—*L.G.*) and many encores with inimitable perfection and brilliance. The artist proved by this that the prognoses which had appeared in the press stating that his talent was on the wane were groundless, or at least premature. No! Ysaÿe is so far the brightest star in the firmament of violinists, one that has not been outshone. The enthusiasm evoked by his playing became at times a clamor that I had not heard for a long time."[177]

Thus, in the memory of the grateful Russian public, Ysaÿe has remained the great artist, the inspired musician, the master vir-

Mischa Elman: Ysaÿe was enchanted with Elman's rendition of the Tchaikovsky Concerto.

tuoso. The great Belgian violinist who loved and appreciated Russian music and musicians took away with him the best memories of Russia. In the future, too, when the circumstances of his life (two American tours, World War I and illness) put an end to his Russian concerts, he used to think of his Russian friends, was always glad to meet them abroad and often played with them at his summer residence "La Chanterelle" at Le Zoute.

As has been remarked at the beginning of this chapter, Ysaÿe maintained close friendly ties with many Russian musicians—composers, performers and critics. He corresponded with some of them and made music with those whom he met abroad. Thus, Sergei Rachmaninov appeared at the Ysaÿe Concerts in Brussels as did some other Russian musicians. Matvei Pressman, a well-known pianist and pedagogue, like Rachmaninov, a former pupil of Nikolai Zverev, wrote that finding himelf abroad in 1913 he appeared together with Eugène Ysaÿe, playing with him a Beethoven sonata, Mendelssohn's Concerto and some other works.[178]

Ysaÿe's friendships with Russian violinists deserve special mention. The Belgian master held a high opinion of the Russian violin school, whose representatives were famous for their artistic interpretation, high culture, expressive tone and virtuosity.[179]

We have already seen that Ysaÿe expressed his friendly feelings and admiration for the celebrated Russian violinist Vasily Besekirsky; he spoke with real enthusiasm about Mischa Elman, an alumnus of the St. Petersburg Conservatoire, who enchanted him with his rendition of the Tchaikovsky Concerto, and he praised warmly the playing of Boris Sibor.

Ysaÿe expressed approbation of other graduates of the Russian conservatoires who came to consult him, for instance, Michael Press,[180] Michael Erdenko, Adolph Metz, Leo Strokov and Mikhail Zakharevich, all of whom became his friends.

We should mention the Belgian artist's interest in the violins made by Russian builders D. P. Tomashov, D. K. Chernov and E. F. Vitaček: he knew their instruments and liked them.

There are many exciting passages in the history of the Russo-Belgian musical contacts. Suffice it to mention the visits to Belgium of our classical composers Alexander Borodin and Nikolai Rimsky-Korsakov, whose works were successfully performed there, the fruitful work in Russia of the famous Belgian violinists

Charles de Beriot, the founder of the Belgian school of violin playing. Courtesy of Arazi. On the facing page, his beautiful wife, Maria Garcia Malibran, the legendary soprano in a rare illustration.

Charles de Bériot and Henri Vieuxtemps, the numerous appearances in Belgium of the violinists Vasily Besekirsky and Stanislav Taborovsky and of the excellent Russian cellists Matvei Vielgorsky and Karl Davydov. Then there were Tchaikovsky's translation into Russian of François Gevaert's *Traité d'Instrumentation* and the enthusiastic popularization of Russian music by the Belgian musician Marie Mercie d'Argenteau, to mention only the best-known instances.

The eminent representative of the Belgian art of violin playing, the inimitable performer, conductor and musical worker Eugène Ysaÿe made a valuable contribution towards furthering the Russo-Belgian musical contacts by his numerous appearances in Russia, his performance of Russian music and his friendly ties with Russian musicians.

NOTES

[92] Voicech Glavac (Vojtéch Hlaváč—1849-1911), a prominent Czech pianist, organist and conductor who settled in St. Petersburg in 1871.

[93] Among them were the violinists Nikolai Dmitriyev-Svechin, Konstantin Pushilov, Henryk Wieniawski, Leopold Auer, Frantisek Onricek and Mischa Elman, the cellists François Servais, Alexander Verzhbilovich and Semyon Kozolupov, the pianists Nikolai Martynov, Vasily Sapelnikov, Sophie Menter, Vladimir Horwitz, Leonid Nikolayev and Yelena Bekman-Shcherbina, the singers Ivan Yershov, Medea and Nikolai Figner, Fyodor Chaliapine, and many other artists.

[94] See Findeisen, N.F., *Pavlovski muzykalni vokzal. Istoricheski ocherk (k 75mu muzykalnomu sezonu), (The Pavlovsk Kursaal. (For its 7th Musical Season)*, St. Petersburg, 1912, pp. 50-51.

[95] *Muzykalny mir*, 1882, No. 2.

[96] *Peterburgski listok*, 1882, No. 198. The program of this concert featured also the overtures by Goldmark, Schumann and Godard, and Tchaikovsky's *1812*.

[97] *S.-Peterbugskiye vedomosti*, 1883, No. 15.

[98] *Kievlyanin*, 1883, No. 78.

[99] See Paul de Stoecklin, "Eugène Ysaÿe," *Le courrier musical*, 1928, No. 3, p. 234.

[100] See *Centenaire de la naissance de Eugène Ysaÿe*, Liège, 1958, p. 27.

[101] See *Kievlyanin*, 1883, No. 96.

[102] *Kievlyanin*, 1883, No. 100.

[103] *Odesski vestnik*, 1883, No. 197.

[104] *Novorossiiski telegraf*, 1883, No. 2472. Ysaÿe also gave two concerts in Kharkov (see *Kharkovskiye gubernskiye vedomosti*, 1883, No. 1104).

[105] Vasily Besekirsky was a pupil of Rudolf Slavik, brother of the famous Czech violinist Josef Slavik, in Moscow and later, in the fifties, of Hubert Léonard (1819-90) in Brussels.

[106] Besekirsky, V.V., *Iz zapisnoi knizhki (From My Notebook)*, St. Petersburg, 1910, pp. 143-44.

[107] Vasily Besekirsky's scrap-book is preserved at the State Central Bakhrushin Museum of the Theater, Moscow (No. 19365). At the end of his life Besekirsky wrote about Ysaÿe, describing him as a brilliant virtuoso with a beautiful tone, full of temperament, who played with inspiration and was "an artist violinist."

108 Eugène Ysaÿe was 37 at the time, and Vasily Besekirsky 60.
109 *S.-Peterburgskiye vedomosti*, 1885, No. 33.
110 The letters are preserved at the Central State Archives of Literature and Art of the USSR (fond No. 786, descriptive list 1, bit of storage No. 62).
111 Vsevolod Cheshikhin, *Otgoloski opery i kontserta. Zametki muzykalnogo literatora (Echoes of Operas and Concerts. Notes of a Music Writer)*, St. Petersburg, 1896, p. 224.
112 *Ibid.*
113 *Moskovskiye vedomosti*, 1895, No. 313.
114 *Russkoye slovo*, 1895, No. 308.
115 *Moskovskiye vedomosti*, 1895, No. 326.
116 *Russkaya muzykalnaya gazeta*, 1895, No. 12.
117 *Novosti i birzhevaya gazeta*, 1896, No. 5.
118 Chausson's *Poème* was first performed in St. Petersburg on December 15, 1907.
119 A copy of the program is preserved in the Sergei Taneyev Archives at the State Museum of Literature in Moscow.
120 The letter is in the same archives.
121 *Russkiye vedomosti*, 1900, No. 60; *Russkaya muzykalnaya gazeta*, 1900, No. 11.
122 *Moskovski listok*, 1900, No. 61.
123 Vieuxtemps composed his romantic and poetic Fourth Concerto in Russia. Tchaikovsky spoke of it in very high terms.
124 *Moskovskiye vedomosti*, 1901, No. 334.
125 *Russkiye vedomosti*, 1901, No. 330.
126 V.G. Belinsky, *Polnoye sobraniye sochineni (Complete Works)*, edited by S.A. Vengerov, Vol. III, p. 224.
127 This work was given a memorable performance in London by Ferruccio Busoni, Eugène Ysaÿe and Hugo Becker in 1902.
128 *Russkiye vedomosti*, 1903, Nos. 75 and 79; *S.-Peterburgskiye vedomosti*, 1903, Nos. 329 and 333; *Moskovski listok*, 1903, No. 343; *Russkoye slovo*, 1903, Nos. 76, 81, 335 and 337; *Novoye vremya*, 1903, No. 997, and other newspapers.
129 *Russkoye slovo*, 1903, No. 81 (the article by L.A. Maximov who used the pen-name "Dinoel").
130 See *S.-Peterburgskiye vedomosti*, 1903, Nos. 329 and 333.
131 *Russkoye slovo*, 1903, No. 76.
132 *Russkaya muzykalnaya gazeta*, 1903, No. 51.
133 Igor Grabar, *Valentin Alexandrovich Serov. Zhizn i tvorchestvo (Life and Work)*, Moscow, 1913, pp. 162-164.
134 Glazunov's Violin Concerto in A minor, Op. 82, was completed at the end of the summer 1904.
135 The letter is preserved in the Nikolai Rimsky-Korsakov Archives at the MS Department of the Saltykov-Shchedrin Public Library in Leningrad.
136 The letter is preserved at the MS Department of the Library of the Rimsky-Korsakov Conservatoire in Leningrad.
137 *Moskovski listok*, 1906, No. 320.
138 Jan Kubelik (1880-1940), a famous Czech violinist of the virtuoso school; composed the *American Symphony*.—*L.G.*
139 *Russkoye slovo*, 1906, No. 303.
140 Maria Kerzina (1864-1926), founder, with her husband Arkady Kerzin, of the Society of Russian Music-Lovers in Moscow.
141 Josef Hofmann (1876-1957), a famous Polish pianist; since 1899 resided in the USA; headed Curtis Institute, Philadelphia (1924-38).—*L.G.*
142 C.A. Cui, *Izbranniye pisma (Selected Letters)*, compiled by I.L. Gusin, Leningrad, 1955, p. 367.
143 *Muzykalny truzhenik*, 1908, No. 1, p. 10 (the review by P.Ye. Vasilkovsky, signed "Svetozar").

¹⁴⁴ Eugène Ysaÿe at a moment's notice deputized for Boris Kamensky, who had fallen ill, at the concert of the Herzog von Mecklenburg-Strelitz Quartet on December 13, 1906.—L.G.

¹⁴⁵ Although Saint-Saëns's violin pieces are certainly inferior, as regards depth of idea, to the works of Bach, Mozart and Beethoven, still they hold their own in the violin repertoire and should hardly have been denounced in such strong terms.—L.G.

¹⁴⁶ Pour out all your soul in creation.

¹⁴⁷ *Slovo*, 1906, No. 29.

¹⁴⁸ *Russkoye slovo*, 1906, No. 303.

¹⁴⁹ *Ibid.*

¹⁵⁰ *Russkaya muzykalnaya gazeta*, 1907, No. 50, pp. 1164-65.

¹⁵¹ *Russkaya muzykalnaya gazeta*, 1907, No. 1, pp. 31-35.

¹⁵² This classic work, Viotti's Concerto No. 22 in A minor, of which Eugène Ysaÿe was a brilliant exponent, was a set piece in the program of the International Ysaÿe Competition in 1937.

¹⁵³ *Golos Moskvy*, 1907, No. 290.

¹⁵⁴ *Russkoye slovo*, 1907, No. 286.

¹⁵⁵ See *Teatr*, 1910, No. 738; *Golos Moskvy*, 1910, Nos. 258 and 265; *Russkoye slovo*, 1912, Nos. 8 and 21; *Studiya*, 1912, No. 16.

¹⁵⁶ *Russkiye vedomosti*, 1910, No. 14.

¹⁵⁷ See *Russkoye slovo*, 1910, No. 13; *Russkaya muzykalnaya gazeta*, 1910, No 5; *Utro Rossii*, 1910, Nos. 83-50, and other newspapers.

¹⁵⁸ *Russkiye vedomosti*, 1910, No. 15.

¹⁵⁹ With the composer at the piano, Ysaÿe played Fauré's *Berceuse* and cellist Anatoly Brandukov, his *Elégie*.

¹⁶⁰ *Apollon*, 1910, No. 6, p. 18.

¹⁶¹ *Russkaya muzykalnaya gazeta*, No. 50, p. 1141.

¹⁶² See, for example, *S.-Peterburgskiye vedomosti*, 1910, Nos. 256, 258, 262, and *Golos moskvy*, 1910, Nos. 258 and 270.

¹⁶³ *Muzyka*, 1911, No. 56, p. 1276.

¹⁶⁴ See, for example, Yu. Sakhnovsky's review in the *Russkoye slovo* newspaper, No. 8, 1912.

¹⁶⁵ *Utro Rossii*, 1912, No. 9.

¹⁶⁶ *Russkiye vedomosti*, 1912, No. 14.

¹⁶⁷ *Russkiye vedomosti*, 1912, No. 14.

¹⁶⁸ *Utro Rossii*, 1912, No. 13.

¹⁶⁹ *Russkiye vedomosti*, 1912, No. 21.

¹⁷⁰ *Russkaya Muzykalnaya gazeta*, 1912, No. 6/7, p. 72.

¹⁷¹ *Russkoye slovo*, 1912, No. 21.

¹⁷² *Studiya*, 1912, No. 17, p. 14.

¹⁷³ Fritz Kreisler, too, expressed his approval of Sibor's *Technical Exercises for the Violin* (see this publication).

¹⁷⁴ Boris Sibor held a professorship at the Moscow Conservatoire from 1923 to 1950. Sibor was the son-in-law of Leopold Auer. His original name was Lifshitz; he simply scrambled his first name for a surname.

¹⁷⁵ Adolph Metz (b. Dubossary, 1888) received his musical training at the Odessa Music School and the St. Petersburg Conservatoire, graduating from Leopold Auer's class in 1904. Then he studied with Ysaÿe (the summers of 1903-6). He settled in Moscow, teaching at the Philharmonic Music School and appearing in concerts. Subsequently he was Professor of the Riga Conservatoire; he died there during the fascist occupation of Latvia.

¹⁷⁶ Ysaÿe's last appearance in St. Petersburg took place on January 22.

¹⁷⁷ *Utro Rossii*, 1912, No. 23.

¹⁷⁸ *Vospominaniya o Rachmaninove (Reminiscences of Rachmaninov)*, compiled and edited by Z. Apetyan, Vol. 1, Moscow, 1957, p. 235.

[179] Here we must express our disagreement with Antoine Ysaÿe, son of the great violinist, who, on pp. 456-458 of his book, *Eugène Ysaÿe, Sa vie...*, 1947, acknowledged, for some obscure reason, only the technical achievements of the Russian violin school. In reading these pages one gets the impression that the Moscow school (whose head is stated to be the eminent musician Leopold Auer, who actually was the head of the St. Petersburg school) had laid particular emphasis on technique, paying insufficient attention to musical expressiveness. Another disputable point (on p. 474 of that book) is the statement that Vieuxtemps was the founder of the Russian violin school. As a matter of fact, before Vieuxtemps' arrival in Russia in 1845, the Russian school had advanced such acknowledged masters as Ivan Khandoshkin (1747-1804), Gavrila Rachinsky (1777-1843), Andrei Polyakov (1792-1867), Afanasy Amatov (1796-1848), Ivan Semyonov (1798-1870), Alexei Lvov (1798-1870), Artemy Shchepin (1819-1878), Nikolai Dmitriyev-Svechin (1824-63), Nikolai Afanasyev (1820-98) and some others, of whom Lvov, Shchepin and Dmitriyev-Svechin had appeared with success in West-European countries.

[180] There is a photograph at the Central Glinka Museum of Musical Culture in Moscow, showing Eugène Ysaÿe and Michael Press with their violins in their hands. The photograph (fond 129, No. 430) bears the date "September 13, 1909."

One of the last portraits of the Master.

Chapter 10

Conclusion

"The best pacifist propaganda on the part of an artist consists in spreading his art whose language reaches every heart," Eugène Ysaÿe used to say.[181]

In Ysaÿe's opinion, the spread and development of the profoundly humanistic art of music must be promoted through the creative communion of musicians from various countries, in particular, by means of international music competitions. It was on his initiative and according to his plan that the International Eugène Ysaÿe Competition was instituted in Belgium. The competition held regularly, as well as the Music Foundation initiated by Ysaÿe, were intended to help young musicians, to remove from their road towards extensive concert activities the difficulties which he himself had experienced in his youth. Besides, he must have foreseen the significance of such creative competitions on an international scale for the friendship and mutual understanding between musicians from different countries.

Already participating in the First International Eugène Ysaÿe Competition held in Brussels in 1937, were five representatives of the Soviet violin school: David Oistrakh, Yelizaveta Gilels, Boris Goldstein, Marina Kozolupova and Mikhail Fichtenholz. All of them won prizes, David Oistrakh carrying off the Grand Prix.[182]

The world of music regarded the results of the Competition as the triumph of the Soviet school. Thus, the famous French

The winners of the First Ysaÿe Competition in Brussels, 1937. From left to right: Odnoposoff, Reyes, Lisa Gilels,

Champeil, Fichtenholz, Oistrakh, Kozolupova, Goldstein, Bobescu and Virovai.

Above: Ysaÿe's familiar New York portrait. On the facing page: Moscow celebrated Ysaÿe's 100th birthday with a special concert in which famous violinists played most of Ysaÿe's pieces. The author, L. Ginsburg, gave the opening speech about Ysaÿe's life and works.

МОСКОВСКАЯ ГОСУДАРСТВЕННАЯ ФИЛАРМОНИЯ
КОНСЕРВАТОРИЯ имени П. И. ЧАЙКОВСКОГО

МАЛЫЙ ЗАЛ КОНСЕРВАТОРИИ
ул. Герцена, 13

Эжен И З А И
(К 100-летию со дня рождения)

Среда, 17 декабря

Сезон 1958—1959 гг.

БАХ — Соната № 2 си минор
    Largo
    Allegro
    Andante — Менуэт
    Аллегро. Менуэт прощания
    Рондо
  Исполняет В. Данченко
  Партия фортепиано — И. Коллегорская

ИЗАИ — Соната № 4 ми минор для скрипки соло (посвящается Ф. Крейслеру)
    Аллеманда
    Сарабанда
    Финал
  Исполняет А. Пелех

ИЗАИ — Экстаз
  Исполняет Р. Файн
  Партия фортепиано — И. Коллегорская

ИЗАИ — Соната № 5 соль мажор для скрипки соло (посвящается М. Крикбуму)
    L'Aurore
    Danse Rustique (Сельский танец)
  Исполняет В. Пикайзен

ИЗАИ — Мазурка си минор
  Партия фортепиано — И. Коллегорская

ИЗАИ — Колыбельная
  Соната № 6 ми мажор для скрипки соло (посвящается М. Квироги)
  Исполняет В. Климов
  Партия фортепиано — В. Ямпольский

Начало в 8 часов вечера

Цена 50 копеек.

Тираж 250
Тип. «Красная звезда». Варшав. Часовня, 33. Заказ 1252

The original poster shows the music foundation established by Queen Elisabeth.

violinist Jacques Thibaud, who was a member of the jury, stated after the results of this representative contest had been announced: "I warmly congratulate the Soviet music school, which has trained the violinists who are the pride of the world violin school."[183] That was a victory not merely for the Soviet violin school but for the whole system of education in the land of socialism.

After the Henryk Wieniawski International Competition in Warsaw, 1935, the Ysaÿe Competition in 1937 was the biggest international contest of violinists. This proved highly conducive to the creative contacts between musicians from all parts of the world, both its young participants and members of the jury, among whom were many prominent musicians of the older generation such as Désiré Defaus, Mathieu Crickboom, Georg Kulenkampf, Arrigo Serrato, Joseph Szigeti, Jacques Thibaud, Jindrich Feld, Carl Flesch, Abram Yampolsky and others. This, too, was a positive result of the competition founded according to Ysaÿe's project.

Professor Abram Yampolsky, a member of the jury, rightly referred to this competition as "the artistic treatment of the great master to the young generation of violinists."[184]

In speaking of the significance of the Ysaÿe Competition for young musicians who come up against many difficulties in the realization of their creative plans in capitalist countries, Victor Buffen, Chairman of the Jury, justly emphasized the noble aims which prompted the aged and infirm Ysaÿe to aid young artists. He said: "At a time of life when many people are plunged in melancholy regrets of the past, Ysaÿe was thinking of the future in store for the youth. Upon graduation from the conservatoire young artists find themselves let loose in the world, all on their own, without aid from any quarter. The most difficult period is still before them. Some eke out their existence with lessons, others bury their talents in the depths of orchestras while still others have to play at cabarets. Ysaÿe knew all this better than anyone else, he had vivid recollections of his own ordeals. He advanced several projects to remedy the situation, in the first place, the project of the Music Foundation of which he was Chairman. Unfortunately, ill health prevented him from pursuing his course of which only the first stage had been accomplished. He wished to add to it the organization of an international violin competition."[185]

The Ysaÿe Competition found a sequel in the Queen Elisabeth

Zino FRANCESCATTI | Raymond GALLOIS-MONTBRUN | Franco GULLI

Yfrah NEAMAN | Ricardo ODNOPOSOFF | Igor OISTRAKH

Dmitri TZYGANOV | Eugénia UMINSKA | Carlo VAN NESTE

*e outstanding
 which judged
 1976 Queen
sabeth (Ysaÿe)
mpetition in
gium.*

Marcel POOT
Président

Toshiya ETO

Leonid KOGAN

Alberto LYSY

Yehudi MENUHIN

nens QUATACKER

Maurice RASKIN

Berl SENOFSKY

Leonid Kogan and David Oistrakh, 1974 (From The Way They Play*).*

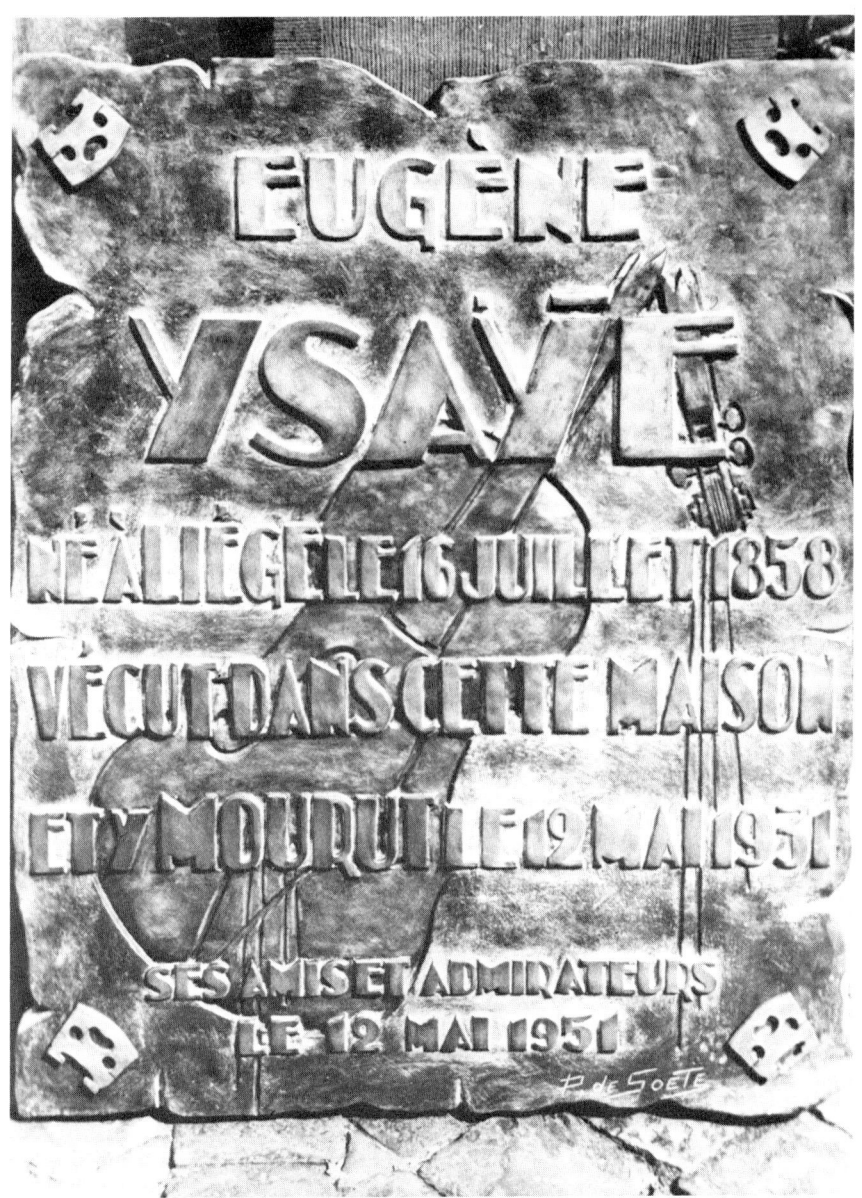

On 12 May 1951 Queen Elisabeth inaugurated the house in which Ysaÿe lived for 40 years, with this plaque.

Philip Newman (1904-1967), one of Ysaÿe's close associates (1950). Courtesy of Arazi.

Competitions, among whose prize winners are many Soviet violinists headed by Leonid Kogan (First Prize, 1951).

Eugène Ysaÿe's works have been published in the Soviet Union and are performed on the concert stage and over the air; some have been recorded and some others are included in music school curriculums.

The celebrations of the Eugène Ysaÿe centenary further strengthened Soviet-Belgian music contacts. In the concerts held on this occasion in Belgium,[186] the celebrated Soviet violinists David Oistrakh and Leonid Kogan participated. The outstanding foreign musicians who participated were: violinists Carlo Van Neste, Zino Francescatti, Arthur Grumiaux, Isaac Stern, Joseph Szigeti, Nathan Milstein, André Gertler, Philip Newman, Lola Bobescu, and Berl Senoffsjki.

The hundredth birthday of the great Belgian musician was celebrated in the Soviet Union as well. On his birthday, July 16,

Zino Francescatti (From The Way They Play, *Applebaum and Roth).*

Igor Oistrakh. He became one of the world's leading violinists after the death of his father.

The modern generation of Belgian violinists lists Arthur Grumiaux as its star.

Efrem Zimbalist autographed this photo to Prof. Auer in 1920.

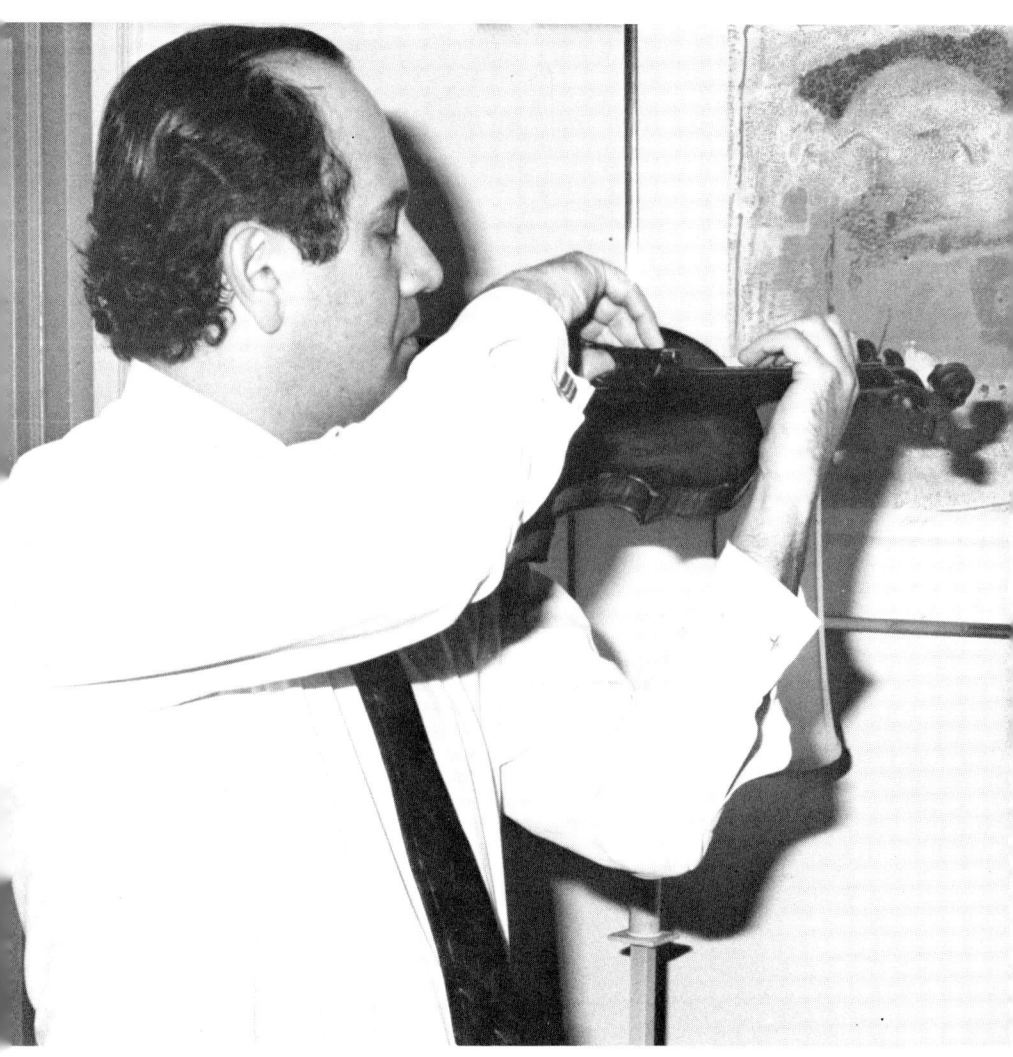

Igor Oistrakh often plays Ysaÿe. (From **The Way they Play**, *by Dr. Samuel Applebaum and Henry Roth).*

Ysaÿe recovering under the loving care of his young wife, Jeannette Dincin. Photo by Queen Elisabeth.

A relief medallion of Ysaÿe dated 1925. It is on display in the Ysaÿe Museum in Liege.

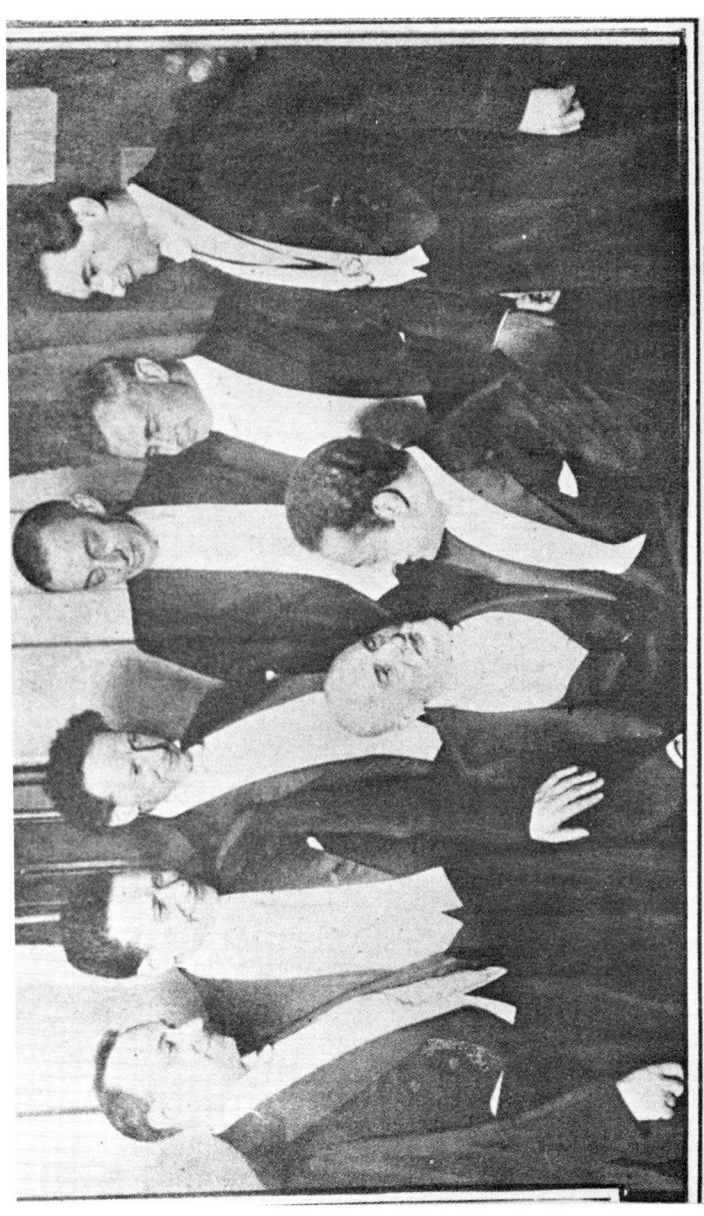

Leopold Auer sits with Jascha Heifetz

Ysaÿe with unidentified members of his family.

1958, the Soviet-Belgian Friendship Society and the Music Section of the Union of the Soviet Societies for Friendship and Cultural Relations with Foreign Countries organized a gala concert in Moscow to commemorate this date. Articles on Eugène Ysaÿe appeared in Soviet newspapers and journals and there were radio and television broadcasts dedicated to the great Belgian artist.

The concert of Ysaÿe's works, sponsored jointly by the Moscow Conservatoire and the Moscow Philharmonic on December 17, 1958, was a major musical event. A talk on Ysaÿe's life and work by the author of this book was followed by a concert of his music performed by international prize winners—students and postgraduates of Professor David Oistrakh, one of the best interpreters of Eugène Ysaÿe's compositions.

This concert, a rare, if not unique opportunity of hearing Ysaÿe's best works in one evening (including all of his six violin sonatas), aroused the keenest interest of Moscow's music lovers.

Soviet musicians honor the memory of the great Belgian violinist and composer, they highly appreciate his art and the contribution he has made towards the Russo-Belgian musical contacts.

The Eugène Ysaÿe Foundation, the list of whose honorary members includes Albert Schweitzer and Pablo Casals, Alfred Cortot and Lionel Tertis, Joseph Szigeti and Efrem Zimbalist, Yehudi Menuhin and Isaac Stern, Zino Francescatti and Henryk Szeryng, David Oistrakh (Honorary President to the end of his days) and Leonid Kogan, Yelizaveta Gilels and Igor Oistrakh, founded a Eugène Ysaÿe Memorial Medal in 1967. The medal has been awarded to many outstanding musicians, among them quite a few Soviet performers and pedagogues.[187]

NOTES

[181] Ernest Christen, *Ysaÿe*, Genève, 1947, p. 220.
[182] The placing of the winners was as follows: David Oistrakh (USSR), 1st prize; R. Odnoposoff (Argentina), 2nd prize; Yelizaveta Gilels (USSR), 3rd prize; B. Goldstein (USSR), 4th prize; Marina Kozolupova (USSR), 5th prize; M. Fichtenholz (USSR), 6th prize; Lola Bobescu (Rumania), 7th prize; P. Makanowitzki (Sweden), 8th prize; F. Virovai (Hungary), 9th prize; R. Brengola (Italy), 11th prize, J. Champeille (France), 12th prize. At the International Ysaÿe Piano Competition which was held in Brussels the following year two Soviet pianists won prizes: Emil Gilels received 1st prize and Yakov Flier, 2nd.
[183] See *Sovetskiye laureaty mezhdunarodnykh muzykalnykh konkursov (Soviet Prize Winners of International Music Competitions)*, Moscow, 1937, p. 127.
[184] A.I. Yampolsky, "International Eugène Ysaÿe Competition of Violinists," *Sovetskaya muzyka*, No. 8, 1937, p. 29.
[185] *Ibid.*
[186] Gala concerts dedicated to Eugène Ysaÿe took place in Liège in May 1958 and an International Eugène Ysaÿe Violin Festival was held at Spa in July of that year. A special brochure, a series of postcards and postage stamps with his portrait were issued for the Ysaÿe centenary.
[187] The author of this book, Professor Lev Ginsburg, is an honorary member of the Ysaÿe Foundation and its representative in the Soviet Union.—*Editor's note.*

Above, a caricature of Ysaÿe in London, 1914. Drawn by W. Barton Wilkinson. On the facing page: an autographed letter from Ysaÿe signed to Pier Adolfo Tirindelli, followed by an English translation.

Bruxelles le 16 octobre 1929.

Mon cher vieil ami,

Ce me fut un grand plaisir de recevoir de tes nouvelles, d'apprendre par toi-même que la providence te tient en bonne vie et en santé; depuis longtemps je pensais à toi me demandant ce que tu devenais et où tu avais planté ta tente; me voilà rassuré complètement, et je suis heureux que tu m'aies gardé ton souvenir et ton amitié. En effet, mon cher Vieux, il y a deux ou trois ans, je devais reparaître en Italie, mais les circonstances ne l'ont pas voulu, et depuis lors le diabète m'a tellement malmené qu'on a dû – il y a trois mois, me couper le pied droit !!! —

La commanderie de la Légion d'Honneur, que le Président vient de m'apporter, n'a pas beaucoup soulagé ma jambe gauche qui supporte à elle seule tout mon poids, mais cela m'a fait plaisir tout de même... Ah! l'Italie, ce pays unique où les chefs-d'œuvre foisonnent, combien je voudrais y retourner et même m'y implanter! — Mais il me faut d'abord attendre qu'un pied artificiel me permette de marcher, et puis il me faudrait un engagement pour diriger surtout, car, ne pouvant jouer debout, je ne joue plus guère.

Ma femme (une jeune américaine) vient d'écrire à Mlle Weertz qu'elle l'entendrai avec plaisir elle devra me téléphoner pour prendre rendez-vous et je tiendrai compte de son avis sur son talent et sur sa recommandation; elle a joué, en effet, pour notre Reine et S.M. en dit beaucoup de bien. Et Vanda! comment, veuve depuis 4 ans, pauvre chère, n'a-t-elle cependant fait grand-Père? et Medame? fait-elle le Macaroni comme on le faisait jadis à Cincinnati? — Enfin j'espère que Toi et ton cher entourage se portent comme d'anciens Romains?... Écris-moi de temps en temps et rafraîchissons notre vieille amitié; c'est en vieillissant qu'on fait le compte exact de ses bons amis et qu'on désire s'en rapprocher pour que les souvenirs lointains se réveillent et redonnent à l'homme, à l'Artiste un peu de la vigueur d'antan.

Je t'envoie le meilleur de mes sentiments affectueux et tu les partageras avec Vanda et Madame.

Au revoir, mon cher Tiri, je t'embrasse de tout mon cœur et prie le bon Dieu qu'il me donne l'occasion de te revoir.

Tout à toi

Ysaÿe

94 Avenue Montjoie
Bruxelles

Autographed letter, signed to Pier Adolfo Tirindelli (1858-1937), Italian Violinist and Composer. Taught at Cincinnati Conservatory, 1896-1920, 4 pages.

Brussels, Oct. 16, 1929

My dear old friend;
It was a great pleasure to receive news of you. I learn through you, yourself, that providence is keeping you in good life and health. For a long time I have thougt of you, wondering what was happening to you and where you had staked your tent; here I am completely reassured, and I am happy that you have kept me in memory and in friendship.

As a matter of fact, my dear old friend, two or three years ago, I was to go back to Italy, but circumstances deemed otherwise, and since then, diabetes mishandled me to such an extent that three months ago they had to **cut off my right foot!!!**
The Commander of the Legion of Honor that the President has just brought me did not relieve my left leg much, which alone has to support my entire weight, but it did give me pleasure just the same . . . Oh! Italy, that unique country where masterpieces abound. How much I would like to return there and even implant myself!—But first I have to await an artificial foot to allow me to walk, and the **above all** *I need an engagement to conduct, as not being able to play standing up, I am not playing any more at all.*

My wife (a young American) has just written to Miss T(?) Wearly that I will hear her (play) with pleasure, she is to telephone me to arrange an appointment and I shall keep in mind your opinion of her talent and your suggestion: as a matter of fact she has played for our Queen and SM (Her Majesty) speaks very well of it. and Vanda! Now, four years a widow, the poor dear. Did she at least make you a Grand-Father? and Madame? does she prepare macaroni as we formerly did it it Cincinnati?—Lastly I hope that Tia (?) and her dear ones are carrying on as ancient Romans? . . .

Write to me from time to time and let us refresh our old friendship, it is during the aging process that one takes an exact account of one's good friends and that one wants to become closer so that the far off memories re-awaken and bring back to the man to the artist a little of the firmer vigor.

I send you the best of my affectionate regards and you divide them with Vanda and Madame.
Au revoir, my dear Tiri, I kiss you with all my heart and pray the good God that He grant the opportunity to see you again.
        All yours,
        E. Ysaye
        94 Ave. Montjoie,
        Brussels.

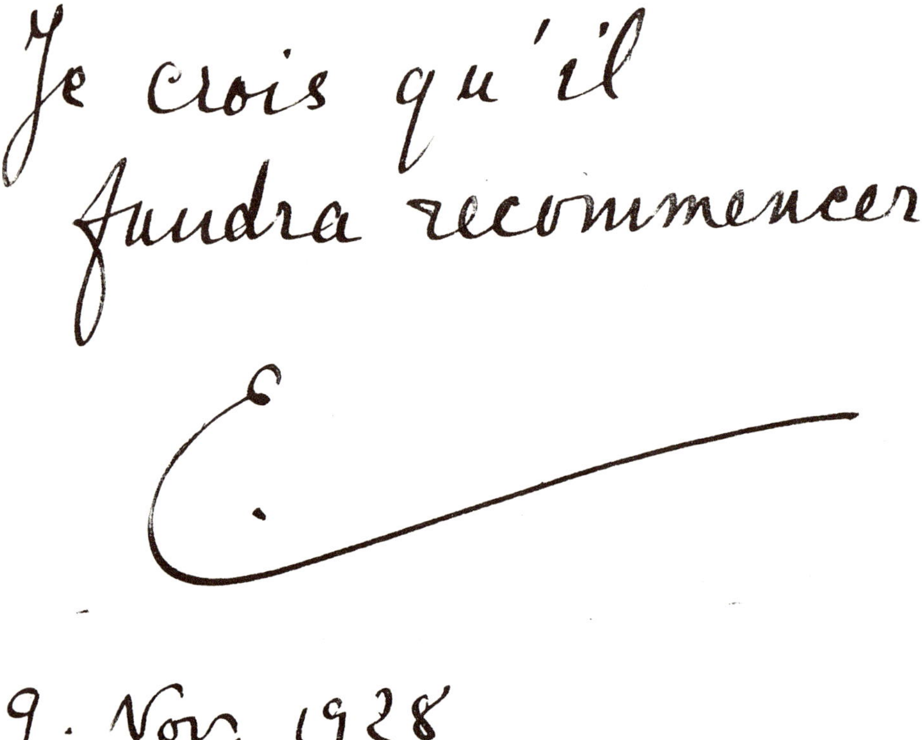

Je crois qu'il faudra recommencer

E.

9. Nov. 1928

Ysaÿe's signature.

A caricature of Ysaÿe.

Madame Eugene Ysaÿe, the second wife of Ysaÿe. She was also his student and took care of him in his later years.

Chapter 11

Addenda

Eugène Ysaÿe as a Teacher

By Jeannette Ysaÿe
(Mme. Eugène Ysaÿe)

Jeannette Ysaÿe, widow of the celebrated violinist, Eugène Ysaÿe, was born in Brooklyn, New York. The daughter of a physician, she showed marked aptitude for the violin at an early age and while still in her teens, was accepted as a pupil by Kneisel, Auer, and Sevčik. Through friends, her talent was brought to the attention of Eugène Ysaÿe during the time (1918-1922) that he served as conductor of the Cincinnati Orchestra. Ysaÿe heard the young lady play and allowed her to study with him. When he gave up his American post and returned to Europe, he suggested that she continue her work with him there. Although Ysaÿe's crowded concert schedule left but little time for regular teaching, she had occasional lessons with him, and launched her own career under her maiden name of Jeannette Dincin. In 1924, Ysaÿe's first wife died and three years later, in his sixty-ninth year, the great violinist married his young pupil. From 1927 until the time of Ysaÿe's death in 1931, the two carried on their separate careers, and occasionally appeared together for performances of two violins.

When Ysaÿe's last illness was upon him, his young wife helped him, assisting with the lessons of Queen Elisabeth of Belgium, and finally taking over the royal teaching herself. One of Ysaÿe's wishes was that his wife should appear publicly under his name. Except for visits here, Mme. Ysaÿe remained abroad until 1939, when she returned to America to resume her career in concertizing and teaching.

Today, some ninety years after his birth, Eugène Ysaÿe lives on among the legendary figures of music. Except for Paganini and perhaps Ole Bull, no violinist has retained a comparable hold on the imaginations of music lovers. I have often been asked to characterize the specific qualities of his art which enabled him to achieve such enduring fame; and think as I will, I can find no better analysis of his genius than that it flowed directly from his complete goodness. Eugène Ysaÿe was essentially a simple man, kindly, helpful, warm, full of love for his fellow men. These traits shone out through his playing and won people's hearts.

MUSICAL EMOTIONS PICTURIZED

The outstanding feature of his own playing was his constant endeavor to *picturize* his musical emotions—to draw from the music he played a concrete image of what went on in his mind. He was born with natural technique; he never had to think about his *vibrato*, his bowing, or any of the purely technical details which can assume such vast proportions in the work of the average violinist. All this was simply born into him. Naturally, my own knowledge of Ysaÿe was limited by the fact that I came to him when he was nearly sixty-four; his struggle years, his conscious working-out of techniques and methods lay behind him. Still, I well remember his talking about all this, even though it took place many years before I knew him. By the time I came to Ysaÿe, he had formulated his musical philosophy into a simple code which he expounded to all his pupils. He would often say, "If you can get to the point where you need do no conscious thinking of fingering and bowing; if you can get away from all that goes on around you; if you can rise to the mood of thinking only of the flow of the music you play, using it to reveal both the soul of the composer and your

Ysaÿe is compared with Paganini in terms of his hold on the imagination of music lovers. There is little doubt that Paganini, Ysaÿe and Heifetz drew the largest audiences and the largest fees!

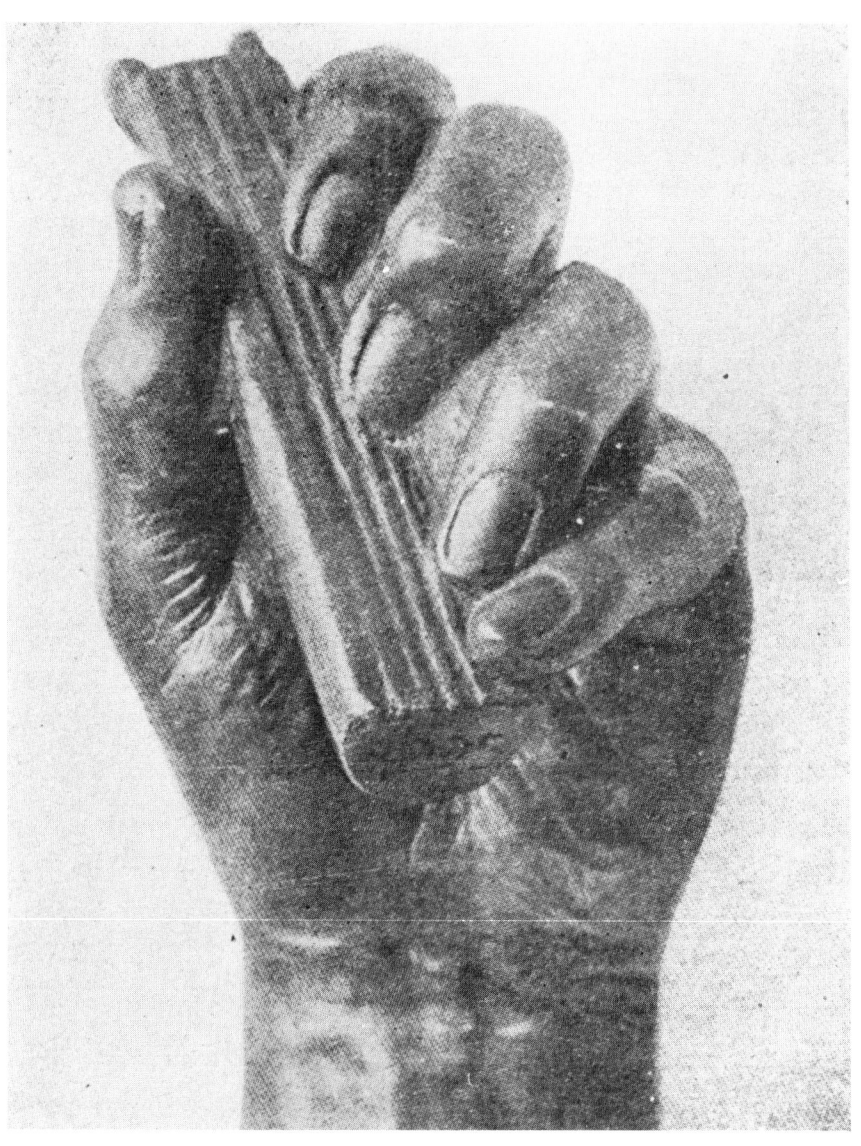

A photograph of Ysaÿe's left hand. This is a cast which shows how Ysaÿe compensated for a short fourth finger.

own soul as you speak for the composer—then you *begin* to find yourself on the right track!"

That was the spirit of his teaching. He knew no other "method." Those who worked with him—and the number included such distinguished pedagogues of today as Edouard Déthier, Lea Luboshutz, and Louis Persinger—soon caught the spirit of Ysaÿe's desire to *make concrete* a tonal image of deep musical thought, and to introduce it into their own work. Lessons with Ysaÿe were magnificent and stimulating. Naturally, he accepted only artist pupils, and with them he spent no time on the working out of technical problems that should have been mastered before the advanced stage. If a pupil had deep-rooted technical difficulties, however, Ysaÿe always encouraged him to discuss them and together, they would work out a personal and individual solution of personal and individual problems. In the beginning, I sometimes wondered at Ysaÿe's unwillingness to *generalize* on those matters of techniques and skills that loom so large on the student's horizon. Could not a master of such powers easily formulate rules and systems from his own experience? Once I summoned up courage to ask him about this and he gave me an answer I shall never forget. Holding out his beautifully formed left hand, he made me look at the third finger. It was not quite straight—not quite normal! Slight as the irregularity was, it was there. "So you see," said Ysaÿe, "it would be impossible for me to set forth any general rules; I do most of my own playing with my first and second fingers!" The fingered editions which Ysaÿe prepared offer strong corroboration of this. At the time, I was dumfounded—to think of an artist with a slight finger irregularity rising to such heights of playing perfection! The incident cured me, though, of seeking any definite short-cuts of "method."

HOW HE TAUGHT

When one came for a lesson, Ysaÿe always held his violin in his arm. He would play for his pupils, allowing them to watch his bowings, and fingerings. His chief occupation, however, was to play the orchestral accompaniments of the student's lesson concerto. He could—and did—actually reproduce the full orchestral part on his violin; and when he had not fingers enough to give sound to the effects he wanted, he would sing! The effect of this remarkable

Léa Luboshutz, a famous violin teacher and a student of Ysaÿe (1920). Courtesy of Arazi.

solo accompaniment was such that even the least gifted of the students would suddenly come to life and play his solo part brilliantly.

Ysaÿe believed, with his own great teacher, Vieuxtemps, in always using the open strings whenever possible. He was deeply devoted to Vieuxtemps and seldom gave a concert without including one of his works—even the works that had not been published. Strange as it may seem, it is difficult for me to think back to specific teaching routines that Ysaÿe used—because he used none at all! I do remember that he disliked the words "teacher" and "pupil"—he preferred to speak of "master" and "disciple," feeling that those terms freed the association from authoritarian pedantry, and gave it the light of a coming together for the purpose of making music.

COMMON-SENSE ESSENTIALS

Ysaÿe thought much about the responsibilities of teaching. Until the demands of his career intervened, he had served for thirteen years as professor at the Royal Conservatory of Brussels, in his native Belgium. He used to say that far too much importance was laid upon the master, in the master-disciple relationship; that the main effort lies with the disciple who must draw from the master the knowledge and experience he has gathered! Certainly, that is an original viewpoint. It is a helpful one, however, in that it stimulates the disciple to an awareness of his own responsibilities. No teacher can pump knowledge into a pupil; unless the pupil is alert to his own needs and determined to serve them, the best teaching in the world will be of little value.

Ysaÿe had no teaching tricks or devices; he did insist, however, on a few common-sense essentials. He held that a pupil needs nothing more than to have his weak points called to his attention. For instance, he believed that the right arm (the bow) was just as important as the left hand (the fingers) and that one of the commonest errors of the player was to allow the bow to become weak at the tip.

His great point was "correct practice." By this he meant only one simple thing: the *slow* practicing of every detail, with complete and alert *concentration* on every detail. Ysaÿe held that, to practice properly, one must have a mental concept of the exact effect desired—after which, one simply listened for that exact effect and brought every tone a shade nearer its realization. Practice without alert thought—even of technical drills—he held to be quite valueless. Another great maxim of Ysaÿe's was that no really fine playing can be done unless the player is relaxed—not only relaxed in his playing mechanism, but in his entire being! When one is worried or hurried, when one has his mind on problems and difficulties, not only playing but even practice becomes tense. And the only way to get rid of tensions (over and above sane and normal living) is to discipline one's mind to shut out distractions. Indeed, self-discipline was the core of Ysaÿe's teaching.

To one thing he was inexorably opposed, and that was imitation! He would play freely for his disciples, and also advised those who came to him to *listen to* the playing of great musicians—but *never* to imitate them. Everything, to Ysaÿe, had to be settled individually. And it was precisely the way in which a pupil showed his individual conception of the composition he was playing that gave him status in the master's eyes.

Ysaÿe's actual teaching habits can be summed up in a few sound maxims. Technically he believed that it was enough to point out the artist-pupil's weak points and then to let him solve them himself in the light of *knowing what to look out for;* musically, he believed in charting a clear mental concept of the music *before* one played it and then striving to release that concept as graphically as possible. But the heart and soul of Eugène Ysaÿe's teaching lay in no maxims that can be summed up in words. It lay—as great teaching and great art always must lie—in the personality of the man himself. It is no exaggeration to say that he inspired his disciples. I have often seen an artist-pupil come to his lesson, play in a correct but routine way, and suddenly catch fire from the ardor of the inspired handsome man performing orchestrally on his violin. Who can say how or why it happened? Simply the spirit of Ysaÿe reached out and touched his pupils. I think that this is the secret of all fine teaching. It is good to blue-print cures for violinistic defects—it is infinitely better to stimulate the pupil to penetrate into his own defects and to solve them through individual thought and concentration. That was Ysaÿe's way.

Louis Persinger, a follower of Ysaÿe's methods.

From left to right: Ysaÿe, his son Gabriel and Louis Persinger, 1913.

This amusing photo has never been satisfactorily explained. Typical of his colorful, jovial nature, Ysaÿe may have posed for this photo merely as a joke.

Arthur Hartmann

YSAŸE: COLOSSUS OF THE VIOLIN

Sharp Contradictions In Art and Personality of Belgian 'Giant Oak'

By Arthur Hartmann

Ysaÿe—the Gargantuan—the Sublime—Emperor of Extravaganza! Everything about him was on the "gigantesque" and all the Hollywoodian hyper-super-terrifics would have fitted him with the naturalness of his own epidermis! In physical stature as in musicianship, mental power, greatness of heart and, if it must be added, in uncontrollable anger and childishness and pettiness of moral fibre, he was always the Colossus. The French have a saying, well known to all gifted people, the good 'Bohémiens', "to be a great artist, one must be a 'grand cochon'," and this equally applies.

His playing was noble one moment and reeking with sensuality the next: beautiful, ideal, poetic, unmatched in grandeur and delicacy and tenderness, and within the next few boisterous roughness, untrammeled vehemence, the most unbridled gypsified capriciousness of tempi, accents and nuances, and of an extravagance that often made me put my hat before my face in my efforts to restrain open laughter! He was truly Rabelaisian and again as delicate as a brush-stroke by Hokusai. It is neither unkind nor a lack of veneration for the dead and the living to make passing mention of the fact that his personal life was that of an extremist, and that some of his experiences and practical jokes (not always of the most refined nature), would, if recounted, bring roars of merriment and protests of incredulity. Truly, Ysaÿe was unique and should have lived to be at least one hundred years old, for this giant oak at sixty years had more vitality than four men of half his age.

Conflicting Elements in Ysaÿe's Nature

I heard him play more often than all the other great violinists put together and though I never heard him play *one* work exactly as written, I still maintain that he was the greatest violinistic genius since Wieniawski! The apparent contradiction is explained—and justified—by the tremendous and conflicting elements of his nature and individuality. I have seen him conduct (and rehearse from memory) the 'Eroica' and 'La Cinquième (as he and all French musicians call it) and, just then, it was my positive conviction that there was no greater conductor living!

I have never heard greater, more profound or revealing interpretations, and surcharged with his physical magnetism the performances were nothing less than bomb-like in their overwhelming vitality. In the year 1900 (I think it was) I lived in London, in the home of René Ortmans, violinist and ultimately a conductor, a compatriot of Ysaÿe and a life-long friend, their bond dating from their boyhood-days together. Joachim, with his associates forming the celebrated Joachim Quartet, had given an annual series of concerts in London "since time immemorial" as I think one might well way, and that season, Joachim having fallen ill, Chappell suddenly found himself without a quartet-organization. Whatever the reasons, the 'Ysaÿe quartet' was engaged for some twenty concerts, throughout the Fall and Winter. This so-called 'Ysaÿe Quartet' consisted of the great violinist and three colleagues, fellow teachers in the Brussels Conservatory of Ysaÿe's former days. Ysaÿe's all-around musicianship had, of course long ago, given him familiarity with the chamber-music literature, yet I doubt if even the most pervid admirer (such as myself) could have claimed for this "quartet" the homogeneity of an ensemble when the first violinist had, since decades, dotted the maps of Europe and America as a violin virtuoso, interspersed with appearances as guest conductor as well as conductor of the 'Orchestre Ysaÿe' in Brussels.

The concerts took place on Monday afternoons (I think) and also on some Saturday evenings, and it happened more often than not that Ysaÿe was appearing, as violinist, somewhere in England or on the Continent, a day or two before, and would be doing so again within the following few days. There were many concerts I know, that were done without any rehearsing, besides which, his associates came over from Brussels for each concert (or week-end) and returned there immediately after. Because of his many appearances in the British Isles that year, Ysaÿe had taken rooms somewhere in Duke Street, London, and—again if I correctly recall—this was not exactly an "elegant" neighborhood. In these two rooms were large straw hampers full of music (orchestral parts to violin concerti) stores of linen and huge Turkish towels and enormous briar pipes in their enormous étuis, and to top it all, he was then wearing a fur coat and a huge, round fur cap. It is, however, not with proper recognition to their importance to Ysaÿe to mention the pipes casually among other indispensable items, for these more properly belonged at the head of the list.

Ysaÿe's Briar Pipes

After playing a concert, Ysaÿe invariably walked from the dressing room entirely out of the building and only on reaching the curb would ask "Eh bien—ma basse! Qui es-ce, qui a ma basse?" ("Eh bien—my bass! Who's got my bass?"). He knew that he was surrounded by friends and cronies and that some one was bringing his enormous double-case. But I, for one, have never known him to ask, "Where did I leave my pipe?" Whereas I did know that no gift could give him greater pleasure than a briar pipe in the shape and size for which he had a great partiality. These pipes were five inches in diameter. The stem was so carved out of the same enormous block of briar as to be very close to the pipe itself. With the curving amber or hard-rubber mouthpiece then attached, these beautiful pipes suggested nothing so much as a miniature bassoon. There were, of course, individual, becushioned and lined boxes for these, and when Ysaÿe, on coming to the dinner table, would deposit his pipe-étui and the tobacco pouch at its side, the size of them together fully equalled the modern girl's overnight bag.

One night at Pagani's, surrounded by a half dozen musicians, he had been recounting his experiences; as the party finally boke up, he said to Ortmans: "René, you will be kind enough to come and wake me up tomorrow at eleven." He shook hands all around and it seems to me that almost invariably he shook hands with his left and not with his right hand. I lived with the Ortmans somewhere out in West Kensington and the trip down to Duke Street meant the better part of an hour—just "to awaken him at eleven o'clock." Ortmans insisted that I go with him and reluctantly I consented. Arrived at his rooms, we found him not only awake but sitting on a chair in his vast nightgown, pipe in mouth, and playing away for dear life. He told us to disregard him, for he had to do some work as he was playing in Glasgow (which he pronounced Glozgov) the following evening and had to play a concerto he had not played in quite some time. To my inexpressible joy, it was the rarely-heard Concerto in F by Lalo, which I knew, though I had never heard it played.

An Informal Performance

I leaned against a piece of furniture while he, with closed eyes and the huge pipe danglng from the right side of his mouth, was pouring forth his wealth of marvelous tone, staggering me with his mastery of the bow and ease of the left hand. However, there was another thing which dumbfounded me and it was that in the pages of passage-work there were scarcely two consecutive measures which contained the notes exactly as they had been written! Perhaps the composer, who doubtlessly had been an intimate friend of Ysaÿe's, had made a revision of that work, for the passages, were different from the printed notes. Reaching a spot where the orchestra interrupts with loud chords, Ysaÿe relaxed for a moment, lowered his violin and, opening his eyes, winked at me. Then, in a high-pitched, thin voice imitated the "meow" of a cat, re-lighting his pipe, he turned to me and said "Meow . . . eh bien cochon, ça va, hein?" He saw that I was transfixed with joy and as I made no response he guffawed: Well say something! It went well, didn't it? What do you think?" I was too confused to be able to find the right words and dreading to contradict him. I blurted the words which accomplished precisely that! I answered, "Oh, it is marvelous, only it isn't quite right. It isn't that . . . it isn't accurate!"

"What!" he roared like a bull which had just been stabbed, and putting fiddle and pipe down, took his long hair in each fist and bellowed "René, René, did you hear that? René, this cochon has the effrontery to tell me that it wasn't right!" While he stood there, a fistful of hair in each hand, I begged his friend Ortmans to try explain to him that it was all, of course, marvelous, genial, overwhelming and staggering because he was not playing the actual notes in the pages of figurations, as published by Lalo. It was in vain I tried to tell him that I knew I had been very much out of order to make the comments that I had, that I did not know the French language sufficiently to pick quickly the right forms and words with which, with due apologies, to express my astonishment that a page of artistically woven figurations, so characteristic of Lalo, could have been so similar and yet dissimilar sufficiently to confound me, and so on. But he was too stunned and infuriated to pay any attention to Ortmans and my explanations and, still tearing at his hair, he stood over me menacingly while he kept on repeating: "So you *know* the work—*you* know it? Do you hear that, René? This cochon here knows the Lalo, when I have played it before he was born."

Volatile Temperament

But suddenly his mood changed and with thorough glee at my red-faced humiliation and wretchedness, he roared "René! Now you are going to see something! This cochon is going to play the Concerto in F of Lalo for me!" He winked his eyes, slapped his thighs and seizing his fiddle and bow thrust them at me with terrific imprecations and ordered me to play the pages containing the passage-work in question!

This was an encounter I had not expected, and paralyzed with terror as this infuriated Goliath towered over me, I begged, actually begged tremblingly, to be forgiven and to be allowed to run from that room. But it was useless, for he kept thrusting fiddle and bow toward me and with terrific oaths ordered me to begin. He straddled a chair, turning it around so that his arms rested on its back, his enormous bare legs and thighs exposed to view, and smoking his pipe. I started the concerto, unprepared as I was, to play it. He watched me steadily and when I reached the passages in question, he closed his eyes, squeezing them together very hard, as if to impress something on his brain. Presently he stopped me by holding up his hand, and opening his eyes, he said to me in a normal, quiet voice: "Play that place over again—a little more slowly." Once more the eyes closed, were tightly squeezed, the head nodding. "And now continue," he said, and again all this had to be repeated. When I terminated the first movement, he turned to Ortmans and said in a matter-of-fact voice: "Eh bien, he is right. I must look through the score a little after lunch," and approaching me, he gave me a slap on the back and said "Hm . . . c'ést un brave! He has talent. We will have lunch together, won't we, Cochon . . .?)"

Pulling his night-gown over his head, he told me to continue with the two remaining movements while he dressed. His clothes were strewn all over the place and I can now visualize him sitting there, pausing in the midst of pulling on a sock, or his trousers, while with closed eyes he was again making a mental record of something in the music at that particular point. This experience is not recounted to show that although unprepared and under such demoralizing conditions I did manage to play the concerto with such a colossal violinist and artist watching every finger-move and bow-stroke, but that Ysaÿe, only one day before rehearsing and playing it publicly with orchestra, conceived the work as an entity and thus had woven things (scarcely less genial than those of Lalo himself) around the music, harmonies which he knew were in the background of the score, just as he, through habit, always filled in harmonies in the single-voiced or melodic phrases. This complete musicality of feeling I never knew of in any other violinist, nor the ability to create fullness of sonority through transposition into various registers and—of course—in any and all positions of the violin. It was like Saint-Saëns' gift and musicianship, to be able to play any work of Bach which he knew, in any key whatsoever! That is what I should call musicianship-plus.

Ysaÿe the Violinist

Ysaÿe had the rare power, at times, to inspire himself to such sublime heights that from no other artist have I seen the vistas of majesty, grandeur and nobility so revealed. It is an experience of a life time to see an artist "of the other world" so feel the meaning of a simple line in the slow movement of the Beethoven violin concerto that utterly unconscious of the orchestra, the lights and the thousands of listeners before him, he stands there with tears streaming down his cheeks, and this I have seen more than once! And in the next movement he would sentimentalize with ridiculous mawkishness in one place only practically to double the tempo in another.

Ysaÿe's Grimaces While Playing

It was one of my "parlor-tricks" to imitate his manner of "falling up-stairs" as he came onto the podium and more especially to mimic his great variety of grimaces while playing. These were an inseparable part of his great artistry, born of absorption and intensity of emotions. But, be it said, when the real feeling was not present, the grimaces were, and perhaps to an even greater extent, for Ysaÿe was not only a born actor but also knew the value of gestures, expressions and poses! Often it was downright funny to see him frantically whipping himself into trying to produce a trill with fingers that were exhausted beyond his will and control: to see him, in a cantilena place assume the poses and grimaces of his inspired "moments of communing" and to know, as soon as one listened without looking, that his playing was lusterless, full of freakish absurdities, cleverly faked in passage-work and interspersed with a chain of unexpected momentary lapses of memory from which he always masterfully extricated himself. These lapses of memory were not entirely due to the fact that he never practiced, though he had an enormous repertoire, but also more generally, because he knew every work so completely that he would lose his part in the whole, and might very likely emphasize something in the horns or in the strings or the reeds.

Right here is where mention should be made of a phenomenal manifestation of this extraordinary artist, one so fantastic that only those who have witnessed and heard it can fully believe, and furthermore never cease to marvel at. Ysaÿe was the violin itself and, so far as I have ever heard, the only one to whom the violin sufficed as a medium of expression of all music. Thus, he accomplished the unbelievable, for with his huge pipe hanging out of the right corner of his mouth, with fiddle tucked side-ways against his shoulder and bow, he would accompany any concerto, giving the fullest harmonies and the most complete effects of the various elements in the orchestration. Similarly, he would play any symphony or overture, and could as well play the Waltzes of Waldteufel or the latest Jazz.

Ysaÿe the Chamber Musician

When it came to chamber-music, I was less inclined to find things "genial," for his erraticism and fiddleistic virtuosity always made me laughingly think of a mountain-climber leaping from cliff to cliff while his three associates were risking neck-breaking jumps after him and apprehensively wondering where the next slip would occur. Even with music before him, he might make those "musical lapses" and when his bow trembled you could hear his grumbled "Allez-allez!" and the tempo was changed immediately and the succeeding measures "speeded up." Ysaÿe and Pugno were generally accepted as "the ideal combination for sonatas," but, musicians remember with amusement that when Ysaÿe had the theme, in the 'Kreutzer' Sonata, he became majestic, grandiose, sublime and ridiculous from beat to beat, and when his partner took it up, it was at least one-third faster, while Ysaÿe blinkingly made the most grotesque sudden crescendi and banishings within a measure and often within a beat! (Reverting to my "parlor stunts" when I was so disposed, I would give an imitation of how he interpreted the Schumann Piano Quintet when he played the viola to my first violin. Where he had the solo in the 'Funeral March' movement, he would invariably broaden the tempo, and as soon as he was through, he would urge me and the others on, from beat to beat. This imitation of Ysaÿe's tone, comments and blasphemies, the manner in which we would murmur "à moi!" and "trop fort" and "attends-donc, cochon", his grimaces, his urging, urging with his whole body while everyone could hear "allez-allez . . . eh bien, va donc!", has always caused uproarious laughter.)

My opinion of most of these quartet-performances I have already given, and perhaps, at the best, they might have been considered as excellent "sight-reading." One day, after a performance of the Second Quartet of Opus 18 by Beethoven (which was extremely erratic), in answer to the applause, Ysaÿe returned to the platform alone. Suddenly a pianist appeared on the steps leading onto the stage in old St James's Hall, and they played as an encore the 'Obertass' Mazurka by Wieniawski! Inevitably I went back-stage, with Ortmans, and long before reaching the "Green Room" we could hear Ysaÿe's voice, roaring with happiness. In the crowded room, we saw him kissing and embracing every woman. Again taking the widow and daughters of Henri Wieniawski in his arms, he roared "N'est-ce-pas—I told you that when I have the happiness of seeing you in one of my concerts, I'll play something especially for you!"

Ysaÿe the Conductor

I no longer recall whether it was at the end of that season or a year or two later when I was playing in London that Ysaÿe was engaged as Conductor in, I think, a three-day festival. At one concert I played Ysaÿe's tenderly-poetic 'Rêve d'Enfant' (then virtaully unknown) and played it quakingly, for Ysaÿe himself sat in the audience, right there under my nose. Arbos had asked me to use his Guarnerius for "he wanted to hear how it sounds in a hall" and with Arbos sat a wonderful fiddler, Achille Rivarde, a second Sarasate, in my estimation, of whose passing I just read while penning this tribute! The old contact was renewed and with his permission, or rather at his invitation, I attended some of the rehearsals, together with my old friend Ortmans.

Ysaÿe's manner of conducting, as was to be expected, was replete with interesting, individual, magnetic and amusingly contradictory elements. At times he did not conduct at all, was absolutely immobile. At others he would indicate to one section of the orchestra to listen to what, for instance, the flutes were playing. His beats, at times, were tiny or did not cover an area of more than an inch in any direction and then suddenly like a lion he would spring, with both arms in the air, the right foot raised, and when his "mane" fell all over his face and collar, it looked truly like three paws mid-air. These were his gestures at concerts as well as in rehearsing.

Once dissatisfied with the spiccati the violins were playing, in a Schumann symphony, he stopped them in high dudgeon, while in a complaining voice he kept repeating, "Mais non . . . mais non, mais non!" and seizing a violin from under the chin of the player nearest him, meant to demontrate what kind of spiccato he wanted. However, the strange bow did not respond to him immediately and in that attentive silence, he stopped suddenly, scratched his head and exclaimed "Where is Ysaÿe?" and the orchestra roared and applauded.

His manner of starting a rehearsal was extremely funny. In a series of rolling-up-hill falls he would reach the conductor's little platform, waving his greetings to the band. Then seizing a rather small baton, he would stand there blinking hard when suddenly he would touch the iron enclosure around himself as if it were charged with an electrocuting current, for he jumped back . . . away from it, in the same instant. Then with terific strength he hurled shoulders, arms and clenched fists into the air and voilá, we had the first beat to "Betovans Sankiem." In that same work, in the transition from the third to the last movement (where the tympani has the motive and steady pulsations) both hands were held in the air, on a line with his face, without any beat whatsoever, which, of course, held the orchestra to a pianissimo without any nuance whatever, while his facial expressions were conveying what he felt. However, two or three measures before the entrance of the Finale, he had quietly dropped his left arm and had gotten his right arm, very slowly, completely across his body and far past his left shoulder. The crescendo was now made by his bringing the right arm across his body, in a straight line, and as he was shaking with the intensity of what he wanted, he accomplished this in a series of jerky little motions and with such terrific, physical strength that when he suddenly raised his arm for the opening melody, the flexible little baton broke into a good dozen bits of wood about an inch or two long. These the orchestra eagerly gathered, and crowding around him, he was made to autograph each one.

As I have said, I think there were three concerts during which I saw him conduct from memory the two-mentioned Symphonies by Beethoven as also those by Franck and Chausson, the 'Istar' by d'Indy, the Overture 'Lenore' by Duparc, the entire 'La Mer' by Paul Gilson and 'Bruennhilde's Immolation' from 'Goetterdaemmerung' with a "Bruennhilde" of course. His vitality and energy were absolutely inexhaustible, for after one of these concerts, he told me to ' stick around" as there was yet a rehearsal to start at about 11:30 (p.m.), an extra one for the next afternoon's performance. He took about two-fingers of whiskey (for just then he was "on the water wagon") and the orchestra having been reassembled, he started with undimmed fire in his tiger-like leaps and, at times, devastating profanities. After going through one composition, he yelled into the wings, "St. Saëns" and sure enough that marvelous little man with the unique parrot-proboscis emerged and approached Ysaÿe. The latter rose form his seat and seizing St. Saëns under the arms lifted him to his own height and kissed him on both cheeks. Then with a wide wave of the left arm he made the presentation: 'L'orchestre philharmonique . . . St. Saëns!" Thereupon the latter stepped down to the platform which had been extended and which was slightly lower than the stage and Ysaÿe resumed his seat, his back completely turned on the soloist. And without ever once turning around, they rehearsed St. Saëns' fifth piano concerto, 'Africa'.

In all these things Ysaÿe was a self-made musician, a natural one and born with a tremendous instinct, enthusiasm and understanding of music. On the other hand, I think no one would gainsay the fact that as a conductor, generally speaking and more particularly as a disciplinarian, he was utterly beyond seious consideration. For with him it was always the extremes, and when the fires from the mounts of inspiration could not be commanded, the gestures and extravagances became parodies, and the "bigness" became one vast, meaningless space of emptiness. I must not fail to mention the night, about fifteen years ago, when the late Speiring had a "stag" at his home and at which were present Auer, Kreisler, Ysaÿe and a score of other musicians. Towards the end of the evening, I was urged to do my imitations and which consisted of the personal characteristics and peculiarities of style, tone, bowings, fingerings, manner of holding the instrument and entrances, of a number of famous fiddlers of the past and present, today, alas, almost all of them gone . . . the game consisted in the audience's guessing the name of the artist from the time of his entrance through his gait, his bows, tunings and so on. I did Sarasate, Kubelik and the great "Fritzey" himself. Finally, taking my courage in both hands, I ended the show with an imitation of Ysaÿe himself and his roars could be heard above the din of the others. I might add that in listening to the few performances of his unaccompanied Sonatas, which in recent years have appeared on programs at intervals, one might become persuaded into believing them of greater value if the great actor-artist himself were presenting them, for I sadly miss his grimaces. And in termination I crave to repeat that in Ysaÿe were incorporated the heart and soul of the violin. This instrument sufficed him as a medium for the expressions of every human tenderness and greatness of thought and emotions, as it did also in the reproductions of an orchestral palette. To me he remains the synonym for violin!

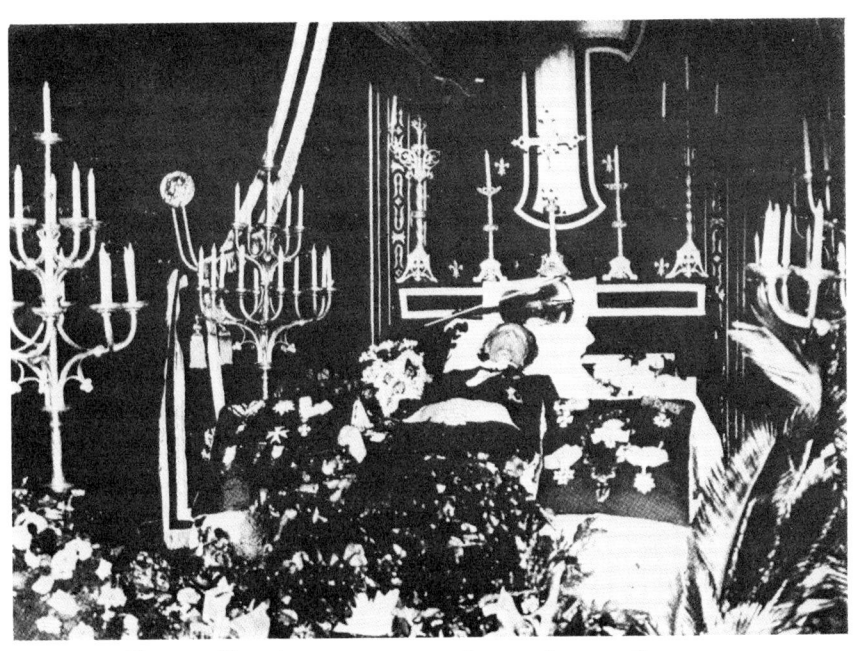

Eugene Ysaÿe lies in state at a huge funeral ceremony on May 17, 1931.

The Ysaÿe Paris Class

By I.S. Arazi

Eugène Ysaÿe's lecture on interpretation took place in an extraordinary atmosphere of affectionate admiration. The hall was packed with violinists: Thibaud, Enesco, Boucherit, Szigeti, Spalding, Hayot, Chailley, Dushkin, Touche, Yvonne Astruc, Mme. Joachim Chaigneau, Nauwinck, Hambourg, Jarosy, Goldberg, Wilkomirski, Boris Schwartz, Dany Brunschwig (I am quoting at random from memory and am sure to have made a few omissions), undisputed masters of today or celebrities of tomorrow; and all the enrolled pupils, some of whom are already appreciated virtuosos. In fact one had the very distinct impression of a collective homage to *one of the most powerful interpreters of all time*, homage put, as it were, in concrete form when at the end of the second class, Enesco gave a magnificent performance of the sonata dedicated to him by Ysaÿe.

FIRST EXCURSUM (Praeludium)

Mes amis from way back, way back ... as I look at you all in this gathering, the first thing that comes to my mind is what a string section you all would make ... and knowing most of you as I do the other thing that comes to mind is "who would be playing second violin or viola?" ... I am so very glad to see most of you again ... under one roof ... and so many of you at the same time ... I would also like to clear up one thing ... this gathering is called a class ... a class to me presupposes that some learning or teaching will be taking place from and between people ... and not only is it a class, but it is also called the Ysaÿe Class. Although this could be classified as a great honor, in my thinking, it is also a great presumption ... because I have been learning from all of you the art for many, many years ... you may not have been aware of it, but I have been putting aside little nuggets of gold from your performances for such a long time, that I now have quite a collection ... of not only how to, but also, how not to ... so, if

I.S. Arazi, student of Ysaÿe, violinist, teacher, musicologist and historian. He supplied many of the photographs which appear in this book.

Albert Spalding.

Prof. Leopold Auer.

Albert Spalding with André Benoist at the piano (from The Accompanist, *Benoist's autobiography).*

it is agreeable to all, we will proceed under the condition that we all take part and share the teaching and the learning that will take place . . . I am in a very fortunate position from a historical point of view . . . I was a disciple of both Vieuxtemps and Wieniawski . . . through Vieuxtemps, I learned about DeBeriot who himself descended from the older Italians . . . Vieuxtemps himself knew Paganini . . . in the History of the Violin I seem to have been positioned in the mainstream . . . and then I also have most of you as colleagues . . . I have many memories and reminiscences . . . I would like to share it all with you.

The tone of this class was simple and direct insofar as this was possible. The method, the same one as that already adopted by Thibaud. First, the performance by the pupil, followed by the master's criticism and commentary.

I will not detail work by work six programs, the contents of which have already been announced; far better, to keep to what characterized the spirit of these lessons most directly.

We shall not dwell very long on technique. In what Ysaÿe asks for one finds the main features of the Franco-Belgian School: AN EASY BEARING, THE VIOLIN HELD HIGH, THE BOW HELD BOLDLY WITH LITTLE OR NO ACTION OF THE UPPER ARM, THE RATHER SPECIAL USE (due to Wieniawski) OF THE POINT IN CERTAIN FORCEFUL PASSAGES WHERE IT IS DRAWN AWAY FROM THE STRING ONLY TO RETURN AND STRIKE IT VIOLENTLY LIKE THE LASH OF A WHIP (Scherzo Tarantelle); FOR THE LEFT HAND, GREAT SIMPLICITY OF FINGERING IN THE STROKES, OFTEN MARKED BY OPEN STRINGS, EVIDENCES OF ACCURACY, AND ELEMENTS OF FORCE AND PERSPICUITY; a complete remoteness from any useless finicky style. And throughout, the concern for continuity and for homogeneousness in the use of the sonorous tints offered by the different strings, in the vibrato, in the dosage of the bow strokes.

As regards the interpretation, this is dominated by a constructive preoccupation of the same order. True, one suspected that Ysaÿe's "Fantasia" was not left to chance. But in the face of the impression of spontaneity given to some of his performances, it would have been difficult to surmise the minuteness with which they had been prepared and the stability of their foundations.

Above all, AN ABSOLUTE RHYTHMIC COHESION; THE IMPORTANCE OF KEEPING ONE'S RHYTHM, OF PROSCRIBING ANY EXCESS OF SHADES, WHETHER AGOGIC (Accelerando, Ritartando) OR DYNAMIC which break the line and disperse interest; in La Folia (Corelli) for instance, where every variation, once its style has been fixed, retains it until the end. Another in the Romance in F (Beethoven) at the end of the tutti as it approaches the minor key (F,C,A-F-E), when care must be taken not to slow down or subdue the sonority, which would at the beginning of the solo, cause an unaccountable break. And Ysaÿe would borrow from Wagner, on the same subject, but this time in connection with the Andante of the Kreutzer Sonata, a judicious remark: ONE CANNOT, AFTER THE CALM RENDERING OF THE THEME, IMMEDIATELY GIVE TO THE FIRST VARIATION ALL ITS VIVACITY AND ALL ITS JAUNTINESS. IT MUST BE PREPARED, THIS DOUBLE FEATURE BEING SLIGHTLY TONED DOWN IN THE BEGINNING. It is for a similar reason connected with balance that in the first movement of the Fifth Concerto by Vieuxtemps, Ysaÿe recommends, on the advice of the composer, his master, to spread oneself somewhat on the transition between the passage which precedes the chant in C Major and the chant itself because this transition is rather short, musically speaking. Similarly, failing a formal intention to establish a contrast, one should not pass quickly (Bach Fugue in G Minor) from the vigorous striking of chords to a spiccato a slight saltato in the first semiquaver episode.

SECOND EXCURSUM (on Vieuxtemps)

I would like to speak to you about my master, Vieuxtemps . . . I often feel that sometimes he is not at all completely understood . . . especially by his own kinsmen . . . he was a great man, the grandeur of whose tradition lives in the whole "romantic school of violin playing" . . . he wrote seven concerti . . . of course they were written for effect, from the virtuoso standpoint . . . and why not? . . . they were conceived and were born on the fingerboard . . . yet how firmly and solidly they are built up . . . I cannot help but think of Beethoven when I think of Vieuxtemps, the composer . . . how interesting and masterly is

Prof. Leopold Auer with Mrs. Wanda Bogutskastein.

their working out . . . and the orchestral score far transcends the mere function of an accompaniment . . . as regards virtuose effect, only Paganini goes side by side with these . . . in wealth of musical and technical development, and in expressiveness, he was a master . . . the proof of this is in the continued endurance of his works . . . he was admired by Joachim, Leonard, Sivori, Wienawski . . . the last used to call him "Le maitre do nous tous" . . . In Paganini and Locatelli, the effect lies in the mechanical and technical innovation for the instrument . . . but in Vieuxtemps, he is the giant who made the violin follow the road of the romanticism which was being blazed by Hugo, Balzac, and Gauthier in literature . . . he knew that the violin was made to charm and to move . . . he felt that the artist must have ideas and emotional powers first and foremost . . . any thoughts and ideas about the mechanical aspect of playing must be so perfected as to be non existent . . . Vieuxtemps wrote in the grand manner and style . . . rich and sonorous . . . the player must reach up to him . . . Vieuxtemps sounds on the violin . . . look at the Fifth Concerto . . . one should have heard Wieniawski play this work . . . it is warm, brilliant, full of fire and temperament, always full sounding, bursting at all times with a con-

tinual, almost unbounded strength . . . his works influenced a large generation of composers to write for the violin, among others, Franck, DuBois, D'Indy, Lekeu, Virene, Ropartz, Lazarri . . . here the violin is very expressive and sings almost continually, yet the technical demands are many and large . . . Vieuxtemps once told me that his greatest moment was at a performance of his fourth concerto, while he awaited his entrance after the long introduction before he played a note, the audience burst into a spontaneous ovation, indicating that they were applauding the composer, not the violinist . . . in his time, he forged ahead with his own brand of technical discovery.

He blazed new paths along with Paganini . . . musical works conceived only from the musical standpoint bring about stagnation . . . and what a violinist at the height of his career!!! He had a bow that seems like 20 kilometers long . . . it almost went around him . . . he could make the instrument sing . . . he often said "Chantez, Chantez . . . Pas de trait pour le Trait (Always sing . . . not runs for the sake of runs)" . . . You should have heard the Beethoven Concerto played by Vieuxtemps and also by Wieniawski . . . they sang this work . . . they expressed themselves without restraint . . . all you heard was the sound . . . everything else vanished before your very eyes . . .

As a corollary to this composition bias, absolute regard for the text: keeping to the written lights and shadows (Winter Song), and to the established and well known traditions like the one initiated by Paganini when playing his Concerto in D on an instrument raised a semitone and demanding to be accompanied by an orchestra performing in E Flat. "PAGANINI," he said word for word, "WAS NOT A POLYPHONIST. HE COMPOSED GUITAR ACCOMPANIMENTS, AND WHEN HE PLAYED HIS PIECE IN D MAJOR WITH AN ACCOMPANIMENT IN THE SAME KEY, HE FOUND THAT THE GUITAR ORCHESTRA WAS TOO LOUD. SO HE CONTRIVED TO RAISE THE ORCHESTRA A SEMI-TONE, PUTTING IT IN E FLAT AND TO RAISE THE PITCH OF HIS VIOLIN A SEMI-TONE, WITH THE RESULT THAT HE HIMSELF STAYED IN D MAJOR. TODAY THE OPPOSITE IS DONE, AND IN ADDITION, A POLYPHONIC ACCOMPANIMENT IS ADAPTED TO THE CONCERTO. JUST ABOUT ENOUGH TO MAKE PAGANINI ROLL OVER IN HIS GRAVE!"

CLARENCE de VAUX-ROYER,
VIOLIN SOLOIST.
Pupil of Ysaye, Halir and Marsick.

Concerts, Musicales and Recitals.

Address care of The Musical Courier.

Instruction Tuesdays and Fridays.

26 East 23d Street, (Madison Sq.), Studio 2, NEW YORK.

Many violinists advertised their connection with Ysaÿe in order to gain stature.

The same scruple for accuracy is found in working out the orchestration. A glance at the original text of Bach's Concerto in E Major reveals the presence of numerous passages figured, not only in the Adagio, but also in the middle, in C-Sharp Minor, of the first Allegro, testifying to the necessary presence of a keyboard instrument, organ or harpsichord which achieves this figuring.

But the adjuration most frequently repeated by Ysaÿe to his disciples is this: "LIVE!!! GIVE ME A RHYTHMICAL ACTION!" A performer may not be content with pouring forth notes without meaning. He must have cultivated his heart and mind, opened his windows to the other arts, read much and visited museums. In practising his profession of musician, the work once acquired insofar as the technique is concerned (and with what care Ysaÿe overhauls it even up to the orchestral accompaniment), he must animate it.

If need be, he must stimulate his imagination by creating a poetic or dramatic fiction. As regards himself, he never played Bach's Chaconne without evoking a procession, the congregation, children throwing flowers as the procession passed, prayers, the vision (in the major key) of the tabernacle, etc. It is a prayer too that suggests to him the Preludium to the First Sonata in G Minor.

As a teacher Ysaÿe was inspiring. He always had his violin in hand and was able to play the accompaniment to absolutely anything on his instrument in such a manner that one felt he surely had a full orchestra supporting him. Once while playing the slow movement of the Bach E major Concerto I thought I was actually being accompanied by an organ, so heavenly were the sounds emanating from his Guarnerius del Gesu. Ysaÿe was most explicit in conveying his ideas. If he thought his student did not fully comprehend his meaning he would play the phrase in question. I recall a tremendous impression still left on me of his playing of the Beethoven "Kreutzer" Sonata—I can still hear it to this day. Apparently I had started the minor variation of the second movement too quickly. Ysaÿe stopped me and asked me to listen while he played it for me. The mood he created, the building of the line, the pathos of the sforzando accents were so stupendous that I was moved to tears! When he had finished playing he asked me to continue. I could not! I was afraid I would lose this wonderful impression if I would so much as touch my instrument.

Ysaÿe was encouraging to his students. He always tried to bring out the best innate qualities in each of us and at the same time was careful to point out the faults. His students were occasionally invited to play string quartets at his home and in these ensembles Ysaÿe would generally play viola. These were inspiring and stimulating occasions—imagine the thrill of an eighteen year old being privileged to play the Franck and Debussy quartets from their original manuscripts!

As a human being Ysaÿe was a kind, devoted and noble man. His heart was as large as his frame and he was six feet five inches tall. His devotion to music, to his friends, to his pupils and his idealism towards the noble, whether it was in music, literature, poetry or human relations, will forever be cherished by those who had the rare privilege of knowing him. These same wonderful qualities were manifest in his violin playing which, for me, represented the ideal. I cherish the memory of this great man and I have endeavored, in my own small way, to carry on his noble tradition of beauty in life and in music.

Antoine Ysaÿe.

Reflections on the Queen Elisabeth Violin Competitions (1937-1976)

By I.S. Arazi

Of all of the violin competitions that have come into being within the past four decades, perhaps the most prestigious is the one that bears the name of the late Queen of the Belgians, Elisabeth, which takes place every fourth year in Brussels. At its inception in 1937, it was called the Ysaÿe Competition, named after the legendary Belgian violinist, Eugène Ysaÿe (1858-1931).

Queen Elisabeth of Belgium was a violinist herself and became a pupil of Eugène Ysaÿe when she first arrived in Belgium from her native Germany. She was related quite closely to King Ludwig II of Bavaria who had been one of Richard Wagner's supporters and benefactors. She had a great interest in all of the Arts in general and Music in particular and became interested in helping talented young people get started on their careers. With Eugène Ysaÿe as her Musical Director and with royal sponsorship and support, she felt that this could be well accomplished. She and Ysaÿe spent much time discussing and planning this competition which would be supported by the Queen Elisabeth Music Foundation which was set up in 1929. This would be the organization which would constitute the framework of the actual competitions themselves. However, the death of the Master in 1931, followed by the death of King Albert in 1934, postponed any initial activity until 1937 when the competition which, was then called the Ysaÿe Competition, first appeared on the musical horizon.

It was held in Brussels and brought into focus the genius and talent of David Oistrakh. It had been decided to award twelve prizes in all so as to not put emphasis on any one individual, but Oistrakh dominated the entire event. Nothing like this could be recalled since the memorable debut in 1918 of Jascha Heifetz, almost thirty years before.

The intervention of World War II caused an interruption that postponed until 1951 the resumption of the Competition which now had been renamed the Queen Elisabeth Competitions and which now had been expanded to include piano and composition within its scope. Its format and structure has been copied a few

Ysaÿe at his desk. Note the picture of Queen Elisabeth, his constant friend and student.

times in various countries, but the Queen Elisabeth Competitions have managed not only to become stronger and more solid, but to increase in magnitude and influence. The combination of the spirit of perhaps the greatest of all the great violinists of all time, combined with the interest and support of the Royal Family, have served well towards this end. Since the death of Queen Elisabeth in 1966, Queen Fabiola has assumed these duties.

VIOLIN PRIZE WINNERS IN THE QUEEN ELISABETH COMPETITION (1937-1976)

1937

1. David Oistrakh (USSR)
2. Ricardo Odnoposoff (Argentina)
3. Lisa Gilels (USSR)
4. Boris Goldstein (USSR)
5. Marina Kozolupova (USSR)
6. Mischa Fichtenholz (USSR)
7. Lola Bobescu (Roumania)
8. Paul Makanovitsky (France)
9. Robert Virovai (Hungary)
10. Angel Reyes (Cuba)
11. Brenzola (Italy)
12. J. Champeil (France)

Ysaÿe during his conductorship of the Cincinnati Orchestra.

Queen Elisabeth of the Belgians spoke many languages—including Russian. She made a very big hit when she supplied autographed photos to the Russian violinists with her Russian inscription and Russian signature.

1951

1. Leonid Kogan (USSR)
2. Mikhail Vayman (USSR)
3. Elise Cserfalvi (Independent)
4. Theo Olof (Netherlands)
5. Olga Kaverzneva (USSR)
6. Heidi Geigler (Austria)
7. Alexei Gorokhov (USSR)
8. Luben Yordanoff (Bulgaria)
9. Fredell Lack (U.S.A.)
10. Pierre Doukan (France)
11. Pierre D'Archambeau (U.S.A.)
12. Kees Kooper (Netherlands)

1955

1. Berl Senofsky (U.S.A.)
2. Julian Sitkovetsky (USSR)
3. Pierre Doukan (France)
4. Mlle Dorfevill-Boussinot (France)
5. Viktor Pikaisen (USSR)
6. Alberto Lysy (Argentine)
7. Marina Iashvilli (USSR)
8. Tessa Robbins (Great Britain)
9. Luben Yordanoff (Bulgaria)
10. Clemens Quatacker (Belgium)
11. Igor Politkowsky (USSR)
12. Marcel Debot (Belgium)

1959

1. Jaime Laredo (Bolivia)
2. Albert Markov (USSR)
3. Joseph Silverstein (U.S.A.)
4. Vladimir Malinine (USSR)
5. Boris Kouniev (USSR)
6. Georgei Minchen-Badev (Bulgaria)
7. Shmuel Ashkenasi (Israel)
8. Desmond Bradley (Australia)
9. Augustin Leon Ara (Spain)
10. Raphael Sobolevsky (USSR)
11. Gerard Kantarjian (UAR)
12. Koji Toyoda (Japan)

1963

1. Alexei Michlin (USSR)
2. Semeon Snitkovsky (USSR)
3. Arnold Steinhardt (U.S.A.)
4. Zariouss Shikhmursajeva (USSR)
5. Charles Castleman (U.S.A.)
6. Masuko Ushioda (Japan)
7. Yossef Zivoni (Israel)
8. Nejmi Succari (Syria)
9. Jean Ter-Mergerian (USSR)
10. Hidetaro Suzuki (Japan)
11. Paul Rosenthal (U.S.A.)
12. Donald Weilerstein (U.S.A.)

1967

1. Phillipe Hirchhorn (USSR)
2. Stoika Milanova (Bulgaria)
3. Gidon Kremer (USSR)
4. Roman Nodel (USSR)
5. Hidetaro Suzuki (Japan)
6. Jean-Jacques Kantarow (France)
7. Nicolas Chumachenco (Argentina)
8. Joshua Epstein (Israel)
9. Endre Granat (Sweden)
10. Josef Ryssine (USSR)
11. Marjeta Delcourte-Korosec (Bel.)
12. Uri Pianka (Israel)

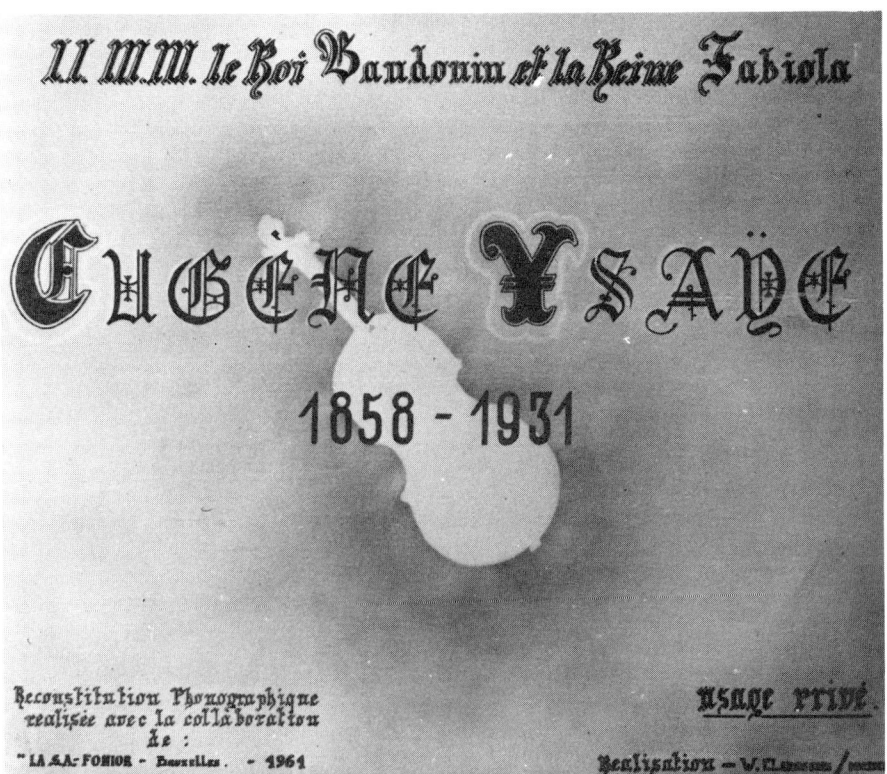

A record issued by King Baudouin, grandson of Queen Elisabeth, and his wife, Queen Fabiola, to commemorate the music of Ysaÿe. Compliments of Arazi.

1971

1. Miriam Fried (Israel)
2. Andrei Korsakov (USSR)
3. Hamao Fujiwara (Japan)
4. Ana Chumachenco-Lysy (Arg.)
5. Edith Volkaert (Belgium)
6. Joshua Epstein (Israel)
7. Rudolf Werthen (Belgium)
8. Zinovy Vinnikov (USSR)
9. Geoffrey Michaels (Australia)
10. Vania Milanova (Bulgaria)
11. Magdalena Rezler (Poland)
12. Zakhar Bron (USSR)

1976

1. Mikhail Besverkhny (USSR)
2. Irina Medvedeva (USSR)
3. Dong-Suk Kang (China)
4. Grigory Jisline (USSR)
5. Shizuka Ishikawa (Japan)
6. Kaja Danczowska (Poland)
7. Marie-Annick Nicolas (France)
8. Eugene Drucker (U.S.A.)
9. Eugene Sarbu (Romania)
10. Tadeuz Gadzina (Poland)
11. Goncal Comelias-Fabregas (Spain)
12. Philip Setzer (U.S.A.)

While compiling this monograph on the Queen Elisabeth Competitions, we one day found ourselves within a hundred or so miles from Josef Gingold, an old friend and one of Ysaÿe's last pupils. On the spur of the moment, we dialed his studio for some information we needed for another monograph we were working on. As we did not tell him from where we were calling, he assumed we were in Bloomington, Indiana and invited us over for some tea that afternoon. On the spur of the moment we accepted, rented a car and zoomed over to the University of Indiana.

His studio had always represented for us a haven for rest and relaxation with its muted interiors, its comfortable hominess, and its extensive gallery of pictures of violinists, not only of our time, but of yesteryear, seemingly on every square inch of wallspace. Ysaÿe was well represented from a giant portrait, to some montages of various poses, to a small gold-framed likeness on the desk. It seemed like we were in Ysaÿe's own workshop in Brussels. And Mr. Gingold, who has assumed a large role in the development of violin players from all over the world, seemed like a true to life replica of his Master.

We spent an hour or so discussing Ysaÿe; the violin Sonatas of Debussy and Bloch; we brought him up to date with the progress we were making with a large scale biography of Bronislaw Huberman and a fair-sized monograph on Ysaÿe, and then we asked him to talk to us about the Queen Elisabeth Competitions.

We furnished him with a small outline, several questions, and switched on the tape recorder:

"No, I don't quite think it's going exactly in the direction Ysaÿe intended . . . I am sure he wouldn't have put all the stress on the virtuoso aspect of the event . . . as I told you once before, when I first met him to more or less audition for the privilege of studying with him, first of all, he made me comfortable and talked to me about many things, viz., studies, hobbies, family, etc. . . . he put me at ease . . . after a little time, we got serious and settled down to business . . . I played what I had prepared . . . Bach, Paganini, etc., followed by the Brahms Concerto . . . although I was more or less relaxed and at ease, I still had the feeling of awe at being there in front of the Master playing for him . . . He had painted such a picture of the violin for me that I was fearful of breaking the magic spell he had cast around the instrument . . . I felt I played well . . . I had quite a degree of composure, I was in control, so to speak . . . I may have been rough with my bow but I projected a convincing Brahms from my point of view . . . At the finish, there was no applause, no "Bravo," no laudatory comment of any kind . . . He merely looked at me and gently said "Now, mon petit, would you please play for me a three octave G major scale and its arpeggio both ascending and descending?" . . . I was a bit stunned because as he uttered these words, the realization suddenly came to me that everything I had played up to now had been a huge praeludium for the MOMENT OF TRUTH which was NOW!!! . . . The meter was now going to start running . . . But, I was prepared . . . and I played what he asked for as he kept glancing at my fingers and bow arm . . . he asked for more and I kept complying . . . in the end, I was accepted . . . I was quite young then and the full import of this didn't strike until years later. . . Ysaÿe was more interested in potential than what was already there . . . he stressed the basic and fundamentals rather than the opposite end of the spectrum . . . if you had these in hand and also the potential, there were no limits   to the distance you could cover . . . the competitions are almost completely becoming virtuoso factories . . . of course they had produced, among others, Oistrakh and Kogan . . . you know these two would have emerged from the crowd sooner or later.

How can you keep genius like this bottled up? . . . the competitions merely acted as a catalyst which hastened the discovery . . . Yes, I am sure Ysaÿe would have been greatly pleased with both of these . . . in fact, sometimes when I listen to Oistrakh play, and close my eyes, I feel like I must be listening to Ysaÿe. . . you know, of course that Ysaÿe and Mischa Elman were great admirers of each other . . . you should have heard the Bach Double concerto played by these two . . . and also just before I

Two views of Mischa Elman. Elman and Ysaÿe were close friends and concertized together. Their famous concert in the New York Hippodrome was given the same night as Heifetz'. See the book **Heifetz** *(Axelrod) for the complete story of that "competition."*

from
Mischa E[lman]

came to Ysaÿe, Nathan Milstein came to Belgium and wanted to study with the Master ... although highly flattered, Ysaÿe told him that he was already a finished product and ready to go forth on his own ... from the listings of the competitions, you notice how the Soviet violinists have dominated the lists since 1937 ... almost one third of all the medals awarded have gone to them ... in the ensuing years, their pupils are following in their footsteps ... the Soviet Government takes a very active interest in these competitions ... there is a very rigorous screening of prospective applicants ... only the top cream is allowed to enter ... every entrant is given the use of a very fine instrument, a whole entourage of coaches, accompanists, instrument maintenance and repair men, doctors, nurses, chefs, etc., is sent to the competition locale weeks before the actual start to let them get accustomed to the new surroundings and atmosphere ... by opening day, everyone is in tip top frame of mind and health ... their output is close to 100% psychologically ... and, bear in mind, they wouldn't be there if they were not ready ... percentagewise, they bring the most entrants ... thus increasing their chance of getting more winners in the final judging ... sometimes, there is a miscalculation ... in one year, they brought along one youngster just for the experience mainly ... he might get one of the lesser prizes if at all, but surely not more ... he fooled them all by playing his heart out and getting the top rating ... there are many side effects that are encountered ... you are judged on what you do there under the lights ... if you have any kind of a reputation and enter, you also are taking the chance that you could be eliminated in the preliminaries for any number of reasons ... nerves, illness, etc ... I once read an observation by a great concert violinist that this career requires the strength of an ox, the endurance of a horse, the tenacity of a bulldog, and the skin of a rhinoceros ... preparation is the key along with the physical staying power ... there are so many variables ... a superb rendition of Paganini in private can disintegrate and fall apart in public . . . conversely, clumsy and very difficult passages that just don't seem to come off in private, somehow come to life with the inspiration of a live audience . . .

There is a circus atmosphere to these playoffs that can make or break a performer . . . it depends on how realistic they are in their thinking and evaluation of themselves . . . I have known of violinists who think only of the prestige to be gained . . . they prepare solely for this particular event . . . nothing will ever take the place of intensive and adequate application after all the problems have been solved . . . the potential and the grounding must be there . . . experience is not something you buy in a store . . . Yes, I have been most gratified and happy to have had some of my own pupils like Jaime Laredo and Joseph Silverstein, both of whom I knew as youngsters, do very well in the competitions, as well as Endre Granat and Miriam Fried who came to me as mature artists . . . about the other side of the coin, so to speak, the judging . . . I am glad you ask me not to tread into any territory which is sacred to me and my many magnificent colleagues over the years . . . you know, my friend, much of the happenings in this area is so inviolate that even after all these years, not one person knows the hows and wherefors of the many decisions I made . . . the competitions usually have three sections, the preliminaries which eliminate quite a few, the semifinals which is the big judgement . . . the first is relatively simple, the next is quite difficult, and the last is the most complex of all . . . the jury is governed by a chairman who lays down the ground rules, confers with the judges, acts as liaison with the higher committees, calls special meetings, arbitrates when the need arises and makes final decisions . . . the judges, after they are apprised of the modus operandi to be employed, are on their own, so to speak . . . they act independently of each other . . . there is no comparing notes, discussions with each other, etc. . . . I would like to say that in all my years as a jury member on many competitions, I have ne-

Mischa Elman, 1918.

ver met a more dedicated group than all of my colleagues . . . some I have met only once or twice, others I run into constantly . . . other than the serious business at hand, we mingle socially and discuss all the goings on in the string world, the developments, the new literature trends, new pedagogic ideas, etc., besides enjoying each other's company at the many social functions that take place . . . the task of judging can be quite a strain . . . how does one differentiate between a 4th, 5th, 6th, or 8th place? . . . there is much balancing to be made.

Sometimes the choice is obvious, sometimes almost impossible . . . in some competitions, sometimes, it is agreed that the standards are not high enough for a first prize winner . . . in which case, it is so judged and the list starts with place number two . . . sometimes, a place is shared by more than one contestant . . . conversely, from the contestant's point of view . . . do they always specify that they were number 4 or number 7 or 9? . . . rather, most always they make a general statement that they were one of the winners . . . you ask about a judge's state of mind after listening to the Bach *Chaconne* or the Mendelssohn Concerto twenty five or thirty times in succession . . . of course we are fatigued . . . sometimes even bored . . . BUT all of a sudden number thirty-one steps up and lays his or her bow on the strings and starts the Bach Chaconne and suddenly the sky opens up . . . you are turned on for possibly the first time . . . all the fatigue is forgotten and you feel elated because a magic spell has taken hold of you . . . this is what you have been waiting for . . . this is the pot of gold at the end of the rainbow . . . you cast a fleeting glance at your colleagues around the room . . . they too are in the grasp of the spell . . . you know without comparing notes that there will be a mutual accord on this one . . . one violinist comes across the footlights to you, another does not . . . Sometimes you discover after the air clears that the winner has a very sketchy background and an even more sketchy repertoire . . . he or she is not ready to go further . . . they have to go back to school, so to speak . . . they

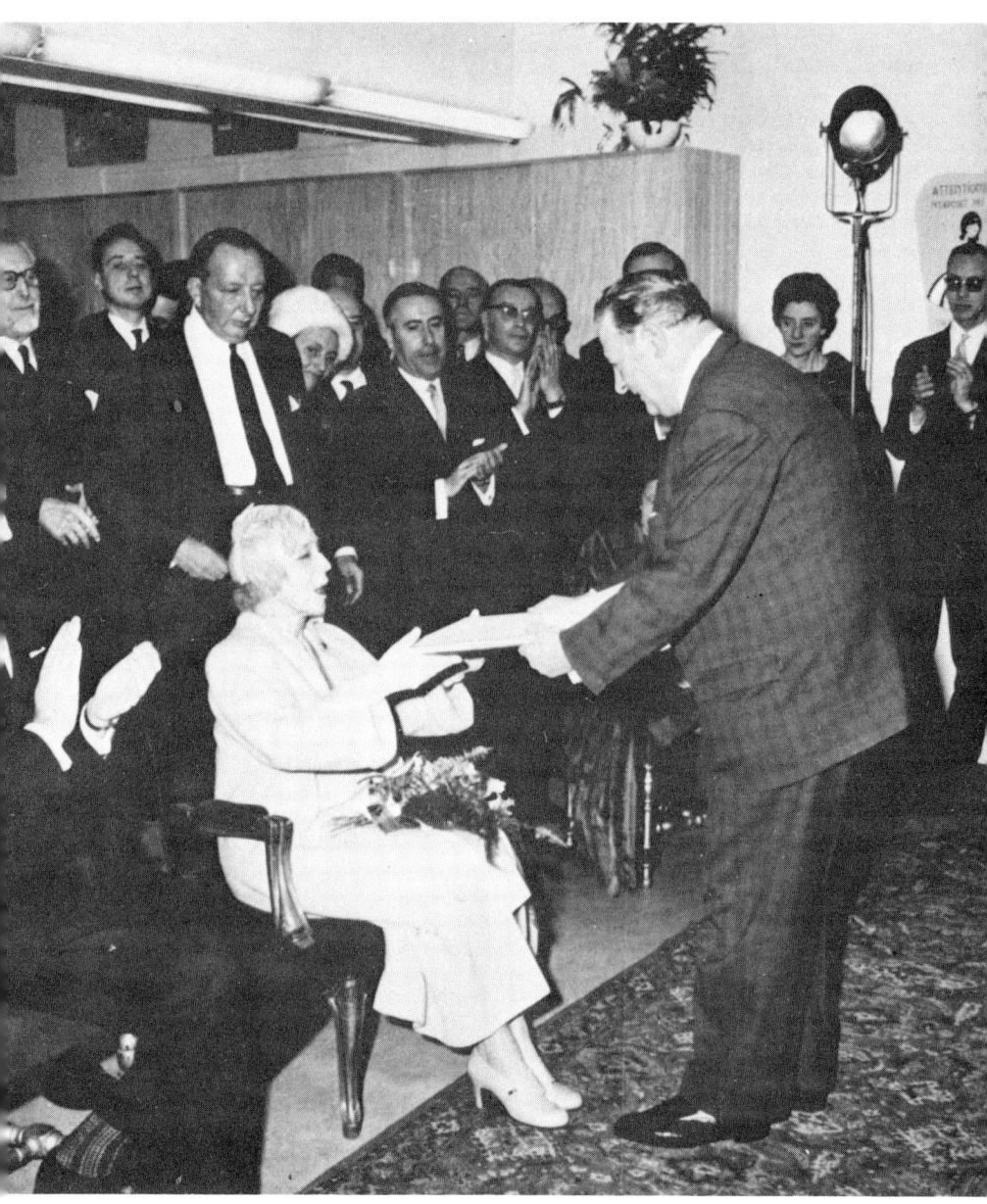

Antoine Ysaÿe presenting Queen Elisabeth with a copy of the Ysaÿe Commemorative Record in 1962.

On the facing page, the Glazunov String Quartet visits Brussels in 1926 to pay their homage to Ysaÿe. Unfortunately he could not be there, but his son Antoine was the center of attention.

just simply prepared for this event . . . if they were offered a concert tour as a result of their performance, they would have to turn it down because they are not prepared . . . some go back and teach, others join a symphony orchestra or a quartet . . . others enter another competition . . . of course times are different now but I am sure Ysaÿe envisioned something else for the chosen ones . . . a career as an interpreter . . . as a performing violinist . . . Yes, to be a juror is an awesome responsibility in all respects . . . it exerts a huge physical drain from one as well as a mental exhaustion . . . yet it is always a great honor and a privilege to be asked to serve . . . if only for the great adventure of possibly being present at a historic discovery of some major, undiscovered talent."

We have been in correspondence with Antoine Ysaÿe, the son of the Master, for five years or so. With the emergence recently of his new Biography of his Father, we wrote and asked him for some similar commentaries from his point of view about the Competitions. His replies are both from his letters and also extracted from his book:

"No, I don't think the direction the Queen Elisabeth Violin Competitions is taking is quite what Ysaÿe had envisioned as far back as 1904 . . . he thought in terms of an extraordinary panel that would uncover a major talent of a qualitative worth . . . and would be of great help to advance the chosen ones in a career . . . the end was not to be in pitting one against another, rather to uphold the best, who have innate gifts implanted by Nature and nurtured and developed by hard work . . . instant recognition by a panel of judges can also result in an opposite verdict that could eliminate one from the lists . . . with few exceptions, notably Oistrakh and Kogan, most of the world's great violinists have not undergone this test . . . Ysaÿe could be called the Messiah of the Violin . . . he had taken part in every type of performance . . . Cafes, theatres, outdoor concert halls, wedding and church performer, chamber musician, quartetist, orchestral player, symphony conductor, supreme concert violinist . . . he liked to think of himself as a simple country fiddler . . . he was more than aware of the vicious circle of circumstances the aspiring artist found himself encircled with . . . "He does not play in public, because he is not known, and he is not known because he does not play in public." . . . he always thought of the listening public as the final supreme judge . . . he always had the welfare of the young, the unemerged in mind . . . he also was not one to be impressed by surface glitter, rather by what could be found beneath the surface . . . in 1904, he wrote a letter to Theodore DuBois, in which he outlined his philosophies about curricula and certificates and diplomas attesting to the assimilation of such curricula by the students . . . he also indicated a desire to have appended to these diplomas a certification of performance which would be a separate entity and would be applied for in due course . . . coming from himself, like most great men, Ysaÿe didn't realize that his set standards would be for giants rather than ordinary mortals . . . During the Vieuxtemps' Centenary, he offered to be an adjudicator at a competition for the Prix Vieuxtemps but his offer was refused on the grounds of impracticality . . . he thought in terms of global rather than regional competition.

. . . It was only with the arrival of Queen Elisabeth and with his own disavowal of residency abroad and his definitive return to Belgium that these plans finally start to take form and shape . . . The Queen was tireless in her efforts to plan and execute the ideas of her Musical Director, for whom she had the greatest admiration . . . in his own humility, Ysaÿe never quite realized the impact and influence he was having on the history of the violin whose image he had raised to the most exalted level . . . while he was making this history, he seemingly was unaware of it . . . in the proposed curricula that he espoused, some of the requirements of the Queen Elisabeth Competitions of today are found, viz., a required reading of a work in manuscript which the con-

Jacques Ysaÿe, who often used the name "Jack Say," was a composer and orchestra leader. He was the son of Antoine, born 12 August 1922. On the facing page is Antoine in 1978, one year before he died. Photos courtesy of Leslie Sheppard.

testant would have to learn and assimilate from the manuscript alone, unadorned as it were with editorial bowings and fingerings, and without the benefit of advice and guidance from a teacher or coach . . . also, the contestant must be possessed of an extensive repertoire of all periods . . . and the contestant must be allowed to play the entire requirements without fragmentation . . . to him, the Violin was King and its Art of Performance should be the noblest and most sacred . . . he imbued his students with his doctrines which they in turn would pass on to their pupils . . . with characteristic simplicity, he once said . . . "History should not pass a judgement on me, rather on my pupils, their pupils and the pupils of their pupils." . . . LONG LIVE THE FIDDLE!!!!!"

The final resting place of Eugène Ysaÿe.

A Tribute To My Master

Written by Josef Gingold shortly before
the celebration of the Eugène Ysaÿe centenary.

July 16, 1958, will mark the one hundredth year of the birth of Eugène Ysaÿe. To the younger generation of violinists he is known as the composer of "Six Sonatas" for unaccompanied violin and other works for this instrument. Perhaps these young violinists may have also noticed that César Franck dedicated his Sonata to Ysaÿe, Chausson his Poeme and Debussy his String Quartet. It was an unforgettable experience to those of the older generation who were fortunate enough to have heard him play. Ysaÿe's violin mastery, his profound interpretation of all schools, his sensitive phrasing, his perfect use of rubato and his ethereal quality of tone plus a sense of rhythm unequaled by any other violinist made him the greatest idol among violinists and music lovers of his age.

It was my good fortune to have studied with Ysaÿe for two and a half years in Bruxelles and at Le Zoute, where he had his summer home. I had come from New York City where I had studied with an Auer pupil, Vladimir Graffman, and had a long string of concert activities under my belt. I prepared the first movement of the Brahms Concerto for my audition with Ysaÿe and was full of enthusiasm for the opening bars of this concerto when Ysaÿe calmly said, "Would you please play a G major, three-octave scale for me?" I was momentarily stunned by this request since all my faculties were concentrated on the concerto, but I did what was asked of me. This was followed by my having to play scales in every conceivable manner of bowing—it seemed like an eternity—when finally I was permitted to play the Brahms. After some encouraging words about my talent the Master agreed to teach me; needless to say, this filled my heart with great joy! He insisted that I get some tutoring in the French language saying that he would speak English to me for only the first two weeks, after that I was expected to converse in and understand the language of his country.

We worked only on string crossings at my first lesson. Ysaÿe found that I had the common fault of using too much wrist in crossing from one string to another and he demonstrated to me the Franco-Belgian method of using the forearm stroke to develop a

In 1968 the whole Ysaÿe family had a reunion and visited Eugene Ysaÿe's final resting place.

more powerful and sustained tone in connecting one string to another. Over a period of two months I studied scales, etudes and the fifth Concerto by Vieuxtemps. Then, only after he was completely satisfied with my bow arm, did I begin the study of repertoire. During the next two years I covered, among other things, the Beethoven Concerto, Bach, Brahms, Lalo, Mozart, Paganini, Bruch—(1st and 2nd and Scotch Fantasie)—Wieniawski, Vieuxtemps, Saint-Saëns, as well as some Sonatas, such as Franck, Beethoven's "Kreutzer," Lekeu, the Bach G minor, B minor, E major and Chaconne. I also studied the Chausson "Poeme"—and what inspiring lessons I had on this piece!—the Saint-Saëns "Rondo Capriccioso" and many other lesser works. I consider it especially good fortune to have been able to study the Six Sonatas and Ysaÿe's other compositions with the composer.

Josef Gingold with Eugene Ysaÿe. Gingold studied with Ysaÿe. On the facing page Gingold with Pavel Kogan and Kogan's star student Tiinaa-Kariina Tampere.

Joseph Szigeti. Ysaÿe dedicated his first solo sonata to Szigeti.

Ysaÿe's Solo Violin Sonatas

By Josef Gingold

The name of Eugène Ysaÿe (1858-1931) is hardly known to the younger generation of concert goers and musicians, yet in his day he was considered the world's greatest violinist. Besides being a supreme artist and a great virtuoso, he also possessed an extraordinary personal magnetism. A mysterious power seemed to flow from him, as it did from Paganini. But he was no little man, like the great Italian, thin and cadaverous, with the devil plainly visible behind him guiding his bow. Rather, he was a mountain of a man, six feet five inches tall, with a full mane, and a commanding presence.

The impression an artist makes upon his listeners somehow cannot be expressed to others. Books and articles can only attempt to describe it—they are unable to recreate it. One way a virtuoso can perpetuate the particular qualities of his art is by composing, by setting down on paper the musical symbols that can make it possible for succeeding generations of players to see the bare bones of his magic and cover them through their own intuition and the sense of style inherent in a carefully written musical text. Such violinists as Tartini, Corelli, Paganini, Spohr, Wieniawski and Vieuxtemps retain their influence over us in direct ratio to the vitality of their works. Present-day artists have the advantage of the recording medium with which to leave a lasting impression of their playing.

Ysaÿe has suffered the temporary setback that overtakes many composers and authors in the decade or two after death, but it is my opinion that his works will eventually become better known to us. It may be that certain of his shorter pieces or his arrangements will enjoy more or less success, but it is the *Six Sonatas for Violin Alone, Op. 27,* that will perpetuate his name. These sonatas were composed in 1923, and they have not yet received the general acceptance of the public or the attention they deserve. I can recommend them heartily to any violinist of virtuoso technique for his professional appearances. Any one of them would add both solid fare and novelty to his recital programs, as well as help him to develop the technical resourcefulness of his own playing. They

The author, Prof. Dr. Lev Ginsburg knew all the famous musicians who came to Russia. Top, facing page, with Joseph Szigeti; bottom facing page with Pablo Casals; above with Shostakovich and Karajan.

The Kreisler Quartet, 1935.

would also make excellent study material for artist students. The *Sonatas* are beautifully printed by Schott Frères in an edition authorized by the composer's son, Antoine, and distributed in America by the Peters Edition ($5.00). To the best of my knowledge, only one of the *Sonatas,* the first, has been recorded. That was by Zimbalist, some ten years ago, but it has since been withdrawn from the Victor catalogue. Here is an inviting field for some violinist and recording company seeking fresh repertory.

It was the young Joseph Szigeti's playing of a Bach Sonata that moved Ysaÿe to compose his sonatas. He told of the experience: "I found in Szigeti that rare combination of the musician and the virtuoso. As an artist he seemed conscious of a high mission into which he put all his faith, and he placed his technique entirely at the service of musical expression. When one hears such an artist who is able to accommodate his playing to the rectangular lines of the great classics as easily as he can to the expressive melodies of the romantics, one feels how absorbing it would be to compose a work for the violin while keeping ever before one the style of one particular violinist."

The latter remarks were made during a motor journey from Brussels to his country place in the Belgian coastal resort, Le Zoute. Upon his arrival there that evening he shut himself in his study. His meals were sent up and he worked steadily. The next evening he emerged radiant. "There," he exclaimed, "I have sketched ideas for six violin sonatas!" The final copies must have been completed with comparable dispatch, for his son tells us that "during the following days" they were finished and sent to the printer.

Each of the six sonatas is dedicated to a celebrated violinist. The first bears the name of Szigeti, who inspired the whole set. The models that are always in the background are, of course, the great unaccompanied violin sonatas of Bach, and Ysaÿe uses the same keys which Bach used in four of the set. The six Ysaÿe sonatas require a powerful bow arm on the part of the performer as well as a highly developed and sensitive ear.

The spirit of Bach hovers over the first sonata with its slow and stately beginning, its *Fugato,* its *Allegretto,* and *Finale.* Of peculiar interest is the whole-tone scale in sixths for which Ysaÿe was the first to discover the only really practical fingering. The printed music contains not only the fingering, as one would expect from a pioneering violinist who was bent on extending the technique of his instrument, but every possible accent, expression mark, and a series of original signs which are listed on the flyleaf. There are striking ponticello effects accompanied by left hand pizzicati, the grand arpeggios, prodigious double stopping, and chordal passages over three strings which must be played simultaneously.

The second sonata, dedicated to Jacques Thibaud, has an opening movement of great originality. Bach's influence had become so overwhelming that Ysaÿe could not shake himself free from it. He was on the point of giving up the whole project when he realized that the solution was not to reject Bach but to embrace him. His brilliant idea was to quote fragments of Bach's "Prelude to the Partita in E Major" with his own vigorous protest to his "Obsession"—for so he called the movement, which gradually progresses from exasperation to a lofty affirmation. The *Dies Irae* also has its place, as it does in each of the three succeeding movements of the sonata, notably in the magnificent coda of the demonic finale entitled "The Furies."

The shortest of the sonatas (it is only 8 minutes in length) and the most original of them all is the third, dedicated to Georges Enesco. For anyone who heard Ysaÿe play, this sonata would come closest to showing his approach to the violin. It is titled "Ballade," and its single movement opens with an introduction in the style of a recitative which is typical both of the way in which Ysaÿe would improvise and of the improvisatory quality he would bring to the music of other composers, making it sound new and fresh at every performance. The main movement shows the strong rhythmic impact of his playing, and the whole work is characteristic of his beauty and grace, the ease with which he could encompass the fingerboard and bring out inner voices. It was my privilege to give the first Brussels performance of this sonata in 1928, while I was studying with Ysaÿe, and I had the honor to introduce it to New York two years later.

Ysaÿe's favorite among the sonatas was the fourth, which he dedicated to Fritz Kreisler. It follows the Eighteenth-Century pattern of a series of dance movements and is tailor-made to exhibit the special qualities of Kreisler's art, the singing tone, the charm, and rhythmic incisiveness. The finale makes gracious and artful

Eugène Ysaÿe, from a photograph made during his conductorship of the Cincinnati Symphony in 1931.

reference to Kreisler's so-called classical transcriptions which he actually composed himself.

The first four sonatas are the most important of the set and the most likely to win a permanent place for themselves in the repertory. The least interesting is the fifth, dedicated to Ysaÿe's pupil and friend, who became second violinist of his quartet, Mathieu Crickboom. It may be called a study in sonority. One important feature is the use of quarter-tones which also appear in several of the other sonatas. The sixth, dedicated to the Spanish violinist Manuel Quiroga, is a *tour de force* of virtuosity. It makes use of the habañera rhythm and like the third sonata is in a single movement.

These sonatas are creations of monumental virtuosity. Their musical content, though not profound, is of excellent quality, interesting, and full of inspiration. The style is always noble, and the lofty musical purpose is aided—and never hindered—by the wonderful exploitation of the resources of the violin.

Ysaÿe always kept abreast of the foremost musical currents of his time. It was for him that Franck wrote his Violin Sonata, Debussy his Quartet, and Chausson his "Poème." In his capacity as Conductor of the Cincinnati Symphony Orchestra from 1918 until 1922, he was one of the first to introduce the orchestral works of Stravinsky, Malipiero, Schönberg, and Bartók. He believed it important to assimilate the new music of his time and to add its new principles to the body of technique at the disposal of musicians. He was a leader in the field of musical performance the like of which our generation does not know. Perhaps these sonatas can bridge the ever-widening gulf between the old and the new schools of technique so that our instrumentalists today may have the necessary equipment to progress along with our modern idiom.

The Final Homage

And now there remains only the final homage, the good-bye of Ysaÿe's own people, of the Belgian nation—for he was a national figure. He was even more, for his death marked the end of a period of history. If it is possible to determine the precise moment when the great romantic period which began with Paganini came to an end, that moment was on the 12th May, 1931. It had blossomed under Liszt; Ysaÿe gave it extended life and it died with him. Its end had indeed begun in August, 1914, but it had lingered as the autumn lingers, hoping not to die.

Everything about Ysaÿe was romantic: the little boy practising in the cellar at Liége and being overheard by Vieuxtemps, the young man throwing his boots into the fire as he undresses after hearing "Tristan and Ysolde," the bridegroom playing the Franck Sonata at his own wedding, his first glorious success in Paris, with Colonne embracing him and the audience gone mad, his passionate love of Louise—and his other loves, his musical compositions, his thoughts, his language, his appearance, his very death, with young Philip Newman arriving just in time to play one of his own Sonatas to him from the landing. And Newman, as though catching something of his hero's spirit, took off the strings from his violin after that last recital so that no music should ever sound from them again, and used them to bind the wreath he placed upon Ysaÿe's grave. It was a gesture after Ysaÿe's heart.

Ysaÿe when he was conductor of the Cincinnati Symphony.

After his death Ysaÿe's body lay in state for three days at his home while a continuous stream of people filed past to pay their respects. Then, on the 17th May, 1931, he who had played as a grimy little boy round the pit-heads of Liége and had grown up to conquer the world with a violin, was carried to his burial place in the cementery of Ixelles with all the pomp and splendo r of a State funeral. Slowly down the avenue goes the hearse drawn by four plumed horses, and followed by Ysaÿe's three sons. Vincent d'Indy and Jacques Thibaud, representing the French Government, Joseph Jongen and François Rasse, representing official music, Dr. Laruelle and Monsieur Maurice Vauthier, Belgian Minister of Arts, are the pall-bearers. Queen Elisabeth, his pupil, is there—"today the Queen came for her lesson and brought me a pot of caviare"—and members of the Belgian Court and Government. His decorations are carried ceremoniously on cushions, his violin is carried by his latest pupil, Remo Bolognini, the band of the

Regiment des Guides de la Garde Royale intones Beethoven's Funeral March. Half the population of Brussels is in the streets and the crowd so dense outside the church of La Sainte Trinité that the procession is held up until the gendarmerie can clear a way for it. Within the church a group of the master's pupils play the Adagio from his Poème Elégiaque.

Thus all that a nation can do to mourn a great man his own nation did for Eugène Ysaÿe. It ensured that his passing should be solemn and splendid. He was more than worth the gesture, for he had raised the name of Belgian music and musicians very high in the estimation of the World.

Honours and Decorations of Eugène Ysaÿe

Maître de Chapelle to His Majesty King Albert of the Belgians
Grand Officer of the Order of Leopold
Commander of the Legion of Honour
Grand Officer of the Order of Wasa
Grand Officer of the Order of the Nile
Grand Officer of the Order of Dannebrog
Commander of the Order of Christ of Portugal
Commander of the Crown of Italy
Commander of the Crown of Rumania
Commander of the Order of Isabella the Catholic
Gold Medal of the Philharmonic Society
Officer of the Academy
Knight of the Order of the Oak
Rumanian Medal of the Arts

Above and the facing page: **Le Soir Illustre** *ran a double-page spread covering the Ysaÿe funeral.*

Pendant plusieurs heures, la foule fut admise à défiler devant la dépouille d'Eugène Ysaye, dans la chapelle ardente.

Le lourd cercueil d'acajou est hissé sur le corbillard.

A gauche du corbillard : les cordons sont tenus par Vincent d'Indy, De Laruelle et Jacques Thibaud.

Derrière le corbillard, deux infirmières, puis les décorations du maître sur deux coussins, enfin un disciple d'Ysaye, M. Bolognini, portant le violon du grand virtuose.

Eugène Ysaye et son frère Théo.

Groupe fait à Liège, lors de la séance inaugurale du nouveau Conservatoire : de g. à dr. César Thomson, Martin Marsick, Eugène Ysaye ; assis, Massard qui fut le professeur d'Ysaye.

YSAŸE IS DEAD; MASTER VIOLINIST HAD DEBUT AT 7
N.Y. Herald Tribune May 13, 1931
***
Virtuoso Succumbs in Brussels at 72 After Premiere of Opera in March
***
First Visited U.S. in 1894
***
Wed Brooklyn Girl He Met While Conducting in Ohio
***

BRUSSELS, May 12—Eugene Ysaÿe, the great violinist who broke most musical traditions to become one of the foremost masters of that instrument, died at 4:30 a.m. today, after a long and wearing illness. He would have been seventy-three years old on July 16.

Death came two months after one of the greatest triumphs of his musical career—the debut of his opera, "Peter the Miner," written in Walloon dialect and presented at Liege in March. He himself was unable to attend, but Queen Elisabeth of the Belgians, who did go, arranged a radio broadcast so he could listen to the opera from his bedside.

Opera Received Ovation

The work received an ovation. Between acts Ysaÿe, speaking into a microphone in his room, thanked the performers for their interpretation of his work and the public for its enthusiastic reception of it.

As early as in the middle of 1928 Ysaÿe was suffering from phlebitis, and a year after had to undergo amputation of the right leg. He seemed to recover, but in 1930 became ill again. At the time of the presentation of the opera he was thought to be on the road to recovery but recently took a sudden turn for worse and failed to rally.

Funeral services will be held on Saturday.
***
(Reprinted from yesterday's late editions)
First Appearance at Seven

Eugene Ysaÿe, violinist and conductor, was seven years old when he made his first public appearance. For two years previously he had been instructed by his father, Nicolas Ysaÿe, and when he entered the Liege Conservatory he studied the violin under Massart and harmony with Dupuis. In the conservatory exercises, however, he won only the second prize, and as a youth he did not attract much attention.

He was born at Liege in July, 1858. When he was fifteen he had the good fortune to study under Wieniawski, and later he came into contact with most of the great masters of the nineteenth century. His individual technique brought him enemies as well as friends, and it was many years before his title to fame was assured. Cesar Franck, however, dedicated his only sonata to Ysaÿe for whom it had been composed. Joseph Joachim, the greatest master of the violin in his generation, listened in silence when Ysaÿe first played before him and remarked: "I never heard the violin played like that before."

Aided by Government

After three years with Wieniawski, Ysaÿe had a stroke of good fortune when Henri Vieuxtemps heard him play one of his concertos at Antwerp. The master was so impressed with the young man's talents that he used his influence to obtain a special government subsidy that enabled Ysaÿe to continue his studies three years longer.

In 1879 Ysaÿe played at concerts in Cologne and Aix-la-Chapelle and made the acquaintance of Ferdinand Hiller, the distinguished pianist and composer, who took a great interest in him and obtained for him an engagement to play Mendelssohn's concerto at a festival of the Gurzenich concerts at Cologne. In 1880 he was appointed leader of the Bilse Orchestra in Berlin.

In 1883 he settled in Paris, where he enjoyed the friendship of Franck and Vincent d'Indy, but after three years he accepted the post of violin professor at the Brussels Conservatoire, where he remained intermittently until 1898.

It was in this period that he formed his famous quartet with Marchot, Van Hout and J. Jacob and founded the Ysaÿe Orchestral Concerts at Brussels which considerably augmented both his reputation and his finances. He first visited America in 1894, and toured here subsequently with great success. He declined an invitation to succeed Seidl as conductor of the New York Philharmonic in 1898, but accepted the leadership of the Cincinnati Symphony Orchestra in 1919. He remained in this position three years, but resigned when dissension arose among members of the orchestra because of alleged favoritism.

He first succeeded in impressing the Berlin critics in 1899 by a striking performance of Bach's Concerto in E, at a Philharmonic concert conducted by Nikisch. His free rendering of Bach was recognized as containing elements of beauty which attracted even audiences accustomed to the more austere rendering of German artists. His famous rendering of Beethoven's Concerto in D, which won him admirers in every musical center in Europe, is an equally fine illustration of his distinctive talent. He made his first appearance in England in 1889 with this piece.

In 1913 Ysaÿe was appointed musical director to the Belgian court, and in the early days of the war he fled before the invasion of the German armies. He returned to Brussels after his resignation of the leadership of the Cincinnati Orchestra.

Modest and Unspoiled

When Ysaÿe first appeared in America he was a mature artist, recognized leader of the Brussels school of violinists, and honored by many decorations bestowed by royalty. But with it all he was modest and unspoiled. While he was touring California he was asked for an autograph copy of a few measures of his original cadenza to the Beethoven Concerto, but he declared that he disliked the idea of an original cadenza to Beethoven's work—that it was much better to omit it as it was no part of the concerto. "In original cadenzas by virtuosi," he said, "we find too much violin and too little music."

His compositions include six violin concertos, variations on a theme by Paganini and a number of smaller violin pieces. He owned a fine collection of French violins, and at one time played a Stradivarius, which was, however, stolen from him in the artists' room of a concert hall in St. Petersburg in 1908. When he first appeared in a New York concert he played a G.B. Guadagnini of exceptional merit, but for some years past his solo instrument was a very fine J. Guarneri del Gesu.

Ysaÿe married twice. His first wife, daughter of a Belgian army officer, died unexpectedly in Brussels February 13, 1924. He was married again July 9, 1927, at Le Zoute, Belgium, to Miss Annette Dincin, forty-four years his junior, the daughter of Dr. Herman Dincin, of 125 Prospect Park, Brooklyn. Miss Dincin met Ysaÿe in 1920 while he was conductor of the Cincinnati Symphony Orchestra. She became one of his pupils and has appeared in concerts both in the United States and abroad.

Ysaÿe had three sons, Gabriel, Antoine and Theo, and a daughter, Carrie. Another daughter died several months ago.

Ysaÿe in 1929.

YSAŸE'S FATHER-IN-LAW
PAYS TRIBUTE TO VIOLINIST
★★★
Dr. Dincin of Brooklyn Says Daughter Will Carry on Work

Dr. Herman Dincin, father-in-law of Eugene Ysaÿe, said yesterday at his home in Brooklyn: "His death grieves me very greatly as it must every music lover in the world. I had so looked forward to seeing him on these shores, as he had promised me faithfully he would visit America this year. My daughter will carry on for him. What he left unfinished, she will try to complete."

Since his daughter married the great violinist, the two had worked at their music together, he said, and she assisted Ysaÿe materially in the writing of his last opera. The two appeared together in Germany and Spain and once gave a series of concerts in Switzerland. Both Ysaÿe and his wife were soloists with the symphony orchestra which Ysaÿe directed and gained distinction for the presentation of the Bach Concerto.

"Ysaÿe," Dr. Dincin continued, "was a lovable as well as a great man. He was a gentleman of great knowledge and it was a pleasure to talk to him about anything. He seemed to sense that the end was coming, for up to the very last day, my wife said, he continued to work in a feverish haste, trying to finish unfinished music. I am sad that he couldn't have made his last appearance in this country. He always was so well received here. In 1912, he gave 118 concerts in America during one tour. Kreisler said one time that he was the greatest of the living violinists. Ysaÿe dedicated one of his operas to him."

Dr. Dincin plans to go to Brussels by the next liner.

EUGENE YSAYE, VIOLINIST, DEAD
New York Sun May 12, 1931
World Renowned Musician Passes Away in
Brussels in His Seventy-third Year.

BRUSSELS, May 12 (A.P.).—Eugene Ysaye, who broke most of the traditions of the violin to become one of the world's great masters of that instrument, died at 4:30 A.M. today after a long and wearing illness. He would have been 73 years old July 16.

Death came two months after one of the greatest triumphs of his career as a musician, the debut of his opera, "Peter the Miner," written in Walloon dialect, at Liege last March. He himself was unable to attend but Queen Elisabeth, who did go, arranged a radio broadcast so that he could hear the opera from his bed. The work was given an ovation.

As early as the middle of 1928 Ysaye was suffering from diabetes phlebitis, and a year later had to undergo amputation of his right leg. He seemed to recover, but late in 1930 became ill again. At the time of presentation of his opera he was thought to be on the road to recovery, but recently took a sudden turn for the worse from which he never rallied.

Married Brooklyn Girl

Ysaye was married twice, his first wife dying in 1924. His second wife was an American girl, forty-four years his junior, Miss Annette Dincin, daughter of Dr. Herman Dincin of 125 Prospect Park West, Brooklyn. He took her first as a pupil and later married her at Le Zoute, a Belgian seaside resort, on July 9, 1927.

Miss Dincin met Ysaye in 1920 while he was conductor of the Cincinnati Symphony Orchestra. After hearing her play, her aptitude for the violin was so evident to him that he

Two ancient photographs of Joachim.

invited her to become one of his pupils. Miss Dincin continued her studies in the United States for two years and then went to Brussels to begin her instruction with Ysaye.

Although he made his first public appearance as a violinist at the age of 7, Ysaye as a youth did not attract much attention.

There was some difference of opinion as to whether the young musician possessed extraordinary ability and talent. Opinion still was divided after Ysaye appeared for the first time before Joseph Joachim, often called in his time "the greatest of living violinists."

Ferdinand Hiller, celebrated pianist, recognized genius in Ysaye, introduced him to Joachim, and arranged to have the young man play for the great master. Hiller accompanied his protege. Joachim listened in silence and when Ysaye concluded, his only remark was "I never heard the violin played like that before."

It was an ambiguous comment, but whether it was tinged with praise or blame it was regarded as illustrating the salient feature of the art of Ysaye—his originality in technic and in his conception and treatment of music.

Born at Liege

Ysaye was born July 16, 1858, at Liege in a district of Belgium, the inhabitants of which displayed much predilection for string music. His early lessons were given him by his father, Nicolas Ysaye, beginning when the son was 5 years of age. Later he studied at the conservatory of his native town, the violin under Rodolphe Massart and harmony under Michael Dupuis.

After three years with Henri Wieniawski the young violinist struck his first bit of good fortune when Henri Vieuxtemps heard Ysaye play one of his concertos at Antwerp. The master was so impressed with the young man's talent that he used his influence to obtain a special Government subsidy that enabled Ysaye to continue his studies three more years. During that time he received many private lessons from Vieuxtemps.

The rise of Ysaye to a place of eminence among the masters of the violin began with his leadership in 1880 of Bilse's orchestra in Berlin. The success of the orchestra added to his reputation and after a year he appeared in concert until 1886. Then he became professor of violin at the Brussels Conservatory and remained in that position ten years. Meanwhile he founded the Ysaye Orchestral Concerts, which achieved artistic and financial success.

Conducted Cincinnati Symphony

Ysaye made his first trip to the United States in 1894. He was engaged as conductor of the Cincinnati Symphony Orchestra in 1919 and remained for three years. Dissension arose among the members of the orchestra because of alleged favoritism shown to some by the conductor. His answer was his resignation which was a surprise to the directors who had just voted him an increase in salary. Returning to Brussels, Ysaye resumed his work at the conservatory of that city.

During his frequent tours Ysaye met many who appeared as musical enemies because of his original style of playing and he often was referred to as a musical colorist. He played almost invariably from memory and was known on many occasions to memorize a new piece with no further knowledge of it than that gained from a few hours of reading the manuscript.

Ysaye composed a number of concertos for violin as well as numerous less pretentious numbers as violin solos.

In February of this year Ysaye was appointed inspector-general of Belgium's four State-subsidized theaters and of the country's sixteen recognized symphonic societies. He also held the title of Chapel Master to the Queen.

Ysaye's first public appearance after amputation of his leg was as honor guest at a dinner given by King Albert at the royal palace, at which president Doumergue of France was present. The French president conferred upon him the decoration of Commander of the Legion of Honor. About a year before Queen Elisabeth of the Belgians had decorated him with the cross of a grand officer of the Order of the Nile, which King Fuad of Egypt had conferred upon him when he was visiting Belgium.

Funeral services for the great violinist will be held on Saturday.

Ysaye Planned Trip Here

The death today at Brussels of Eugene Ysaye, one of the world's greatest violinists, canceled his long anticipated visit to this country.

Dr. Herman Dincin, Brooklyn physician, and father-in-law of the artist, said today that his daughter Annette and the violinist had planned a trip to America since a year ago, but the health of the violinist forbade it.

Since the successful debut of Ysaye's opera, "Peter the Miner," hailed as one of the major triumphs of his musical career, Ysaye and his young wife have worked on its translation into French hoping to present the work before American audiences.

Dr. Dincin said that since their marriage Ysaye and his wife have worked together and she assisted him materially with his last opera. They also appeared together in the musical centers of Germany and Spain, etc. They gained particular distinction for their presentation of Bach Concerto for two violins.

"My daughter will carry on for Ysaye. What he left unfinished she will try to complete," said Dr. Dincin, today. "Ysaye's death grieved us very greatly, as it must every music lover in the world. I had so looked forward to seeing him on our shores, as he had promised many faithfully he would visit America this year."

The Recordings of Eugène Ysaÿe

By John Anthony Maltese

Yehudi Menuhin once remarked that the violin playing of Eugène Ysaÿe was "as exuberant, as flamboyant, as elegant in his phrasing, and as incredibly charming and alluring as only the fusion of the Belgian and French schools could produce." Indeed, Ysaÿe is recognized as one of the landmark violinists of his time. Pablo Casals is even reported to have said that he had never heard a violinist play in tune until Ysaÿe.

The great British playwright and music critic George Bernard Shaw (alias Corno di Bassetto) described Ysaÿe's playing as "bumptious." That very self-assertive, extravagant style is, in fact, quite evident in his recordings. Ysaÿe recorded only fifteen selections (and only thirteen of those were released to the public). The recordings consist of relatively minor works. The short playing time of each disc prohibited any lengthy selections from being considered. The only offering of a truly major work is the Finale (Allegro molto vivace) from the Mendelssohn violin concerto. And even that is cut and played with quite dazzling speed so as to fit into the alloted time.

The recordings were made by Ysaÿe in New York City for the Columbia Record Company in 1912. For many years Ysaÿe had steadfastly refused to record. When he finally acquiesced it was for the munificent sum of thirty-thousand dollars in addition to 33% of the profits. The money, he said, was for his grandchildren.

Ysaÿe's son, Antoine, recalled in his book, *Ysaÿe*, that his father was quite taken by these recordings. He was, said Antoine, "often found by his family listening to his own records. 'Listen,' he would say, 'I missed the cut there, but you see how I returned to the beat?' Or again, when listening to his playing of the last movement of the Mendelssohn concerto: 'I never thought I played it as well as that! Listen. Most violinists rush it, they will take the finale too fast—like a breathless gallop, too wild altogether. What is needed is the maintenance of a steady rhythm, and a careful observance of the time. Try it with a metronome and you will see what I mean. You will find that I am steady throughout."

Yehudi Menuhin when he was presented to Ysaÿe. 1931.

The Cincinnati studio of Rudolf Wurlitzer. Efrem Zimbalist is shown here with the Vuillaume he just purchased from Wurlizter. Ysaÿe and Wurlitzer were very close friends at the time of his conductorship in Cincinnati.

From the Ysaÿe scrapbook made available by Marianne Wurlitzer.

Ysaÿe's accompanist for these recordings was Camille Decreus, a noted pianist who studied under Saint-Saens and others at the Conservatoire in Paris at the same time as another noted accompanist, Andre Benoist.

Ysaÿe had first come to the United States in 1894. In a letter to his wife from New York City (dated November 26) Ysaÿe spoke of his success: "I am advancing along a flower-strewn path from triumph to triumph. My success has been brought home to me in countless ways; both big and little things seem to prove to me that I have now reached the point at which I aimed. I am not making any concessions to taste. I am playing all the most important works, and it is perhaps just that that has enabled me to conquer the American public . . . I can't give you any idea of . . . the emotion with which I am filled at every concert, but I want you to know that if it is true that the public has been conquered by me, it is even more true that I have been conquered by it, completely and absolutely."

Ysaÿe returned to America again in 1897, when he gave a series of concerts with the great pianist Raoul Pugno. In 1898 he was offered the position of conductor of the New York Philharmonic (to succeed Anton Seidl), but he refused. He returned to Belgium that summer and did not return to the United States again until 1904. That tour consisted of one hundred and twenty concerts. He toured again in 1912-13 and 1913-14, but by now he was beginning to be plagued by arthritis. When he came back for his final American tour in 1916 the difference in his playing was quite noticeable. The difficulties he was experiencing with his bow arm and left hand led to his decision to accept the position of conductor of the Cincinnati Symphony Orchestra in 1918.

It was in this capacity as conductor that he returned to the recording studios. He made a series of records for Columbia with the Cincinnati Symphony. In fact, their recording of Rimsky-Korsakoff's "Scheherazade" included a violin solo played by Ysaÿe himself, although the record made no note of that. At the end of his contract with Cincinnati in 1922, Ysaÿe returned to Europe. There he occasionally played the violin and conducted some concerts, but his health was rapidly failing. He died on May 12, 1931.

★★★★★★★

Sources of Information:
Antoine Ysaÿe and Bertram Ratcliffe. *Ysaÿe: His Life, Work and Influence.* London: William Heinemann, Ltd., 1947.

James Creighton, Archivist at the University of Toronto.

★★★★★★★

Jacksonville, Alabama
December 1978

The Recordings of Eugène Ysaÿe

Part I: The Solo Recordings (Commercial Releases)
BRAHMS, JOHANNES—Hungarian Dance no. 5, in F sharp major (arr. Joachim). Camille Decreus, piano. 78 RPM: Columbia 7106 and 36524; LP: Delta TQD-3033.
CHABRIER, EMMANUEL—Scherzo-Valse (arr. Loeffler). Camille Decreus, piano. 78 RPM: Columbia 7111 and 36514; LP: Delta TQD-3033.
DVORAK, ANTONIN—Humoresque (arr. Wilhelmj). Camille Decreus, piano. 78 RPM: Columbia 7102 and 36908; LP: Delta TQD-3033.
FAURE, GABRIEL—Berceuse. Camille Decreus, piano. 78 RPM: Columbia 7112 and 36519; LP: Delta TQD-3033.
KREISLER, FRITZ—Caprice Viennois. Camille Decreus, piano. 78 RPM: Columbia 7115 and 36525; LP: Delta TQD-3033.
MENDELSSOHN, FELIX—Concerto in E Minor: Allegro molto vivace (3rd movement). Camille Decreus, piano. 78 RPM: Columbia 7108 and 36520; LP: Delta TQD-3033.
SCHUBERT, FRANZ—Ave Maria. Camille Decreus, piano. 78 RPM: Columbia 7103 and 36907; LP: Delta TQD-3033.
VIEUXTEMPS, HENRI—Rondino. Camille Decreus, piano. 78 RPM: Columbia 7110 and 36523; LP: Delta TQD-3033.
WAGNER, RICHARD—Albumblatt (arr. Wilhelmj). Camille Decreus, piano. 78 RPM: Columbia 7114 and 36526; LP: Delta TQD-3033.
WAGNER, RICHARD—Prize Song (arr. Wilhelmj). Camille Decreus, piano. 78 RPM: Columbia 7107 and 36513; LP: Delta TQD-3033.
WIENIAWSKI, HENRYK—Mazurka No. 1, in G major ("Obertass"). Camille Decreus, piano. 78 RPM: Columbia 7109 and 36521; LP: Delta TQD-3033.
WIENIAWSKI, HENRYK—Mazurka No. 2, in D Major ("Dudziarz"). Camille Decreus, piano. 78 RPM: Columbia 7109 and 36521; LP: Delta TQD-3033.
YSAŸE, EUGÈNE—Mazurka No. 3, in B Minor ("Lointaine-Passe"). Camille Decreus, piano. 78 RPM: Columbia 7113 and 36516; LP: Delta TQD-3033.

Part II: The Solo Recordings (Unissued Discs)

SCHUMANN, ROBERT—Abendlied (arr. Wilhelmj). Camille Decreus, piano. 78 RPM: Columbia 36515 (unissued).
YSAŸE, EUGÈNE—Reve d'enfant. Camille Decreus, piano. 78 RPM: Columbia 36522 (unissued).

(a) The Published Works of Ysaÿe

Name		Opus	Publisher
Two Mazurkas		10	Schott Freres, Brussels
Poème Elégiaque	Violin and Orchestra	12	Breitkopf, Leipzig
Lointain Passé		13	Breitkopf, Leipzig
Scène au Rouet	Violin and Orchestra	13	A. Ysaÿe, Brussels
Chant d'Hiver	Violin and Orchestra	15	Enoch, Paris
Rêve d'Enfant	Violin and Orchestra	16	A. Ysaÿe, Brussels
Méditation	Cello and Orchestra	16	A. Ysaÿe, Brussels
Trio de Concert	Two Violins and Viola	19	A. Ysaÿe, Brussels
Berceuse	Violin and Orchestra	20	A. Ysaÿe, Brussels
Extase	Violin and Orchestra	21	A. Ysaÿe, Brussels
Sérénade	Cello and Orchestra	22	A. Ysaÿe, Brussels
Les Neiges d'Antan	Violin and Orchestra	23	A. Ysaÿe, Brussels
Divertimento	Violin and Orchestra	24	A. Ysaÿe, Brussels
Exil.	For Strings without Basses	25	A. Ysaÿe, Brussels
Amitié	Two Violins and Orchestra	26	A. Ysaÿe, Brussels
Six Sonatas for Violin solo		27	A. Ysaÿe, Brussels
1. G Minor	J. Szigeti		
2. A Minor	J. Thibaud		
3. E Minor	G. Enesco		

4. D Minor	F. Kreisler		
5. G Major	M. Crickboom		
6. E Major	M. Quiroga		
Sonata	For Cello	28	A. Ysaÿe, Brussels
Poème Nocturne	For Violin and Cello	29	A. Ysaÿe, Brussels
Harmonies du Soir	Quartet	31	A. Ysaÿe, Brussels
Fantaisie	For Violin and Orchestra	43	A. Ysaÿe, Brussels
Caprice d'Après l'Etude en Forme de Valse de Saint-Saëns		—	Durand, Paris
Paraphrase of a theme of Mendelssohn			A. Ysaÿe, Brussels

(b) Arrangements made by Ysaÿe

Name		Publisher
1. Nardini-Ysaÿe	Sonata in D Major	A. Ysaÿe, Brussels
2. Chopin-Ysaÿe	Eight Waltzes	A. Ysaÿe, Brussels
3. Handel-Ysaÿe	Aria	A. Ysaÿe, Brussels
4. Bach-Ysaÿe	Aria	A. Ysaÿe, Brussels
5. Pasquali-Ysaÿe	Sonata in A Minor	A. Ysaÿe, Brussels
6. Locatelli-Ysaÿe	Sonata au Tombeau in A	A. Ysaÿe, Brussels
7. Bach-Ysaÿe	Inventions	A. Ysaÿe, Brussels
8. Vivaldi-Ysaÿe	Sonata	A. Ysaÿe, Brussels
9. Vivaldi-Ysaÿe	Concerto in G Minor	A. Ysaÿe, Brussels
10. Viotti-Ysaÿe	Cadenza for Concerto No. 22.	A. Ysaÿe, Brussels

Works not included in this list are in MSS. only.

THE RECORDED COMPOSITIONS OF EUGENE YSAŸE

Compiled by John and John Anthony Maltese

The most complete set of Ysaÿe compositions available in one collection is found in EMI's release entitled "The Belgian Violin School" (C161-95897/900). Several violinists share the billing in this set with Edgard Doneux and the Orchestre de Chambre de la R.T.B. One should note that this recording is an import and therefore not widely distributed in this country. A fine recording which is easily obtainable is Ruggiero Ricci's performance of the complete sonatas (opus 27) for unaccompanied violin. These are Ysaÿe's most important (and most recorded) works. Each was dedicated to a fellow violinist (Joseph Szigeti, Fritz Kreisler, etc.). The third sonata is the most popular, an individual recording of which is available in this country by David Oistrakh (on Westminster). As one will note by scanning the discography, the majority of Ysaÿe's recorded compositions have been released in Europe. An excellent recording of the second sonata by Cornelia Vasile may be obtained on a Deutsche Grammophon import. A number of other performances are available from the Musical Heritage Society, and on such imports as Mezhdunarodnaya Kniga, Melodyia, Muza, and Qualiton.

The following discography is a collaborative effort between father and son. Much of the preliminary research was provided by my father, John, who utilized his vast collection of violin recordings in Jacksonville, Alabama. Without his generous assistance I could never have found the time to compile the following pages.

The compositions are listed alphabetically in bold print. Listed under the title are the individual recordings of that work, arranged alphabetically by the principal performer's last name. To the right may be found the names of assisting artists, the record's label, and the catalogue number of the recording. The country in which the record is released is listed in parentheses (except in the case of the United States). Unless otherwise noted all recordings are LPs.

Durham, North Carolina
December 20, 1979

BERCEUSE DE L'ENFANT PAUVRE, OP. 20
(1) Bezrodny, I. (violin); A. Makarov (piano). Mezhdunarodnaya Kniga D3400 (Russia).
(2) Raskin, M.; Orchestre de Chambre de la R.T.B., E. Doneux (conductor). EMI C161-95897/900 (France).

CHANT D'HIVER, OP. 15
(1) Debot, M. (Violin); Orchestre de Chamber de la R.T.B., E. Doneux (conductor). EMI C161-95897/900 (France).
(2) Rosand, A.; Radio Luxembourg Symphony Orchestra, L. Froment (conductor). Candide CE 31054.

CONCERTO D'APRES DEUX POEMES, OP. 18/19
(1) Raskin, M. (violin); Orchestre de Chambre de la R.T.B., E. Doneux (conductor). EMI C161-95897/900 (France).

EXTASE IN E FLAT (POEME NO. 4), OP. 21
(1) Fain, R. (violin); I. Zaitseva (piano). Mezhdunarodnaya Kniga D5572/3 (Russia).
(2) Fain, R.; Moscow State Philharmonic Symphony Orchestra, K. Kondrashin (conductor). Mezhdunarodnaya Kniga D016148, S01004 (Russia).
(3) Oistrakh, D.; V. Yampolsky (piano). Bruno BR14018.
(4) Oistrakh, D.; V. Yampolsky. Angel 35354.

FANTAISIE, OP. 32
(1) Sroubek, K. (violin); J. Hala (piano). Supraphon SUA10580, SUAST50580, SV8169 (Czechoslovakia).

HARMONIES DU SOIR, OP. 31 (FOR 2 VIOLINS, VIOLA, CELLO AND STRINGS)
(1) E. Koch and H. Koch (violins); P. Lambert (viola); G. Mallach (cello); Les Solistes de Liege, Lemaire (conductor). Alpha CL 3007, CL4007 (France).

LES NEIGES D'ANTAN, OP. 23
(1) Werthern, R. (violin); Orchestre de Chambre de la R.T.B., E. Doneux (conductor). EMI C161-95897/900 (France).

Ruggiero Ricci was the only person (up to 1980) to record all of the Ysaÿe sonatas for solo violin. Ricci has recorded more music than any other violinist up to date. His technical and interpretative powers are legend.

A reproduction of the album cover for Ricci's recording of Ysaÿe's 6 Sonatas for Violin Solo, Op. 27.

MAZURKA NO. 1, IN G MAJOR, OP. 11 (DANSE SOUVENIR)
(1) Danchenko, V. (violin); M. Khylstov (piano). Mezhdunarodnaya Kniga D021594 (Russia).
(2) Snitkovsky, S.; L. Iosiovich. Mezhdunarodnaya Kniga D08788 (Russia).

MAZURKA NO. 2, IN A MAJOR, OP. 11
(1) Danchenko, V. (violin); M. Khylstov (piano). Mezhdunarodnaya Kniga D021594 (Russia).
(2) Kogan, L.; A. Mitnik. Mezhdunarodnaya Kniga D5072, D028117/8 (Russia).

MAZURKA NO. 3, IN B MINOR, OP. 11 (LOINTAIN-PASSÉ)
(1) Bouissinot, M. (violin); G. Defresne (piano). Festival FCD84 (Australia).
(2) Danchenko, V.; M. Khylstov. Mezhdunarodnaya Kniga D021594 (Russia).
(3) Odnoposoff, R.; with piano. HMV C2966 (England-78 rpm).
(4) Oistrakh, I.; N. Zertsalova. Mezhdunarodnaya Kniga D08831/2, S0225/6 (Russia).
(5) Pikaisen, V.; L. Kollegorskaja. Mezhdunarodnaya Kniga D2807 (Russia).
(6) Pikaizen, V.; Moscow State Philharmonic Symphony Orchestra, D. Oistrakh (conductor). Mezhdunarodnaya Kniga D023102 (Russia).
(7) Werthen, R.; Orchestre de Chambre de la R.T.B., E. Doneux (conductor). EMI C161-95897/900 (France).
(8) Ysaÿe, E.; C. DeCreus. Columbia 7113, 36516 (78 rpm); Delta TQD 3033 (England); Masters of the Bow MB-1026 (Canada).

POEME ELEGIAQUE IN D MINOR, OP. 12 (POEME NO. 1)
(1) Markov, A. (violin); O. Yablonskaya (piano). Mezhdunarodnaya Kniga D08265/6 (Russia).
(2) Mikhlin, A.; Y. Seidel. Mezhdunarodnaya Kniga D019331 (Russia).

(3) Oistrakh, D.; V. Yampolsky. Bruno BR14018; Decca DL9882; Mezhdunarodnaya Kniga D5082, D028807/8 (Russia).
(4) Petrosyan, I.; with piano. Mezhdunarodnaya Kniga D024381/2 (Russia).
(5) Raskin, M.; Belgian National Orchestra, Defossez (conductor). Decca FA143337 (France).
(6) Van Neste, C.; Orchestre de Chambre de la R.T.B., E. Doneux (conductor) EMI C161-95897/900 (France).

REVE D'ENFANT, OP. 14

(1) Debot, M. (violin); Orchestre de Chambre de la R.T.B., E. Doneux (conductor). EMI C161-95897/900.
(2) DeGroot, D.; P.B. Kahn (piano). HMV C903 (England-78 rpm).
(3) Dubois, A.; F. Goeyens. Columbia D15175 (78 rpm).
(4) Elman, M.; M. van Gool. HMV DB1594 (England-78 rpm); Victor 7574 (78 rpm).
(5) Grumiaux, A.; D. Varsi. Phillips 6500814.
(6) Odnoposoff, R.; with piano. HMV C2966 (England-78 rpm).
(7) Ricci, R.; K. Furstner. HMV DB4622 (England-78 rpm).
(8) Ysaÿe, E.; C. Decreus. Columbia 36522 (78 rpm); Masters of the Bow MB-1026 (Canada).

SCENE AU ROUET, OP. 13 (POEME NO. 2)

(1) Kogan, L. (violin); A. Mitnik (piano). Mezhdunarodnaya Kniga D7863, D028117/8 (Russia).
(2) Sroubek, K.; J. Halla. Supraphon SUA10580, SUAST-50580, SV8169 (Czechoslovakia).

(6) SONATAS, OP. 27 (VIOLIN UNACCOMPANIED) (COMPLETE)

(1) Bress, H. (violin). Alpha DB132 (France).
(2) Ricci, R. Candide 31085.

SONATA NO. 1, IN G MINOR (Á JOSEPH SZIGETI), OP. 27

(1) Danchenko, V. (violin). Mezhdunarodnaya Kniga D17635/6 (Russia).

(2) Octors, G. Gramola GLP2510 (Belgium).
(3) Zimbalist, E. HMV ED263/4 (England-78 rpm); Victor set M669 (78 rpm).

SONATA NO. 2, IN A MINOR (À JACQUES THIBAUD), OP. 27

(1) Castillo, J.F. del (violin). Fundacion Mito Juan Pro-Musica (Vol. I) (Venezuela).
(2) Grumlikova, N. Supraphon SUA10520, SV8252 (Czechoslovakia).
(3) Isakadze, L. Mezhdunarodnaya Kniga D021449/50 (Russia).
(4) Jakowicz, K. Muza SXL0522 (Poland).
(5) Kogan, L. Melodya CO719-20 (Russia).
(6) Mikhlin, A. Mezhdunarodnaya Kniga D019331 (Russia).
(7) Szenthelyi, M. Qualiton LPX11677 (Hungary).
(8) Vasile, C. Deutsche Grammophon 642106 (Germany).

SONATA NO. 3, IN D MINOR ("BALLADE") (À GEORGE ENESCO), OP. 27

(1) Accardo, S. (Violin). Victor SL20245 (Italy).
(2) Dembeck, J. CBC Radio Canada SM27 (Canada).
(3) Dubois, A. Columbia LCX104.
(4) Granat, E. Orion 73128.
(5) Gutnikov, B. Mezhdunarodnaya Kniga D010224, D010-325/8 (Russia).
(6) Gyarmati, V. Qualiton LPX1152 (Hungary).
(7) Harth, S. Iramac 6523 (Netherlands); Musical Heritage Society MHS 1531.
(8) Jakowicz, K. Muza SXL0522 (Poland).
(9) Lubotsky, M. Mezhdunarodnaya Kniga D014587/8 (Russia).
(10) Odnoposoff, R. Concert Hall CHS1175.
(11) Oistrakh, D. Colosseum CRLP150; Vanguard VRS6024.
(12) Oistrakh, D. Philips PHM500112, PHS900112.
(13) Oistrakh, I. Mezhdunarodnaya Kniga D08831/2, S0225/6 (Russia).
(14) Rabin, M. Angel 35305.
(15) Raskin, M. Decca FAIX3337 (France).
(16) Vinnikov, Z. Mezhdunarodnaya Kniga D21386 (Russia).

SONATA NO. 4, IN E MINOR (À FRITZ KREISLER), OP. 27
(1) Kocsis, A. (violin). Qualiton LPX1148 (Hungary).
(2) Malinin, V. Mezhdunarodnaya Kniga D6013 (Russia).
(3) Odnoposoff, R. HMV (unissued; England-78 rpm).
(4) Odnoposoff, R. Concert Hall CHS1175.
(5) Rabin, M. Angel 35305.

SONATA NO. 5, IN G MAJOR (À MATHIEU CRICKBOOM), OP. 27
(1) Granat, E. (violin). Orion 73128.

SONATA NO. 6, IN E MAJOR (À MANUEL QUIROGA), OP. 27
(1) Klimov, V. (violin). Supraphon SUF20004; Ultraphon DM5541 (Czechoslovakia).
(2) Lubotsky, M. Mezhdunarodnaya Kniga D014587/8 (Russia).
(3) Mikhlin, A. Mezhdunarodnaya Kniga D15343/4 (Russia).
(4) Petronio, F. Alpha DB34 (France).
(5) Sitkovetsky, J. Melodyia 06829/30 (Russia).
(6) Voicu, I. Electrecord ECE086 (Rumania).

SONATA, OP. 28 (FOR CELLO UNACCOMPANIED) (1928)
(1) Frezin, A. (cello). Protone 131.
(2) Sylvester, R. Desto 7169.

SONATA NO. 1, IN C MAJOR (FOR TWO VIOLINS)
(1) L. Kogan and E. Gilels (violins). Columbia CX1887, FCX-984 (England); Mezhdunarodnaya Kniga D012691/2, S0719/20 (Russia).

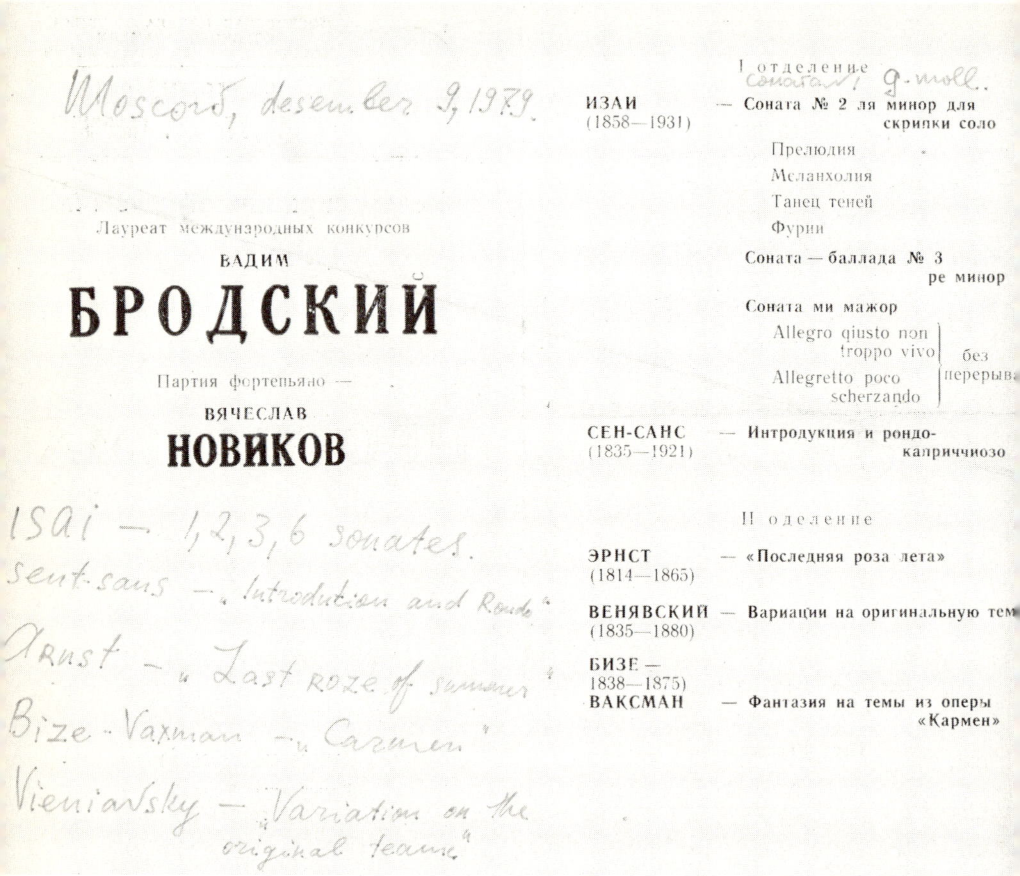

Handwritten annotations:

Moscow, desember 9, 1979

Isai — 1,2,3,6 sonates.
sent-sans — "Introdution and Rondo"
Arnst — "Last roze of summer"
Bize-Vaxman — "Carmen"
Vieniawsky — "Variation on the original team"

Printed program (Russian):

Лауреат международных конкурсов
ВАДИМ
БРОДСКИЙ

Партия фортепьяно
ВЯЧЕСЛАВ
НОВИКОВ

I отделение

(handwritten: sonata No 1, g-moll)

ИЗАИ — Соната № 2 ля минор для
(1858—1931)   скрипки соло
  Прелюдия
  Меланхолия
  Танец теней
  Фурии

Соната — баллада № 3
ре минор

Соната ми мажор
  Allegro qiusto non
    troppo vivo   без
  Allegretto poco   перерыв
    scherzando

СЕН-САНС — Интродукция и рондо-
(1835—1921)   каприччиозо

II отделение

ЭРНСТ — «Последняя роза лета»
(1814—1865)

ВЕНЯВСКИЙ — Вариации на оригинальную тем
(1835—1880)

БИЗЕ — Фантазия на темы из оперы
1838—1875   «Кармен»
ВАКСМАН

Vadim Brodsky, one of Russia's superstar violinists, winner of the Wieniawski Competition in 1977 and prize winner in the Tchaikovsky Competition of 1974, played this impossibly difficult program before Moscow's discerning musical public. The handwriting is Brodsky's and the program, which was performed to rave reviews in Moscow on December 9, 1979 consisted of four of Ysaÿe's Sonatas; Ernst's Last Rose of Summer, Etude No. 6; *Saint-Saëns' Introduction and Rondo Capriccioso, Bizet-Waxman Carmen Fantasy and Wieniawski's Variations on an Original Theme. Two of the Ysaÿe Sonatas were performed as encores.*

Facing page: Vadim Brodsky with conductor Arvid Jensen after their performance of the Tchaikovsky and Paganini concerti in 1974 in Moscow.

Eugene Ysaÿe, avid exponent of Brahms, photographed while recording one of the difficult passages of a Brahms' composition. Note the horn at the right used to convey the music to the recording apparatus which later enabled millions of people to hear the wonderful art of this great artist. Photo courtesy of Wurlitzer-Bruck, New York.

Index

Page number references set in italics, refer to illustrations.

A

Arazi, Ishaq, *16*, *486*, 487, 498
Auer, Leopold, 93, *97*, 178, *284*, 285, 393, 420, *455*, 467, 484, *489*, 492
Axelrod, Herbert R., *10*, 11, *14*, 97, 148, *149*, 360

B

Bach, Johann Sebastian (personal references and illustrations), 35, 53, 191, 291, 339, 367, 381, 382, 387, 391, 399, 403, 405, 425, 482, 504, 521, 530
Bach, (references to music pieces)
First Sonata for Solo Violin, 41, 335
Chaconne, 73, 294, *309*, 382
Concerto, 185, 288
Partita, 199
Concerto in E Major, 285, 288
Prelude of "Obsession", 335, 531
Six Suites for solo cello, 341
Fugue in G minor, 367
Fugue, 369
E Major Partita, 379
Sarabande, 381
Gigue, 381
Concerto in E Major, 387, 391 408
Sonata in F minor, 391
Double Concerto, 391, 397
Chaconne, 403, 415, 419, 495, 511
Double Concerto, 403, 415, 420
Fugue in G Minor, 492
Bach Concerto in E Major, 495, 496
Double Concerto, 505
Sonata, 530
Concerto in E, 539
Concerto, 541
Bachmann, Alberto, 73
Bartók, Béla, 533
Bauer, Harold, *212*
Beethoven, Ludwig van (personal references), 35, 63, 107, 191, 291, 345, 356, 367, 382, 388, 391, 399, 405, 408, 415, 484, 493, 521
Beethoven (references to music pieces)
Romances, 41, 189
Fidelio, 107
Concerto, 227, 230, 279, 283, 285, 379, 391, 397
Sonata in C-sharp minor, 362
Romance in F Major, 367
Seventh Quartet, 369
Romance, 387, 388
Rondo from Beethoven Concerto, 401, 403
Concerto, 415, 419
Beethoven Concerto, 494
"Kreutzer" Sonata, 496, 521
Funeral March, 535
Concerto in D, 539
Belinsky, 267
Benedetti, René, 73
Benoist, André, *490*, 547
Berlin Philharmonic Orchestra, 41
Berlioz, Hector Louis, 356
Bernhardt, Sarah, 267
Besekirsky, Vasily (personal references), 373, 427, 430
Besekirsky, (reference to music piece), Prélude du Poème Concertant, 373

Bilse, Benjamin, 35, 41, 45, 47, 291, 356, 539
Bordes, Charles, 53
Bordes-Pène, Marie, 57, 132
Borodin, Alexander, 63, 384
Brahms, Johannes (personal references and illustrations), 35, 107, *119*, 191, 291, 294, 345, 382, 399, 408, 411, 420, 520, 521
Brahms (references to music pieces),
  Concerto for Violin and Cello, 221
  Hungarian Dance, 301
  Double Concerto, 321, 419
  Sonata in D minor, 407, 408
  Concerto, 505, 520
Brandukov, Anatoly, *176-177*, 267 321, 373, 387
Brodsky, Vadim, 561
Bruch, Max (personal references and illustrations), 107, 288, 291, 380, *381*, 382, 387, 391, 415, 521
Bruch (references to music pieces)
  Concerto in G minor, 291
  Second in D minor, 291
  Scottish Fantasia, 380
  Concerto in G minor, 408
Brunschwig, Dany, 73
Brussels Conservatoire, 31, 63, 73, 375, 479, 539, 543
Bull, Ole, *137*, 468
Bülow, Hans von, *398*, 399
Burmester, Willy, 93, *115*, 141, 163, *169*
Busoni, Ferruccio, 63, *66*, 73
C
Capet, Lucien, 63
Casals, Pablo, 63, *71*, 73, 107, *121*, 210, *215*, *218*, 221, *223*, *225*, 227, 230, 267, *320*, 321, 393, 407, 411, 415, 419, 420, 457, 527, 544

Castillon, Alexis de, (personal reference), 96
Castillon, (reference to music pieces), Quartet, 132
  Quintet, 382
Cheshikhin, Vsevolod, 379
Cézanne, Paul, 57
Chabrier, Emmanuel, 53
Chausson, Ernest, (personal references and illustrations), 53, 96, 105, *127*, 132, 135, 142, 291, 484, 520
Chausson, (reference to music pieces), *Poème*, 53, 135, 142, 283, 314, 382, 411, 521, 533
  Concert, 132
  Poème de l'Amour et de la Mer, 142
  Concert in D, 142
Cherynskevsky, Nikolai, 21
Chopin, Frédéric (personal references), 191, 342
Chopin, (references to music pieces), *Funeral March*, 275, 483
  Sonata, 283
Cincinnati Symphony Orchestra, 205, 467, 533, 539, 541, 543, 548
Colonne, Edouard, 47, 107, 356, 533
Corelli, Arcangelo, 525
Cortot, Alfred, 63, 73, 107, 210, 227, 230, *231*, 457
Covent Garden Theatre, 107
Crickboom, Mathieu, 63, 73, 331, *333*, 441, 532
Cui, Ceasar (personal references and illustrations), 283, 291, 373, 375, *376*, 382, 384, 397
Cui (references to music pieces)
  Cantabile, 283
  Berceuse, 375, 379
  Tarantella, 375
  Twelve Miniatures, 379
  Concert Suite, 379

D
Dalcroze, Emile Jaques, 135, *143*, 271
Damrosch, Walter, 302
d'Argenteau, Marie Mercie, 430
Davydov, Karl, 283, 430
de Beriot, Charles, *428, 429*, 430 491
Debussy, Claude (personal references and illustrations), 63, *152*, 153, 154, *155, 156*, 157, *160*, 161, 288, 353, 496, 504, 520
Debussy, (references to music pieces) *Nocturnes*, 53, 153, 161
Pellèas and Melisande, 154
Quartet, 533
Decreus, Camille, 547
Defaus, Désiré, 441
Déthier, Edouard, 471
Dincin, Dr. Herman, 539, 541, 543
Dincin Jeanette, 210, *237*, 344, *452, 466*, 467, 539, 541, 542, 543
d'Indy, Vincent (personal references and illustrations), 53, *55*, 63, *64*, 96, 105, 243, 381, 534, 539
d'Indy (references to music pieces) *Quartet*, 53
Piano Quartet, 132, 382
'Istar', 484
Dukas, Paul, *Sonata for Violin and Piano*, 53
Duparc, Henri (personal references and illustrations), 96, *102*
Duparc (reference to music piece), Overture 'Lenore', 484
Dvorak, Antonin, 107, 301

E
Eberhardt, Goby, 285, 291
Elgar Concerto, 63, 163, 178
Elman, Mischa, 93, *97, 136*, 163, *170, 172*, 178, 185, 426, 427, 505, *506, 507*, 510
Erdenko, Michael, 73, 373, 427
Ernst, Heinrich, *Hungarian Airs*, 356
Enesco, Georges, *70*, 73, 93, *136*, 221, 267, 285, 288, 331, 487, 531
Engel, Julius, 387, 388, 391, 407

F
Fauré, Gabriel (personal references and illustrations), 53, 63, *65, 177*, 291, 381, *410*, 411
Fauré (references to music pieces), *Piano Quintet*, 53
Piano Quartets, 132, 382
Flesch, Carl, 73, 163, *166, 173*, 178, 185, 285, 288, *292*, 294, 441
Francescatti, Zino, *136, 442*, 446, *447*, 457
Franck, César, (personal references and illustrations), 53, *54*, 57, 63, 96, 153, 257, 288, 291, 313, 408, 415, 484, 494, 496, 520, 538, 539
Franck (references to music pieces), Sonata for Violin and Piano, 53, 96, 283, 381, 382
Quartet and Quintet, 132
Sonata in A Major, 407
Sonata, 411
Violin Sonata, 532, 533
Fried, Miriam, 509

G
Gailliard, Jacques, 321
Galkin, Nikolai, 356
Gérardy, Jean, *117, 131, 147*, 315, 321, *334, 417*
Gevaert, François, *Traité d'Instrumentation*, 430
Gilels, Yelizaveta, 344, 435, 457
Gilson, Paul *Fantasia on Canadian Folk Themes*, 233
Gingold, Josef, *10*, 11, *14*, 73, 322, 504, 520 *522, 523*, 525

Ginsburg, Lev, 11, *12*, 13, *14*, 15, *526-527*
Glavac, Voicech, 356, 362
Glazunov, Alexander (personal references and illustrations), 63, 107, *125*, 291, 356, 384, 391
Glazunov (references to music pieces), *Meditation*, 384
Suite *From the Middle Ages*, 384
Concerto, 393
Solemn Overture, 403
Glazunov String Quartet, 513
Godowsky, Leopold, *280*
Goldenweiser, Alexander, 105, 373, 407, 408
Gogol's *Inspector General*, 279
Gorky, Maxim, 260
Gounod, Charles François, *Faust*, 367
Granat, Endre, 509
Grieg, Edvard, 45, 107
Grumiaux, Arthur, 446, *449*
Guarnerius del Gèsu, *24*
Guide, Arthur, *34*, *36*

H
Halir, Karel, 35, 63
Handel, George Frideric (personal reference), 382
Handel (reference to music piece), *Aria*, 407
Hartmann, Arthur, *478*, 479
Heifetz, Jascha, 63, 93, *136*, *148 149*, *286*, *455*, 498
Hekking, André, 321
Hekking, Anton, *318*
Hekking, Gerard, *196*
Henryk Wieniawski International Competition, 441
Heynberg, Désiré, 24
Hindemith, Paul, Sonata Op. 25, 341
Hollmann, Joseph, 120, *316*, 321, *335*
Hubay, Jenö, 93, *103*

Hubermann, Bronislaw, 63, 397, 504
Hugo, Victor, 401

I
Igumnov, Konstantin, 267
Impressionism, 349, 353
International Ysaÿe Competition of Violinists, 233, 243, 435, *436-437*, 441, 498
Ippolitov-Ivanov, Mikhail, *371-372*, 373

J
Jacob, Joseph, 63, *79*, 539
Jensen, Arvid, *561*
Joachim, Joseph, 41, *42*, 93, *94*, 107, *137*, *266*, 279, 283, 285, 294, *299*, 367, *368*, 369, 395, 399, 479, 492, 538, 542
Joachim Quartet, *112-113*, 479
Jongen, Joseph (personal references) 63, 233, 243, 534
Jongen (reference to music piece) *Impressions d'Ardennes*, 233

K
Kamensky, Boris, 373, 382
Kashkin, Nikolai, 285, 387, 395, 397, 401, 405, 407
Kneisel, Franz, 467
Kodaly, Zoltan, Sonata Op. 8, 341
Kogan, Leonid, 344, *443*, *444*, 446, 457, 505, 514
Kogan, Pavel, 521
Kreisler, Fritz, 63, *68*, 73, 93, 107, *111*, 133, 163, *165*, *175*, 178, *179*, 185, 221, 230, 285, *286*, 331, 415, 484, *528-529*, 531, 532, 541
Kubelik, Jan, 93, 107, *110*, *394*, 395, 397, *418*, 420, 484
Kuznetsov, Konstantin, *Lullaby*, 283

L

"La Chanterelle", 73, 187, *189*, 205, 210, 427
Lachaume, Louis, *131, 147*
Lalo, Edouard (personal references and illustrations), 63, 288, *290*, 291, *386*, 481, 521
Lalo's (references to music pieces)
Symphonie espagnole, 47, 382, 387, 420
Concerto, 78, 233
Concerto in F, 480, 481
La Monnaie Opera House, 233
Laredo, Jaime, 509
Laub, Ferdinand, 279, 285, 301, 395
Lekeu, Guillaume (personal reference), 63, 96, 291, 411, 521
Lekeu (reference to music piece)
Sonata for Violin and Piano, 53
Lemaitre, Frédéric, 267
Leschetizky, Theodore, 47
Liège Conservatoire, 27, 50, 538
Liège Théatre Royal, 233
Lindenlaub, Theofile, *52*, 161, 321
Liszt, Franz, 31, *38, 39*, 41, 47, 309, *310*, 533
Locatelli, Pietro, 291, 345
Luboshutz, Léa, 471, *472*

M

Macmillen, Francis, 144, *145*
Marchot, Alfred, *37*, 73, 288
Marsick, Martin, *30, 50*, 379
Marteau, Henri, *131, 147*, 163, *168*
Massart, Rodolphe, 24, 27, *29, 37, 50*, 538, 542
Mendelssohn, Felix (personal references), 35, 63, 288, 291, 307, 356, 362, 367, 382, 391, 399, 411, 415, 544
Mendelssohn Concerto, 294, 359, 369-370, 379, 408, 427, 511
Mendelssohn Trio, 419
Mengelberg, Willem, 63
Menter, Sophie, 47
Menuhin, Yehudi, *443*, 457, 544, 545
Meunier, Constantin, 57, 105, 106, 243
Milstein, Nathan, 210, 446, 508
Monet, Claude, 57
Morini, Erica, 136
Moscow Conservatoire, 73, 279, 456
Moscow Philharmonic Music School, 373
Moscow Philharmonic Society, 373, 387, 405, 456
Mottl, Felix, 63
Mozart, Wolfgang Amadeus (personal references), 63, 191, 291, 349, 382, 397, 399, 401, 405, 408, 521
Mozart (references to music pieces), Concerto No. 3, 345
Sonata in D Major, 407
Concerto in G Major, 419
Musin, Ovide, *34, 36, 251*, 252, 253, 254

N

Nardini, Pietro, 345
Nedbal, Oskar, 356, *361*
Newman, Philip, 296-297, *446*, 533
Nikisch, Artur, 63, 163, *164, 167*, 294, 539

O

Oistrakh, David, 285, 331, 349, *351*, 435, *436-437, 444*, 446, 456, 457, 498, 505, 514, 552
Oistrakh, Igor, *442, 448, 451*, 457
Ondricek, Franz, 93, 107, *108*
Ortmans, Réne, 479, 480, 481, 483

P

Paganini, Niccolò (personal references and illustrations), *137,* 260, 267, 331, 349, *350, 365,* 468, *469,* 491, 492, 494, 504, 508, 521, 525, 533, 539
Paganini (reference to music piece), Caprice No. 4, 41
Parent, Armand, 96, *104,* 105
Paris Conservatoire, 96
Partello, Dwight, J., *180-181*
Partello Collection of Violins, 182-*183*
Pasquali, Nicolò, 349
Pavlovsk Concerts, 356
Persinger, Louis, *72,* 73, 471, *475, 476*
Piatigorsky, Gregor, *148*
Pierret, August, 132
Pisarro, Camille, 57
Pollain, Férnand, 315, 321
Polyakin, Myron, 93, 285, *287*
Popper, David, 47
Press, Michael, 73, 163, *171,* 427
Pressman, Matvei, 373
Primrose, William, 73
Prix International Ysaÿe, 21
Prokofiev, Sergei, 107
Pugno, Raoul, 63, *69,* 73, 105, 107, *109, 117,* 321, *414,* 415, *417,* 482, 548
Pushilov, Konstantin, 356

Q

Queen Elisabeth of the Belgians, *193,* 199, 233, 344, 441, 468, 498, *501,* 504, 513, 515, 534, 538, 541, 543
Queen Elisabeth (Ysaÿe) Competitions *442-443,* 498, 449, 502, 503, 514, 515
Queen Fabiola, 499, 503
Quiroga, Manuel, 331, *332,* 532

R

Rachmaninov, Sergei, (personal references), 63, 78, 107, 267, 373, 387, 419, 427
Rachmaninov (reference to music piece), Piano Concerto Op. 18, 384
Radoux-Rogier, Charles, 345
Radoux, *Berceuse,* 362
Raphael's, *Triumph of Poetry,* 399
Reger, Max, Three Suites, Op. 131, 341, 399
Im alten Style, 382
Reicha, Antonin, 96
Ribaupierre, André de, 73
Ricci, Ruggiero, 552, *554,* 555
Rimsky-Korsakov, Nikolai (personal references), 47, 153, 291, 393, 427
Rimsky-Korsakov (reference to music pieces), *Fantasia on Russian Themes,* 384
Russian Easter Overture, 384
"Scheherazade", 548
Rodin, Auguste, 57, 105
Rolland, Romain, 47, 96, 107, 127
Royal Conservatory of Brussels, 473
Royal Philharmonic Society, 107
Rubinstein, Anton (personal references and illustrations), 31, *33,* 41, 45, 78, 93, 267, 279, 283, 355, *364,* 367, 372, 373, 375, 382, 391, 397, 399
Rubinstein, Anton (reference to music piece), *Ivan the Terrible,* 356
Rubinstein, Artur, 210
Russian Music Society, 373, 375, 407, 408

S

Saenger-Sethe, Irma, 294
Safonov, Vasily, 373, 380
Saint-Saëns, Camille (personal references and illustrations), 47,

51, 53, 63, 93, 107, *118,* 120, 127, 288, 291, 362, 367, 380, 381, 382, 388, *389, 390,* 391, 399, 419, 482, 484, 521
Saint-Saëns (references to music pieces), *Rondo Capriccioso,* 41, 107, 120, 372
Jeunesse d' Hercule, 107
Sonata for Violin and Piano, 120
La Muse et le Poete, 120, 321
Piano Trio, 120
Rondo Capriccioso and Introduction, 356
Prelude from *The Deluge,* 362
Violin Concerto, 380
Third Concerto, 380
Rondo Capriccioso, 387, 388, 408, 415, 420, 521
Trio, 415
Salle Pleyel, 132, 156, 288
Sarasate, Pablo de (personal references and illustrations), 47, 93, *95,* 107, *137,* 260, *261,* 294, *295, 299,* 301, 367, 369, 379, 381, 395, *396,* 397, 420, *421,* 483, 484
Sarasate (reference to music piece) *Zigeunerweisen,* 381
Sauret, Emile, 93, *98*
Seidel, Toscha, *26*
Serov, Alexander (personal references and illustrations), 267, 283
Serov, (reference to music piece), *Zaporozhye Cossack Dance,* 356
Serov, Valentin, 392, 393
Servais, Joseph, 321
Sevcik, Ottokar, *26,* 467
Seydel, Irma, *26*
Schradieck, Henry, 26
Schubert, Franz, 35, 63
Schumann, Clara, 41
Schumann, Robert, 307
Schumann Third Symphony, 233
Schumann Piano Quintet, 482

Segovia, Andres, 63
Shchepkin, Mikhail, 279
Sheppard, Leslie, *357*
Shostakovich, Dmitri, 107, *422,* 527
Sibor, Boris, (personal references), 373, 408, 419, 420, 427
Sibor (reference to music piece), Technical Exercises for the Violin, 420
Siloti, Alexander, 373, 384, 411
Siloti Concerts, 387, 393, 403
Silverstein, Joseph, 509
Simonetti, Achille, *26*
Sitt, Hans, *26*
Sivori, Camillo, *26*
Slavik, Joseph, 260
Spalding, Albert, 73, *76, 136, 286,* 487, *488, 490*
Spohr, Louis, *26,* 525
Soumagne, *23*
Smetana, Bedrich, *Vltava,* 380
Stern, Isaac, 24, 446, 457
St. Petersburg Conservatoire, 356, 427
Strauss, Johann, 356, 382, 415
Stravinsky, Igor, 107, *123*
Strokov, Leo, *423,* 424, 427
Sollertinsky, Ivan, 353
Szeryng, Henryk, 457
Szigeti, Joseph, 73, 210, *219, 251,* 331, 339, 345, *352,* 441, 446, 487, 524, 527, 530

T

Taneyev, Sergei, *Oresteia,* 380, 384 *Reverie,* 384
Concert Suite, 420
Tartini, Giuseppi, *138,* 525
Tchaikovsky, Peter (personal references and illustrations), 35, *37,* 47, 63, 185, 267, 291, 382, 384, 391, 419

Tchaikovsky (references to music pieces), Violin Concerto, 178
Melancholy Serenade, 384
Piano Trio, 388
Tchaikovsky Trio, 419
Tchaikovsky Concerto, 427
Tertis, Lionel, *201,* 457
Thibaud, Jacques, 63, *67,* 73, 93, *138,* 210, *212,* 221, 227, *229,* 230, *231,* 243, 275, 331, 423, 441, 487, 491, 534
Thomson, César, *50, 84,* 93, *101, 138*
Toscanini, Arturo, 107
Twenty Club, *56,* 57, 58, *82,* 105, 127, 132, 154

U

Urso, Camilla, *138*

V

van Hout, Leon, 63, 539
Van Neste, Carlo, 73, *442,* 446
Verhaeren, Emile, 191
Verzhbilovich, Alexander, 373, 382
Viardot, Paul, *138*
Vidas, Raoul, *138*
Vieuxtemps, Henri (personal references and illustrations), 21, 24, 27, *28,* 35, *40, 43,* 93, *137, 174,* 257, 260, 288, 289, 291, 307, 311, 342, 345, 356, 362, 367, 381, 382, 388, 391, 430, 473, 491, 492, 494, 515, 521, 525, 533, 538
Vieuxtemps (references to music pieces), *Fantasia appassionata,* 41
Fourth Concerto, 185, 375, 387
Ballade, 199
Rondino, 301, 369
Duo Brilliant, 321
Ballade and Polonaise, 356
Concerto in D minor, 367
Concerto, 372

Legend, 372
Souvenirs de Russie, 381
Concerto in E Major, 381
Fourth Concerto, 388
Polonaise and Rondino, 408
Ballade and Polonaise, 420
Fourth Concerto, 425
Fifth Concerto, 493
Viotti, Jean Baptiste, (personal references and illustrations), *174,* 347, 382, 411
Viotti (reference to music piece), Concerto No. 22, 345, 405
Vivaldi, Antonio, *138,* 291, 349, 382, 411, 419
Vitali, Giovanni
Chaconne, 189, 382, 411
Von Vecsey, Franz, *138,* 259

W

Wagner, Richard (personal references), 96, 127, 191, 349, 356, 381, 493, 498
Wagner (references to music pieces), *Albumblatt,* 301, 407
Mastersingers of Nuremberg, 381
Parsifal, 381
Walloon Farandoles, 135
Walloon dialect, 538, 541
Weingartner, Felix, 63
White, Josepe, *174*
White, Roderick, *174*
Wieniawski, Henryk (personal references and illustrations), 24, 31, *32,* 93, *137, 174,* 233, 257, 260, 285, 291, 307, 342, 345, 356, 359, 362, 367, 375, 381, 382, 479, 491, 492, 494, 521, 525, 538
Wieniawski (references to music pieces), *Concerto in D minor,* 41
Romanza, 189
Mazurkas, 301
Fantasia, 362
Polonaise No. 2, 367

Variation on a Russian Theme, 369
Legend and Polonaise, 369
Faust Fantasia, 369
Wilhelmj, August, 93, 99, 174, 253
Wolff, Johannes, 174
Wood, Sir Henry, 270, 285, 288

Y

Yesipova, Anna, 47, 355
Ysaÿe, Antoine, 86, 120, *195, 197,* 321, *497,* 512, 513, 514, 530, 539, 544
Ysaÿe, Carry, 233, *235,* 539
Ysaÿe, Eugéne (illustrations), *2-3, 4, 6, 18, 34, 36, 44, 46, 48-49, 50, 52, 59, 64, 69, 83, 87, 88, 92, 106, 116, 117, 124, 126, 127, 128, 129, 130, 131, 133, 134, 139, 146, 147, 150-151, 156, 158-159, 162, 171, 176- 177, 179, 180-181, 184, 186, 188 190, 192, 193, 194, 195, 196, 197, 198, 201, 202, 204, 207, 208-209, 210, 214, 216-217, 220, 222-223, 226, 228, 229, 232, 234, 236, 237, 238-239, 240-241, 244-245, 246- 247, 249, 256, 258, 264, 268, 271, 274, 276, 277, 278, 280, 282, 298, 299, 300, 302, 305, 306, 308, 335, 336-337, 338, 345, 346, 348, 354, 359, 358, 360, 363, 366, 372, 374, 378, 383, 385, 392, 400, 402, 404, 406, 409, 423, 434, 438, 452-453, 454, 456, 458, 465, 476, 477, 485, 499, 500, 522, 532, 534, 536-537, 540, 560*
Ysaÿe (references to music pieces), *Exil,* 203, 313, 321
Amitié and *Poème Nocturne,* 205
Sonatas for Solo Violin, 205
Peter the Miner, 230, 307, 538, 541, 543
Méditation, 233, 313, 315
Poème Elégiaque, 243, 309
Caprice d'après l'Etude en forme de Valse de Saint-Saëns, 294, 344
Sonata to Kreisler, 296-297
Court Joie, 307
Badinage, 307
Perdue and *Retrovée,* 307
Music Example #1. *312,* 313
Poème Elégiaque, 313, 535
Scene au Rouet, 313, 314
Chant d' Hiver, 313, 315
Extase, 313, 315, *322-329*
Amitié, 313, 321
Poème Nocturne, 313, 321
Music Example #2, 313, *314*
Music Example #3, 314, *315*
Music Example #4, 315, *317*
Music Example #5, 315, *317*
Music Example #6, 321, *330*
Serenade, 321
Sonata No. 2, *Prelude,* 335, 339
Music Example No. 7, 335
Sonata No. 1, 335, 339
Sonata No. 3, 339, 340
Sonata No. 4, 339, 340
Sonata No. 5, 339, 341
Sonata No. 6, 339, 341
Music Example No. 8, 339
Sonata No. 2, *Dies irae* theme, 340
Music Example No. 9, 340
Music Example No. 10, 340
Music Example No. 11, 341
Music Example No. 12, 341
Sonata for Solo Cello in C minor, 341
Music Example No. 13, 342
Music Example No. 14, 342
Music Example No. 15, 342
Music Example No. 16, 342, 343

Mazurka Op. 14, 343
Music Example No. 17, 343
Berceuse Op. 20, 343
Les Neiges d'Antan Op. 23, 343
Divertimento Op. 24, 343
Music Example No. 18, 343, 344
Fantasie Op. 32
Sonata for two violins, 344
Dix *Préludes* pour Violin seul. Essai sur le Mécanisme moderne du Violin, 344
Harmonies du Soir, Op. 31 349
Saltarelle carnavalesque, 362
Près d'un berceau, 369
Mazurka, 369
Rêve d'Enfant, 483
Six Sonatas for Violin, 520, 521, 525
Dies Irae, 531
"Ballade", 531
Ysaÿe, illustrations of citations, letters, memorabilia, programs, reviews and scrapbook entries:
Bloomfield bookplate, 23
Wedding invitation, 60-61
Wedding menu, 62
Letter to Louise Ysaÿe, 74-75
Brussels studio, 80-81
Ysaÿe scrapbook, 85
Brussels studio, 86, 90-91
Boston Courier, Ysaÿe/Thomson review, 100
Ysaÿe letter, 114
Fiddle Strings, Ysaÿe master class, 206
Ysaÿe–Kreisler concert program, 211
Times-Star, Ysaÿe review, 213
Concert program (Riga, Latvia), 225
Memorial urn, 248
Ysaÿe tour managed by Johnston, 259
Scrapbook, 262, 263, 264, 265
Musical Courier, Ysaÿe editorial, 269
Scrapbook, 272, 273, 281
The Violinist, Ysaÿe, poem, 303
The New York Times, concert tribute, 319
Barcelona concert program, 347
Ysaÿe medal, *357*, *359*
Letter to Cesar Cui, 377
Moscow concert program (1907), 412-413
Concert program, (1910), 416
Letter to Leo Strokov, 424
Inaugural Plaque, 445
Letter to Tirindelli, 459-463
Ysaÿe commemorative record, 503
Scrapbook, 547
Ysaÿe Concerts, 63, 205, 384, 427, 539, 543
Ysaÿe, Gabriel, *196*, *476*, 539
Ysaÿe, Jacques, 516
Ysaÿe, Joseph, *116*
Ysaÿe, Louise Bourdau, *48-49*, 53 *77*, *128*, *129*, *184*, *190*
Ysaÿe Memorial Medal, 457
Ysaÿe, Music Foundation, 440, 457, 498
Ysaÿe, Nicholas, 21, *25*, *116*, 538, 542
Ysaÿe Publishers, Brussels, 344, 349
Ysaÿe String Quartet, 57, 132, 154, 384, 479
Ysaÿe, Theofile, 105, *116*, *195*, 539

Z

Zimbalist, Efrem, 93, *122*, *174*, *450*, 457, 530, 546
Zimmer, Albert, 321